D1587753

SURVIVOR
FROM A
DEAD AGE

SURVIVOR
FROM A
DEAD AGE

THE MEMOIRS OF
LOUIS LOZOWICK

Edited by
VIRGINIA HAGELSTEIN MARQUARDT

With a foreword by
Milton W. Brown

and a prologue by
John E. Bowlt

SMITHSONIAN INSTITUTION PRESS

Washington and London

Copy Editor: Debbie K. Hardin
Production Editor: Jack Kirshbaum
Designer: Kathleen Sims

Library of Congress Cataloging-in-Publication Data
Survivor from a dead age : the memoirs of Louis Lozowick / edited by
Virginia Hagelstein Marquardt with foreword by Milton Brown ;
introduction by Virginia Hagelstein Marquardt
      p.   cm.
  Includes bibliographical references and index.
  ISBN 1-56098-696-4
  1. Lozowick, Louis, 1892–1973. 2. Lithographers—United States—
Biography. I. Marquardt, Virginia Carol Hagelstein.
NE2312.L69A4   1997
769.92—dc20
[B]   96-18741
British Library Cataloguing-in-Publication Data is available

Manufactured in the United States of America
03 02 01 00 99 98 97   5 4 3 2 1

∞ The paper used in this publication meets the minimum requirements of
the American National Standard for Information Sciences—Permanence of
Paper for Printed Library Materials Z39.48-1984. Printed on recycled paper.

Unless otherwise noted, illustrations are courtesy of Adele Lozowick.

Jacket front: *New York,* oil on canvas, ca. 1924–1926. Walker Art Center,
  Minneapolis, gift of Hudson D. Walker, 1961.
Jacket back: Ralph Steiner, *Louis Lozowick,* 1930.
Frontispiece: Ansel Adams, *Louis Lozowick,* photograph, 1932.
Opposite contents page: *Autobiographic,* ink, 1967.
Fig. 1 Lozowick, date unknown. (page xii)
Fig. 2 *Self-Portrait,* lithograph, 1930. (page xxxii)

To Adele Lozowick

CONTENTS

Part Four. 1924–1945
   Back in America 253

PREFACE

Louis Lozowick's memoirs, which he worked on from approximately 1945 to his death in 1973, are titled *Survivor from a Dead Age*. In the eleven chapters of this manuscript, Lozowick recounts his life as a child in Ukraine, his Jewish upbringing, the pogroms he witnessed as a boy, the Revolution of 1905, and his early training at the Kiev Art School, as well as his years in Paris and Berlin and his first trip to Moscow during the early 1920s.

These memoirs were written during the last years of the author's life and have a fluid, informal style. In editing this manuscript, I have maintained the tone and, as much as possible, the organization of the original, including occasional repetitions of thought. At times Lozowick departs from a strict chronological ordering to comment and make associations as they occur to him; these breaks of thought are indicated by the author's parentheses and the editor's typographical ornaments. Brackets have been reserved for editorial additions, changes, and notes, as well as for references to the illustrative material, which has been added to the manuscript. In places paragraphing has been revised for greater coherence and fluidity of thought. Misspellings and errors of punctuation and grammar have been corrected and complete names of individuals have been provided whenever possible. The transliteration of Russian and Ukrainian has been amended to conform to a modified Library of Congress system except where English-language usage dictates otherwise; for example, Fyodor Dostoevsky, Leo Tolstoy, Petr Tchaikovsky, Wass-

ily Kandinsky, Vladimir Mayakovsky, and Vsevolod Meyerhold. The transliteration of Yiddish is based on the guidelines
of the YIVO Institute for Jewish Research, except in the cases
in which spellings have been adopted in English usage, as indicated by *The New Shorter Oxford English Dictionary* (1994),
Random House Unabridged Dictionary (second edition, 1993),
and *Webster's New Universal Unabridged Dictionary* (second edition, 1983); and transliterations of Hebrew often reflect Yiddish and Ashkenazic pronunciations or the pronunciations
used by the author. The *King James Bible* is used for biblical
references.

Lozowick's memoirs fall into two segments: his youth and
life in Russia, ending with his arrival in America in 1906; and
his years abroad during the early 1920s. The intervening years
(1906–1920) and the years after his return from Europe in
1924 are not directly discussed in this manuscript. Because
these periods are crucial in Lozowick's maturation as an artist,
I have added Part Two, "The Years from 1906–1920," and
Part Four, "The Years from 1924–1945." These sections draw
on interviews with Lozowick conducted by Barbara Kaufman, William C. Lipke, Gerald M. Monroe, and Seton Hall
University students, along with Lozowick's other writings
and archival papers. Intended to bridge the two segments of
the *Survivor of a Dead Age,* these parts include accounts of
Lozowick's associations and activities as well as his artistic
evolution during these periods. Specific events are enumerated in the chronology of this book, which is expanded from
the chronology by Janet A. Flint in *The Prints of Louis Lozowick: A Catalogue Raisonné* (1982).

I would like to acknowledge the many individuals who
have contributed their time, effort, and expertise. I thank
Regina Sara Ryan for her early interest in this project; Lois
Woodyatt of the National Academy of Design and Zachary
Backer of YIVO Institute of Jewish Research for their research assistance; Mary Beth Commisso of Academic Com-
puting at Marist College for her technical assistance; and
Wendy Fell, Margaret Lyko, Michelle Paquette, Carolyn Sut-
ton, Garnet Toritto, and Jennifer Zanetti for their clerical assistance. I am grateful to Monia Bageritz, John E. Bowlt,

Katrine Hecker, Claire Keith, Rabbi Samuel Klein, Stephen Lewis, Benjamin J. Salzano, and Milton Teichman for checking the transliterations and translations of foreign texts. Special acknowledgment is due to Benjamin J. Salzano, Rabbi Samuel Klein, Gail Harrison Roman, and Alison Hilton, who graciously answered my numerous queries about Russian and Jewish history and culture with endless patience.

The editorial, production, and marketing staff members of the Smithsonian Institution Press deserve special recognition for their expertise and professionalism. I especially thank Amy Pastan, Debbie K. Hardin, Jack Kirshbaum, Kathleen Sims, and Annette Windhorn.

I am delighted that Milton W. Brown and John E. Bowlt, both friends of Louis and Adele Lozowick, agreed to write introductory sections. Brown gives a very personal recollection of his family's Russian roots and his warm friendship with Lozowick in the Foreword, and Bowlt provides the historical and cultural context relevant to Lozowick's memoirs in the Prologue.

Foremost, I thank Adele Lozowick, the author's widow, who initiated this project and whose assistance, encouragement, and enthusiasm have been invaluable in bringing it to completion.

Virginia Hagelstein Marquardt

FOREWORD

The publication of Louis Lozowick's *Memoirs* opens an unexpected and welcome new window to the past. Its value to the history of art in our century is obvious, but reading it is also an adventure into another era, another culture, even another world vanished forever.

I am especially pleased, but not really surprised, to be writing this introduction to Louis' memoirs. I seem to have outlived all other logical candidates and my credentials are acceptable: I knew him personally for many years, was even his student for a while, admired his art, and wrote about it early on. Also important, I have known his wife, Adele, for many years, and she graciously asked me to write the introduction. In truth, I would have felt deeply disappointed if she had not, for I have always felt closely attached to Louis.

Louis came to this country as a teenager at about the same time as my parents did. In 1911, when they were all living in Newark, they were introduced by a mutual friend. I do not know what the circumstances were, but one day while Louis was visiting my parents he took a photograph of my mother seated behind a kitchen table, according to her account, the day before I was born. Our relationship is thus, if not preordained, prenatal. Years passed, my family moved to Brooklyn, and, as far as I know, they did not have any close contact with Lozowick, but when I continued to show some inclination and talent for art, they arranged for me to study privately with him.

He was then living in Manhattan on Eighth Avenue just

north of 14th Street, and I came by subway to see him every other Saturday. He criticized whatever work I had done in the interim, which, considering all my curricular and extracurricular activity, was not very extensive. He then set up a still-life for me to paint and after an hour or so he criticized and we discussed what I had done. While I was at work he worked on his lithography, using a zinc plate, as I remember, rather than a stone. He also often worked on retouching blemishes on the prints themselves. I was always amazed at his technical facility, and he explained that he had achieved his very meticulous technique by working as a photo retoucher as a youth. Now having read his memoirs, I would guess that it went as far back as his training in the rigid academic routine of the art school in Kiev. We talked about many things, mostly about art. He lent me books to read, and I was introduced to art history and especially modern art by him. Art history eventually became my vocation, and there is no question that he had a profound influence on my artistic and intellectual development.

I was really quite naive, knew little about art or artists, and did not realize that Louis had some standing in the art world at the time, though he had taken me to Weyhe's book store and art gallery and I knew that they handled his prints. My recollection is that I studied with Louis in 1928–1929 because I remember some of the prints he was retouching, especially the *Checkered Table Cloth,* which is still one of my favorites. It was only in later years, after I had left him to go on to college, to the National Academy of Design, and then to the study of art history, that I realized Louis' status in the contemporary art world and the role he had played in the evolution of the machine image and the Precisionist movement in American art. I remained a friend and a great admirer of Louis over the years, though I saw less of him after the Lozowicks moved to New Jersey.

When I read Louis' memoirs for the first time, I was overcome by an extraordinary sense of predestination. It is not at all strange that my parents' memories of the "old country" and Louis' should have been similar, since they came from the same generation, background, and even region (Ukraine).

But those memories, transmitted to me in my youth, mostly
by my mother, were deeply embedded in my psyche and per-
sonalized by a trip I took to Russia in 1934 to see my mater-
nal grandmother and family and the *dorf* [village] in which
my mother had grown up. It was an experience that left an
indelible impression on me. In a sense the accumulated memories of my mother's *dorf* and my father's *shtetl* [Jewish town
or village] had somehow become my own and when I began
to read Lozowick's account, it was if I was reliving an experience I had already had, except for minor details. His account
struck me as so uncannily evocative that it seemed like déjà
vu. His memories of the *shtetl* and the heder are like my father's, of the *dorf,* like my mother's. Her family also was the
only Jewish family in a peasant village, and curiously enough,
her uncle—like his father—also ran a mill.

Louis' account is a rare treasure; another personal record
of the great migration of Jewish refugees to this country following the Russo–Japanese War and the subsequent period of
reaction and pogroms. It is told with remarkably detailed recall, evoking a vanished time and culture with texture and
resonance. The meagerness and poverty of existence, the
narrowness of vision, the harrowing threat of violence are
palatable, as are the humanity, idealism, and dogged effort at
survival. Louis' vision is broad, humane, historically knowl-
edgeable, and politically aware so that the memoir is not only
interesting but informative. In its spare, factual, almost disen-
gaged telling, it echoes those haunting photographs of our
ancestral past in so many dusty and forgotten albums, the
shadow images that record that epic migration that included
a whole generation of artists who achieved renown in other
lands—Marc Chagall and Chaim Soutine in France; Jacob
Epstein in England; and an especially large contingent in the
United States—Max Weber, Abraham Walkowitz, Samuel Hal-
pert, Isaac, Moses, and Raphael Soyer, William Gropper, Chaim
Gross, Peter Blume, and Ben Shahn, to name only a few.

After so detailed an account of the early years, it is a disappointment to find that Louis left only the barest skeletal
record of his Americanization—joining his brother in
Newark, attending high school, continuing his art studies in

New York at the National Academy of Design, graduating
from Ohio State University, and serving in the army during
World War I. Whether he ever meant to expand that account
or not, we shall never know. Perhaps, in retrospect, he did not
consider that phase of his life to be as important as the early
years, which he seems to have felt were his roots, or his years
abroad, the section that follows, which he obviously considered his formative years as an artist. Louis was clear about his
position and importance in American art. He had, of course,
seen a great deal and written widely and knowledgeably
about art. Critical opinion did not affect him, though he
must have wondered at its vagaries during his lifetime. I don't
think he would have been surprised at his belated recognition.
Although extremely modest, he knew his own value and understood the historic role he had played in American art.

Because Louis never carried his memoirs beyond the
1920s (though he obviously continued to work on them during the years), one is forced to the conclusion that in his own
mind those were the crucial years of his career. He never lost
faith in his talent or his vision and continued to work with
undiminished vigor to the end of his life, but he seems to
have recognized that the experiences of those first years
abroad helped form his artistic vision and style and that was
what he wanted to record.

The story he tells is fascinating and unique as an art historical document. Beginning with Max Weber in 1904, there
were many American artists of his generation who first encountered avant-garde art in Europe. By the time Louis arrived, the new art was no longer a novelty. But Louis had the
particular advantage of being linguistically equipped, in English, Russian, Ukrainian, French, German, and Yiddish, to
deal with a broad spectrum of artists. He also had not come
to Europe to study at any particular school and took the opportunity to spend time on his own schedule in Paris, Berlin,
and Moscow, where he encountered all the current "isms"
and their practitioners. In addition, he came in the guise of a
writer on art with portfolios from *Broom,* one of the leading
avant-garde small magazines in the United States, and the
Jewish *Union Bulletin.* Artists, even then, apparently were sus-

ceptible to the siren song of publicity. As a result, Louis got to meet a great number of people in the cultural world in three of the major centers of Europe; the list is overwhelming, to name only a few: Pablo Picasso, Marc Chagall, Fernand Léger, Constantin Brancusi, and Filippo Marinetti in Paris; László Moholy-Nagy, Theo van Doesberg, and Pavel Tchelitchev in Berlin; and Kazimir Malevich, Aleksandr Rodchencko, El Lissitsky, Vladimir Tatlin, Liubov' Popova, Aleksandra Exter, and Vladimir Mayakovsky in Moscow.

In Berlin, Louis began to work, to develop a theme and a style. He exhibited and received immediate recognition. It was a time in which he had an opportunity to learn about Constructivism from the Russians themselves—Lissitsky, Natan Al'tman, Tatlin, Naum Gabo, and David Shterenberg, all of whom were then in Berlin. His own predilection was for the industrial confluence in Germany at the moment of the Bauhaus, De Stijl, and Constructivism. He could see his own art as part of a larger twentieth-century international cultural wave. Invited to Moscow by some of the Russian artists, he returned home, in a sense, though now an American citizen, to see the revolution and the art that came with it, and to talk to the artists who were responsible. He found, ironically, that Russians, just as all the other Europeans he had met, were interested in him as an American, an exemplar of what they thought of as the most modern and progressive nation in the world, at least in an industrial and technological sense.

Thus, it was Louis who became the earliest connection between the international "Constructivist" or machine aesthetic and the nascent American Precisionist movement already under way in the work of Charles Demuth, Morton Schamberg, Charles Sheeler, and Joseph Stella. In his book, *Modern Russian Art,* published by the Société Anonyme in 1925, Louis introduced the Russian avant-garde and Constructivism to the American scene. In 1927, he played a major role in organizing the Machine-Age Exposition in New York, the first of its kind in this country. This exhibition and the lithography to which he subsequently dedicated himself all were an integral part of the Precisionist movement.

It seems to me that Louis, in the careful, thoughtful way that was his nature, wanted the memoir to serve as a clarification of his life as an artist. He supplies us first with the memories of his childhood, which no one else would know, and then with what he considers the most crucial elements in his formation as an artist. What came later, half of his life, full of world shattering events of which he was part, full of achievement and recognition, were all in the public domain, accessible to historical review. He left us with these fascinating fragments of personal reminiscences, it seems, to make the picture complete and to adjust the perspective.

Milton W. Brown
Professor Emeritus
City University of New York Graduate School

PROLOGUE

Pathos Created by Distance:
The Memoirs of Louis Lozowick

Louis Lozowick's *Survivor from a Dead Age* is a chronicle of
episodes and events, both great and small. As an evocation of
Jewish life in the Ukrainian Pale of Settlement in the late
nineteenth and early twentieth centuries, the memoirs are
both poignant and instructive. They remind us of the constant threat of Tsarist imposition under which the Jewish
populace was forced to live, including enforced conscription
and rampant pogroms, and it reminds us of the persistence of
Jewish ritual and ceremony and the unfailing respect for the
life of the mind in a community where "art was the most
pervasive activity."[1] But the memoirs are also the story of a
liberal bohemian, unbound by religious or familial prejudice
and open to the most varied aesthetic currents in New York,
Paris, Berlin, and Moscow. Lozowick's first manifesto, "Tentative Attitudes" (1917), avoids any reference to the ethnic
traditions that nurtured and molded him. Moreover, Lozowick's description of Paris and Berlin with their Dada poetry
and Zenitist declarations, their cafés and cabarets, and their
ever changing carousel of writers and artists (from Filippo
Tommaso Marinetti to Iwan Goll, from Theo van Doesburg
to László Moholy-Nagy, from Valentin Parnakh to Ivan Puni)
tells us of a thoroughly secular, if not atheist, culture that had
replaced the alchemy of religion with the chemistry of ideology. Lozowick's experience of the new Russia and his en-
counters with the heroes of the Russian avant-garde also
bring a historic moment into relief, even though, curiously
enough, Lozowick the professional artist chose to identify

himself not as a Russian, but as an American, "for reasons of outlook."[2]

Lozowick's memoirs are much more than a travelogue or sentimental reconstruction of the past. They also constitute a linguistic experiment, a political manifesto, and an oracle of parable, functions that perhaps are even more important than the documentary value. This is apparent from one of the remarks that Lozowick made about time and place in the context of his birthplace, Ludvinovka, a *shtetl* south of Kiev:

> For many years of my adult life, I resided in one of the largest, perhaps the largest, city in the world; my childhood was spent in one of the smallest villages in the world. And yet, the miniature Ludvinovka did not leave me entirely unprepared for the giant New York. I am astonished to see, in retrospect, the many points which both places had in common in customs, beliefs, prejudices, and institutions—just a difference in scale and complexity.[3]

Lozowick's comment on the constancy of human society, whether in the remote fastness of Ukraine or the teeming metropolis of New York (or Paris, Berlin, or Moscow) illustrates a distinguishing feature of his memoirs. Lozowick was an acute observer of social and political ritual, an artist who adapted almost effortlessly, it would seem, to the deportments and ceremonies of the most diverse nations—Jewish, Ukrainian, Russian, American, French, German, and even Japanese; and Lozowick captured their physical and psychological traits not only in his paintings and prints but also in his conversations, written critiques, and reminiscences. In spite of the "pathos created by distance,"[4] Lozowick's memoirs are at once past and present, for their sections are interconnected by an uncanny cohesion of theme—an "interactivity"—as if chronological sequence and local space were secondary to some higher, transcendental logic.

Lozowick's narrative proceeds by a curious series of predictions and fulfillments, of foreshadowing and projection: surely, in sketching the steel mills and bridges of New York and Chicago, Lozowick must have been remembering the trestle structure and moving parts of his father's mill in Lud-

vinovka; perhaps his sophisticated window display for the
Lord and Taylor centennial celebration in 1926 was a direct
extension of the primitive signboards of bakers and butchers
that he passed by as a child; perhaps the piglets in Aleksei
Kruchenykh's avant-garde booklet *Porosiata* (Piglets) that so
appealed to Lozowick were a nostalgic reminiscence of the
stray pigs of Ludvinovka "wandering in from the surrounding
peasant households";[5] and perhaps the sober reductions of his
geometric lithographs in the 1920s were paraphrases of the
anatomical analyses and dissections that he undertook at the
Kiev Art Institute. Witness to Lozowick's power of observation is the fact that his interpretation of the church (and synagogue) service as an artistic synthesis anticipated the parallel
and radical conclusion that the philosopher Pavel Florenskii
promulgated in his essay, "The Church Rite as a Synthesis of
Art" in 1922;[6] and perhaps it is from this profound synthetic
impression that Lozowick developed his interest in the *Ge-
samtkunstwerk* (total work of art), especially in stage and book
design.

There are many such intratextual components in Lozowick's memoirs, but perhaps the common denominator
here—to which Lozowick returns again and again—is not a
visual or sociopolitical dimension, but a verbal one. The memoirs emphasize just how important language was to Lozowick,
a fact expressed not only in the clarity and fluency of his style
of writing, but also in his fascination with linguistic exercise.
Lozowick's initial remark on glossolalia and the speaking in
tongues that, as a young boy, he identified with the mutual
incomprehensibility of Yiddish, Russian, and Ukrainian,[7] was
not a casual response, but demonstrated an abiding interest in
what Malevich called the "energy of language."[8] Indeed, those
of us who had the good fortune to talk with Lozowick in
person remember the magic serenity of his conversation and
the special weight that he lent his every word, as if reflecting
on the true meaning of "In the beginning was the word."

Lozowick's discussion of the language of the Russian
Cubo-Futurists and the French Dadaists is especially illuminating, for it emphasizes their indebtedness to the utterances
of children, savages, and other outsiders. No doubt Aleksei

Kruchenykh, the inventor of *zaum* (transrational language)
and coauthor of the topsy-turvy poem *Mirskontsa* [World-
backwards] in 1912, would have been delighted to learn that
the schoolboy Lozowick could recite the Russian alphabet
"backward and forward in one breath."[9] Kruchenykh also
might have agreed that the irrational incorporation of the
word "vakhalaklakes"[10] into a Jewish jingle was an immediate
precursor to his own vowel poem called "Heights (Universal
Language)"—in other words, the famous "e u yu." Lozowick
himself was quite aware of these proto–Cubo-Futurist gestures, implying that the poetical experiments of Rudolf
Blümner, Raoul Hausmann, and Il'ia Zdanevich in the 1920s
(and his own "Néantisme") were only developments of these
primitive, if unintended, examples of avant-garde culture. As
writer and artist, therefore, Lozowick felt a close kinship to
Malevich, the poet and painter, dwelling on the latter's essay,
"On Poetry" of 1919, in which we learn that the highest poetry is one "in which pure rhythm and tempo remain as
movement and time; here rhythm and tempo rely on letters
like signs containing this or that sound."[11]

Malevich examined and applied verbal language as a code
or collection of "sensible" and "nonsensical" phonemes—as
a pictographic and written method and as an instrument for
articulating real and abstract concepts. On this level, then,
Malevich used language as a medium of promotion and persuasion (if not of elucidation) and, like a priest or ideologue,
resorted to metaphors instead of "hard truths." Moreover,
Malevich intermingled Ukrainian, Russian, and Polish (a fu-
sion that must have appealed to Lozowick) and often in an el-
liptical or incomplete fashion, so that the result resembled
zaum or children's language. Obviously, Malevich sympathized with Velimir Khlebnikov's and Kruchenykh's linguistic
acrobatics, especially the latter's push for "slips of the tongue,
misprints, lapsus,"[12] and he even tried to apply the "logic of
zaum"[13] to the inscriptions and descriptions of his paintings.
Malevich, Kruchenykh, and Mikhail Matiushin, the creators
of the transrational opera, *Victory over the Sun,* seemed to be
speaking in tongues and proposing their own glossolalia
when, in July 1913, they proclaimed the "right of poets and

artists to annihilate the lucid, limpid, noble sonorous Russian language."[14]

Lozowick discovered the logic of *zaum* not in Moscow but in Paris just after World War I, and he commented on the curious parallels between what the Russian Cubo-Futurists had been doing in 1913 and the Dada poets in Western Europe in the early 1920s. Lozowick visited Paris in 1920 and 1923 just as the ranks of its foreign community were being swelled by the enormous emigration from Russia, although in general, the Russian colony there had little enthusiasm for the extreme gestures of the avant-garde, giving ready preference to the elegant landscapes and portraits of Aleksandra Benois and Konstantin Somov. The reasons for this may be as much ideological as artistic, because to many émigrés, the post-Revolutionary experiments in abstract and propaganda art were synonymous with the aggression of the Bolshevik regime. That is why the "Erste Russische Kunstausstellung" in Berlin was regarded largely as a "Communist" exhibition, even though the Soviets organized it as a commercial venture and as a means to encourage foreign investment in the new Russia rather than as an ideological vehicle. Still, as Lozowick indicates, Paris in the early 1920s was the axis of the international bohemia, and if the Russian colony consisted more of *fin de siècle* artists than of avant-gardists, there were many other radicals—French, American, Polish—whom Lozowick befriended and appreciated. For example, he was an eager visitor to the various cafés, galleries, and artists' venues that promoted the cause of the new art such as the philanthropic fancy-dress balls organized by the Union des Artistes Russes. Here Lozowick met the "plus grands génies du monde"[15] such as Albert Gleizes, Natali'a Goncharova, Juan Gris, Mikhail Larionov, Fernand Léger, Pablo Picasso, and Il'ia Zdanevich—one of Lozowick's linguistic heroes, who declaimed his glossologic poetry while the jazzman Parnakh clambered over tables and chairs to dance his versions of the foxtrot and the shimmy.

Andrei Belyi's *Glossololiia,* the first Russian treatise on the subject, was published in Berlin in 1922. Lozowick bought a copy when he visited Berlin that year and, as he implies in his memoirs, the appearance of this "poem about sound" was appropriate and opportune, for Berlin was a mercurial and fluid society that communicated simultaneously in German, Russian, Hungarian, and Yiddish. To Lozowick the hybrid Germany even resembled Kafka's *Metamorphosis,* and perhaps because of its flux and diversity it attracted so many Russian émigrés after the October Revolution—more than half a million permanent and temporary émigrés. One result of this invasion was a remarkable constellation of Russian literary, theatrical, and artistic enterprises that played an effective, if ephemeral, role in the evolution of the "other" Russian culture. Natan Al'tman, Marc Chagall, Aleksandra Exter, Wassily Kandinsky, El Lissitzky, and Ivan Puni—not to mention their numerous literary colleagues such as Belyi and Viktor Shklovskii were among the Russians whom Lozowick met in Berlin in the early 1920s. The Russian artists and writers, including Lozowick, frequented particular parts of Berlin such as the Romanische Café, the Café Nollendorfplatz, and especially the Haus der Künste at the Café Léon—which welcomed the most diverse intellectual and aesthetic spirits, from Serge Charchoune to Roman Jakobson, from Vladimir Mayakovsky to Sergei Esenin. One critic observed of Berlin in 1922 that

> If you follow the fate of Russian art abroad, you will be amazed that, in spite of the difficult spiritual and material condition of the emigration, our art is not only not dying, but is gradually winning the ever greater attention of Western European artistic circles.[16]

The efforts of the Russian émigrés led to the establishment of cabarets such as Der Blaue Vogel, of art magazines such as the Constructivist review *Veshch'/Gegenstand/Objet,* and of important exhibitions such as "Die Erste Russische Kunstausstellung." The "Erste Russische Kunstausstellung" at the Galerie Van Diemen in Berlin in 1922 served as an instrument not only for the physical transmission of art works from Soviet Russia to the West but also of people. Although the exhibition was presented as a panorama of new art from Revolutionary Russia, it was accompanied by numerous satellites in the form of curators and consultants, including Al'tman, Naum Gabo, Lissitzky, and David Shterenberg—not all of whom returned home. The Russian cafés, theatres, and cabarets such as Der Blaue Vogel and the Russische Romantische Theater, of which Lozowick was an avid visitor, also played an important role in the emigration, offering a livelihood to many Russian artists, musicians, and actors in those difficult times. Der Blaue Vogel, for example, attracted a number of experimental artists, including Puni and the young Pavel Tchelitchew, whom Lozowick later remembered for his Surrealist *Hide and Seek* at the Museum of Modern Art, New York. The theatrical dimension of Russian Berlin should be underlined, because to artists such as Puni and Tchelitchew Berlin was not only the first station in their journey westward, where they recaptured something of the cultural vitality to which they had been accustomed in St. Petersburg, Moscow, and Kiev, but also a key moment in their artistic development. The sociopolitical reality of Berlin compelled Russian painters to explore new media and métiers, including book illustration, *haute couture,* stage design—and also the movie industry, where Boris Bilinskii and Ivan Loshakov achieved resounding success.

The social and political fabric of the new Moscow, which Lozowick first visited in 1922 was, of course, very different from Paris and Berlin, although certainly not as homogenous and as cohesive as some histories would have us believe. In any case, Lozowick was fortunate to visit the young republic during that time of enthusiasm and expectation and, clearly, with his Socialist commitment, Lozowick felt an immediate sympathy with its "preoccupied restlessness . . . and general excitement."[17] By his very nature, Lozowick was interested in people of radical persuasion, even if they were "against art,"[18] but it would be misleading to assume that all radical painters and poets supported the Marxist idea or that all advocates of Marxism were at one with the cultural avant-garde. If some recognized a direct link between radical art and radical politics, others merely acquiesced to the new political structure, and still others contended that Suprematism, for example, was the remnant of an individualistic, bourgeois consciousness. In xxvi

Prologue

other words, the cultural milieu in which Lozowick found himself in Moscow was neither wholly "left" nor wholly "right," but rather was a plurality of theories and practices represented by the most diverse individuals, from Liubov' Popova to Evgenii Katsman; and the most remarkable aesthetic resolutions could be seen—from Vladimir Tatlin's model for the Monument to the III International to Konstantin Yuon's serene landscapes. In fact, the persistence of traditional styles during the Revolutionary period contributed a great deal to the retrenchment and triumph of Realism in the late 1920s and 1930s, a *volte face* that Lozowick himself witnessed.

In any case, by 1922 Moscow was the cultural axis of the new Russia, symbolized by the activities there sponsored by Anatolii Lunacharskii's Ministry of Enlightenment (Narkompros). With its many sections, including the Department of Visual Arts (IZO) directed by Shterenberg, the Ministry supervised exhibitions, art education, commissions, and research. With Malevich, Aleksandr Rodchenko, and Tatlin among its members, IZO Narkompros did much to promote the cause of the avant-garde artists by appointing them as teachers at SVOMAS/VKhUTEMAS (Lozowick described his visit in detail), allocating their works for museum collections, and sponsoring think tanks such as the Institute of Artistic Culture and the State Academy of Artistic Sciences. Thanks to this liberal environment, Rodchenko and his colleagues could announce the death of painting and the birth of Constructivism on the one hand[19] while the champions of Heroic Realism, the members of AKhRR (Association of Artists of Revolutionary Russia), could reject this as mere "abstract concoction" on the other.[20]

Lozowick's first trip to Moscow left a profound impression on his cultural and ideological world view and, for example, left a discernible influence on his urban prints and inspired several lectures and essays on the new Russian art—culminating in his articles for *Broom* and his monograph *Modern Russian Art* of 1925. Visually, the exposure to the economy and order of Constructivist design identifiable with Lissitzky's typography, Vsevolod Meyerhold's bio-mechanics, and Tatlin's "engineering" informed Lozowick's own artistic explorations. The axonometric cover for his *Modern Russian Art,* for example, indicates a simultaneous debt to Lissitzky's *Prouns,* Rodchenko's linear compositions, and Popova's minimal scenographies. Lozowick himself was quick to admit the impact of the Soviet avant-garde on his own creativity: He admitted that his designs for the 1926 New York version of Georg Kaiser's *Gas* were influenced by Meyerhold's Constructivist productions of *The Magnanimous Cuckold* and *Death of Tarelkin,* and after seeing the experimental productions of *The Sorceress* and *At Night in the Old Market* at the State Jewish Theater, for example, Lozowick recalled their "profound effect. . . . no other plays affected me as powerfully."[21]

Like Alfred Barr, Jr., Fritz Karpfen, and René Fülöp-Miller, Lozowick played a major role in the promotion of early Soviet culture in the West in general and of Suprematism and Contructivism in particular. (Malevich and Rodchenko are well represented in his *Modern Russian Art.)* More than his colleagues, Lozowick also concerned himself with the theories of the avant-garde, acquiring magazines such as *Iskusstvo kommuny* [Art of the commune], radical treatises of Boris Arvatov, Aleksei Gan, Nikolai Punin, and Nikolai Tarabukin, exhibition catalogues, photographs of artists and works, and various publications by or on Exter, Lissitzky, Malevich, Rodchenko, and Tatlin. True, by the time Lozowick returned to Moscow in 1927, Constructivism had lost its impetus and the new Realism was receiving increasing support and popularity, but he still sought—and found—artistic styles and ideas that were original and potential and chief among these was the Society of Studio Artists (OST). Supported by Shterenberg, Lozowick's friend from the Berlin days, Aleksandr Deineka, Yurii Pimenov, and Aleksandr Tyshler, OST depicted the "revolutionary contemporaneity"[22] of industrial progress, sports, and aviation in a dynamic and incisive style that often paid homage to German Expressionism, especially the work of Otto Dix and George Grosz.

Symptomatic of the high regard in which Soviet artists held Lozowick was his invitation to lecture at the State Academy of Artistic Sciences (GAKhN) on December 6, 1927, on

"Contemporary American Painting"; a version of the lecture was published in Moscow the following year.[23] In January 1928 Lozowick, this "active participant in the leftist artistic groups of America,"[24] was honored with a one-man exhibition of his graphic work at the Museum of New Western Art (now the Pushkin Museum of Fine Arts), for which a catalogue was compiled and published. Joseph Freeman, with whom Lozowick collaborated on the book *Voices of October* two years later, published an enthusiastic review of the Lozowick exhibition.[25]

We should not forget that Lozowick was a voice of October, that he regarded art and literature as key weapons in the fight for universal justice, and that the struggle for democracy was of great importance to him (even if "nowadays such sentiments seem almost trite").[26] Obviously, Lozowick saw nothing reprehensible in redirecting his artistic energy from abstract or precisionist compositions to didactic commentaries on urban oppression or the social elite, and he felt a genuine solidarity with those French, German, Hungarian, Italian, Russian, and American artists who adapted their art to the sobriety of Realism and summoned the masses to action. As a founding member of the John Reed Club—and a victim of the chastisement that such an association provoked—Lozowick continued to contribute to Soviet exhibitions that, if not by designation, then certainly by inference, were anti-Capitalist and pro-Communist. Among them were the "Anti-Imperialist Exhibition" in Gorky Park, Moscow, in 1931,[27] "American Artists of the John Reed Club" at the Museum of New Western Art in 1932,[28] "Revolutionary Art in the Countries of Capitalism" at the Museum of New Western Art in 1932–1933, and "Revolutionary Graphics in the Countries of Capital" at the Central Museum of Tatarstan, Kazan, in 1934.

A citizen of many countries and a committed Socialist, Lozowick stood for the cause of international revolution. But in many respects, the real stimulus to Lozowick's universality lay in the weight of his birthright, his Jewish ethnicity, because, to a considerable extent, Lozowick's aspiration toward the ideals of equality and fraternity was conditioned by, or ran parallel to, his physical transference from the confines of the *shtetl* to the larger worlds of Guermanovka, Vasil'kov, Kiev, New York, Paris, Berlin, and Moscow. It was a centrifugal itinerary shared by many Jewish artists and writers and one that affected much of their intellectual and spiritual expression. As at any moment when traditional mores are undermined by demographic shift, modernization and ready exposure to other world views, Russian Jewry at the end of the nineteenth century—when Lozowick was growing up—was confronted suddenly with choice and plurality. The rituals that the Jewish community had conducted for centuries (which Lozowick describes in the early sections of his memoirs) could not always resist secular innovations in science, philosophy, and everyday comportment. Even the patriotic anthropologist An-ski (pseudonym of Semeon Rapoport), who was collecting and cataloging Jewish folklore and artifacts just as Lozowick was shedding the last vestiges of his patriarchal education in the anonymity of New York, acknowledged this development, noting that Jewish society (in Russia and Ukraine) was transferring its "ideological" loyalty from the rabbi to the doctor, the professor, and the writer.[29] Lozowick himself observed that the new generation of assimilated, Russified Jews strove consciously to avoid association with the nation that they had left, even rejecting Yiddish because it was felt to be the "language of kitchen maids."[30] In 1916 the prominent lawyer Maxim Vinaver, member of the State Duma and patron of Chagall, contended that the central place of the synagogue in Jewish life already had been usurped by other institutions—social and cultural clubs, ethnographical museums, art galleries, and literary circles.

The young Lozowick was affected by this sudden displacement in traditional Jewish values, and the very fact that his father allowed him to train as an artist (i.e., to challenge the convention forbidding Jews to make graven images) and to leave home for the Kiev Art Institute indicates that even devout families recognized the force of circumstances and the inevitability of change. In this respect, Lozowick embarked on a journey that many other aspiring Jewish artists also pursued—from the Pale of Settlement to a provincial center

(Vasil'kov) to a regional capital (Kiev) and then to metropolises such as St. Petersburg, Moscow, Paris, and New York. As Lozowick makes clear in his memoirs, Kiev represented his real introduction to the modern urban world, and his tenure at the Art Institute coincided with his coming of age—physically, socially, and politically. The Institute was one of the few state institutions that did not follow the Jewish quota system, and in the early twentieth century it was one of the most "Jewish" art schools in the Russian Empire. During the 1900s and 1910s Abraham Manevich, Isaak Rabinovich, Issachar Ryback, Nison Shifrin, and Tyshler were all students there. Of course, its aesthetic predilections—for the Realism of Nikolai Pimonenko and the "god" Il'ia Repin[31]—were not especially advanced, but thanks to enlightened friends and relatives Lozowick discovered the Decadent painting of Arnold Böcklin and Edward Burne-Jones and the Neo-Byzantine ornaments of Viktor Vasnetsov and Mikhal Vrubel'. Kiev also impressed Lozowick by the wealth of its artistic repositories such as St. Vladimir's Cathedral, the Museum of Art and Antiquities, the Khanenko collection, and so on.

Of course, Lozowick recognized the strength of the Jewish faith, even though his confrontation with the external world soon undermined his blind allegiance to Jewish custom (much to his father's regret). Even so, choosing between an indigenous belief and a universal ideal formed a difficult dilemma, and even in Expressionist Berlin and Constructivist Moscow, Lozowick returned to the ethnic question. He admired Lissitzky's move from Jewish folklore (e.g., his designs for the *Legend of Prague)* to the neutrality of the *Prouns,* and yet he also admired Chagall for his unswerving homage to Jewish ethnic content. Even as an established artist in New York Lozowick maintained the debate, publishing an essay, "What, Then, Is Jewish Art?," as late as 1947.[32] In his rigor of composition, severity of form, and economy of means, Lozowick maintained the Constructivist tradition and, obviously, he sympathized more with Lissitzky than with Chagall. He might even have gone so far as to support the extreme theory elaborated by Boris Aronson and Ryback in 1919 according to which

> The composition of a painting is more important than its idea
> and the richness of color means more than the realistic render-
> ing of objects. . . . Pure abstract form is precisely that which
> embodies the national element. . . . Only via the principle of
> abstract painting, free of any literariness, can the expression of
> ones own national foundation be attained.[33]

Lozowick remembered that Ryback even painted a Cubist
picture, "using Hebrew lettering instead of the French to
prove that the national character of the artist will come to the
surface even in an abstraction."[34]

Lozowick recalled of his boyhood that "to a product of
the *shtetl,* Manhattan was a phenomenon as fantastic and improbable as Istanbul might have been,"[35] and his memoirs describe the long and arduous journey from Ludvinovka to
New York. Ultimately, however, national or ethnic alliance
was of secondary importance to Lozowick, for his home was
both the *shtetl* and the metropolis and anywhere in between.
For Lozowick art, too, was a medium of therapy and tran-
scension that existed beyond material privilege and racial am-
bition, and he spent his artistic talent and intellectual energy
in search of that higher state. But today, in a global village that
derives increasing profit from parochial strife, the pathos of
Lozowick's memoirs is ever more acute and, sad to say, their
distance ever greater.

John E. Bowlt
Director, Institute of Modern Russian Culture
University of Southern California

INTRODUCTION

In his memoirs entitled *Survivor from a Dead Age* and in his interviews, Louis Lozowick documents and comments on many important aspects of early twentieth-century developments in the visual arts and theatre, as well as the social and political arenas in which they occurred. He describes his life as a Jewish boy growing up in the *shtetlach* (Jewish villages) of Ukraine, his formal schooling at the heder, yeshiva, and Kiev Art School, as well as his equally important informal education in Paris, Berlin, and Moscow in the early 1920s. Fact, observation, and personal development are interwoven in this rich collection of reminiscences. Students and scholars of Russian and Jewish history as well as art history will find Lozowick's firsthand accounts and thoughtful commentary of immense value in understanding the early twentieth century in Russia and Europe.

Two areas of his life emerge as the most significant in Lozowick's development as a person and an artist: his Jewish heritage (Chapters 1 through 8) and his education in the heady capitals of Paris, Berlin, and Moscow during the early 1920s (Chapters 9 through 11). Because Jews in Russia were confined to the Pale of Settlement (the area in which Jews were permitted to live), denied admission to certain professions (with art being an exception), and limited in their educational opportunities, it is understandable that Lozowick viewed himself as a Jew, not as a Russian. While he was interested in the political and artistic events occurring in Russia throughout his life, he never identified with Russia as a homeland. It was America, with its freedom of movement and its wealth of opportunities, that became his home.

One reads with great fascination Lozowick's vivid memories of his childhood in the *shtetlach* of Ludvinovka, Guermanovka, and Vasil'kov: his family life; his religious education in the heder and yeshiva; his demeanor as a yeshiva student with earlocks *(peyos)*, yarmulke, and tallith katan; his father's wish that he become a rabbi; his family's observance of the Sabbath; his favorite religious holidays—*Hamisha Asar B'Shevat, Lag B'Omer,* and Purim—with their gastronomic delights; and home remedies concocted for common ailments. In all these accounts, Lozowick warmly conveys love of both Jewish tradition and of family.

Lozowick's memoirs reveal him to be acutely aware of his physical and social surroundings. He describes in great detail the geographic layout of Ludvinovka and his family's house, in which the immense fireplace was the literal center of the two-family dwelling and the site of boyhood games. In his descriptions of the physical setting of the *shtetl* there is also a social dimension. Even as a boy, he was conscious of the contrast between the crowded and impoverished conditions of the Jewish peasants and the gracious homes of the Jewish middle-class *(kulaki)* and the even more marked contrast of the peasants with the landlord Kozar's estate, which was protected by guard dogs and watchmen. He observed similar class distinctions in Kiev where his older brother, a socialist, pointed out the differences between the peasants' outdoor market *(tolchok)* and the fine department stores on Kreshchatik Street. Although the activities of his brother and his socialist friends made Lozowick aware of political radicalism at a young age, it was his own observations of the ruthlessness and capriciousness of Kozar, the raids *(oblavy)* on Jews in Kiev, and the Revolution of 1905 that profoundly affected him, sensitizing him to the social ills that he saw plaguing Germany during the years of the Weimar Republic as well as to the struggles of workers and artists in America during the years of the Depression.

Because the restrictions placed on Jews in Russia included limitations of education and travel, it is understandable that

Lozowick was excited by the diverse people and modernist styles he encountered during his trip abroad in the early 1920s. As an artist, he naturally was interested in the modernist movements of Cubism, Expressionism, and Constructivism. What is not obvious is the basis of his attraction to the Dadaists' phonetic poetry and the Russians' transrational *(zaum)* poetry. It appears that Lozowick was fascinated by the Dadaists' nonsensical forms of expressions, perhaps because of their similarity with the jingles of his childhood and, probably more relevant, with the mystical aspects of Talmudic studies that he had found so ineffable as a yeshiva student. He repeatedly alludes to the potential spiritual dimension of phonetic poetry, which he associates with the Biblical "speaking with many tongues" or glossolalia. It seems fair to say that Lozowick found a religious cord in this modernist poetry.

An additional dimension to the appreciation of these recollections is our knowledge of Lozowick the artist—painter, draftsman, and lithographer. Inevitably one seeks to find in these accounts the sources of Lozowick's preference for the black-and-white medium of lithography, his modernist vocabulary of the 1920s, his preoccupation with the theme of industrialization, and his ideas concerning the social responsibility of art. A modest man, Lozowick speaks only briefly and intermittently of his own development as an artist; nevertheless, his memoirs reveal many of the sources of his mature work.

Lozowick's earliest recollections of artistic activity is that of drawing (not painting). Although he describes the pencil he used as a boy as having red lead at one end and blue at the other, he never mentions these colors as important to his sketches. Although his later paintings, especially the American "Cities," obviously use color—at times the strongly contrasting hues of German Expressionists—it is the precisely delineated geometric shapes and underlying ordering of his compositions that dominate his work. Like Honoré Daumier whom he admired, Lozowick was essentially a draftsman, and like Daumier, his preferred medium was lithography.

Lozowick's description of the systematic progression of education at the Kiev Art School is revealing in understanding the sources of his own technique. As he outlines in Chapter 6, instruction progressed from a mastery of geometric shapes, which were drawn in outline and shaded, to the ornament class, in which photographic exactitude was stressed. Close observation and exact rendering were further perfected in the mask, head, and figure classes. In the life class, the highest and last course, students applied these skills by first blocking in the main areas of the model, then outlining the shapes, and finally shading them in. The emphases on contours and large masses that dominated the curriculum of the Kiev Art Institute remained integral to Lozowick's formal style, as evidenced by the geometric shapes and precise contours of the City compositions (see Figure 5) and his later synthesis of realist detail and semiabstract geometric organizational elements (see Figure 26). His early training in the rendering of lighting effects undoubtedly provided the groundwork for his later interest in textural effects (see Figure 25).

Lozowick's concept of machine ornamentation and his series of "Machine Ornaments" (see Figure 8) clearly have their genesis in the exercises undertaken in the ornament class, where he learned to render precisely decorative elements from various historical periods. His subsequent application of his Machine Ornaments, which he considered to be the prototypes of contemporary applied decoration, to book covers, stage sets, and poster designs (see Figures 14, 16, 17, 18, 19) reflected the ideas of Russian Constructivists, such as Aleksei Gan and El Lissitzky, who were exploring ways in which fine art could be integrated into industrial production. It is noteworthy that Lozowick's ventures in the area of applied design were among his most innovative contributions to America's machine aesthetic.

Although the objective and rational system of art education at the Kiev Art School appears to be in marked contrast to his Talmudic studies, it is important to note that order and discipline underlay both. It is this fundamental rationalism that is the key to Lozowick's precisionistic style of geometric order and linear exactitude. The machine-like quality of Lozowick's technique is matched by his characterization of

America as a terrain of cities, factories, and machines—
images that derived from the cross-country bus trip he took
after his discharge from the U.S. Army in 1919. This trip
brought Lozowick in direct contact with his new homeland
and was crucial to his formation of the concept of the Americanization of art. His subsequent insistence on being placed
in the American sections of international exhibitions further
testifies to his strong identification with his adopted country.

It is also relevant to note that at the time that Lozowick
was an art student in Kiev, the Wanderers *(Peredvizhniki)* were
the popular school of painting. Their belief that artists have a
social responsibility to make their work relevant to common
people certainly would have been recalled by Lozowick when
he, like other artists in America, addressed the issue of the social responsibility of the artist during the years of the Depression. His involvement with the activist organizations of the
New Masses, the John Reed Club, and American Artists'
Congress reflect his continuing sensitivity to social inequities
that he first witnessed in Ludvinovka. Further, the Wanderers' commitment to social content art provided a context for
Lozowick's later receptivity to the call for proletarian and revolutionary art during the 1930s. In his writings on art, from
what he labeled his first "Tentative Attitudes" in 1917 to his
formal, final "Credo" of 1947, Lozowick consistently defined
art through its ability to relate humanity to the environment,
whether that environment be physical geography or social
condition. In his art Lozowick recorded his changing percep-
tion of America's landscape—from the impersonal structures
of skyscrapers, smokestacks, and machines of the early and
mid 1920s (see Figure 5) to the particularized and individual-
ized city streets and construction sites of the late 1920s (see
Figures 4 and 21), and to the strikes, demonstrations, bread
lines, and Hoovervilles of the 1930s (see Figure 25).

Lozowick's evolution from Jewish boy of Ukraine to New
York artist of international repute is remarkable. As he depicts
in his drawing *Autobiographic* (see page vi), Lozowick's life
and his art are rooted in his Jewish upbringing in the *shtetlach*
of Ukraine, cultivated by his contacts with European and

Russian avant-garde poetry and art of the 1920s, and conditioned by his sensitivity to the human condition and his sense of social responsibility. His memoirs and interviews provide insights into the complexity of this important figure in American art of this century.

PART ONE

CHILDHOOD AND LIFE IN RUSSIA, 1892–1906

Fig. 3 Lozowick and his father, ca. 1904–1906.

1

MY "TURKISH" ANCESTRY

Some years ago I visited Istanbul. The city was a visual delight. The magnificent view from the Galatea Bridge across the Golden Horn, scattered minarets soaring into the sky. Walking around and inside the Blue Mosque, its exquisite workmanship; veiled in a hushed twilight, a lone worshiper prayed in a corner. St. Sophia—arches upon arches, one above the other, one inside the other, rising to the dome. Climbing up and down the steep and narrow streets and alleys descending to the sea. Altogether a unique city.

Sauntering in the covered market amidst the pungent smells of various "Turkish delights," blinded by the glitter of jewelry, precious stones, hammered copper vessels, and an endless assortment of other products tempting you with unheard of bargains, I was struck by an improbable thought: What kind of person would I be if I had been born in Turkey? I would speak Turkish, of course, French perhaps, but certainly no Yiddish. If my father were as pious in Turkey as I knew him to be in Russia, he would try to prepare me for the rabbinate. More likely, I would have turned out to be a clerk in this very market. Fantastic? Not as far fetched as it sounds. To explain, I must make a detour of a little more than a century and tell the tale as related to me by several people.

My father was born in the early fifties of the last century, in the time of the Tsar Nicholas I (*y'makh shmo*—May his name be obliterated, as a pious Jew always adds when the name of a fanatical Jew-baiter is mentioned). Nicholas I is remembered by the Jews (and non-Jews as well) for the dreaded

Draft Law of 1827–1855. Briefly, the Law decreed that Jewish boys must serve in the army twenty-five years, beginning at the age of eighteen. However, to give them preliminary training, they were usually drafted at the age of twelve and placed in cantons. Hence, the name "cantonists." In actual practice, the age of twelve was purely theoretical. Children of ten, eight, or even younger were inducted or, more exactly, forced into the service so as to mold them from a tender age to unquestioned obedience and loyalty and, in the process, terrorize them into conversion to Greek Orthodoxy.

■

The noted Russian graphic artist Ivan Nikolaevich Pavlov, a name that could hardly be more typically Russian, says on the first page of his autobiography: "My father was a 'cantonist.' At the age of six he was picked up in the streets of Saratov and converted to Christianity. He was given the name Nikolai Pavlovich in honor of Tsar Nicholas himself." And his last name, Pavlov, was in honor of Nicholas' father.[1]

The picturesque and rebellious Russian sculptor [Ernst] Neizvestnyi is also a descendant from cantonists, and his name (Neizvestnyi—the unknown) tempts one to speculate on its origin—probably a joke perpetrated on a defenseless child by his baptismal godfathers.

■

The boys were farmed out to village estates and workshops, hundreds, sometime thousands, of miles away from home. "The children suffered dreadful tortures from their drunk soldier 'Uncles,' and the brutish employers treated the tots like animals" (G[rigorii] Bogrov, *Memoirs of a Jew).*

Is it any wonder that the Jews looked forward to the conscription of their children with the blackest foreboding and horror? Each Jewish community had to furnish a certain number of recruits yearly, and the decisions were always made by its most respected members—i.e., the pious, the wealthy, and their toadies. The recruits were, therefore, practically always from among the most indigent. The more wealthy could buy themselves exemptions by paying higher taxes, acquiring titles of Guild Merchants (for high fees), or hiring others to serve in their stead. The poor tried everything possible and impossible to cheat their fate. They went into hiding, wandered from place to place, and worse. "Mothers made cripples of their children to make them incapable of serving in the army" (Bogrov).

All these attempts at evasion developed a whole class of spies and kidnappers, "recruit catchers," who carried on a regular traffic in souls. During the recruiting season the hunt was on at crossroads, near schools, and in forests. The recruit catchers would even break into private homes in the middle of the night to snatch children from bed. The boys thus rounded up were herded, taken to some other town to be offered for sale to the highest bidder as army substitutes— sometimes even to the parents for a ransom, only perhaps to be kidnapped again later.

A wide literature on the subject exists in Russian and in Jewish.[2] The great Russian liberal Aleksandr Herzen in *Byloe i dumy [My Past and Thoughts]* describes a chance meeting with a group of young recruits:

> They lined them up front. It was one of the most horrible sights I have ever seen. Poor, poor children; boys of twelve or thirteen managed somehow to hold their bearings, but infants of eight and ten . . . no brush in existence could paint this misery on canvas . . . pale, harried, terrified, they stood dressed in heavy, unwieldy soldiers' uniforms . . . white lips, blue circles under their eyes, indicating fever or chills. . . .

Novels and legends were created around this subject. Here is a folk poem, one among many others:

> Little tots are kidnapped from their heder
> They are fitted out in soldiers' uniforms
> Yankel, the rich man, has seven sons

> Not one of them goes into the army
>
> But widow Leah's only child
>
> Is sacrificed for the community's sins.

They even, as is the custom with Jews, occasionally found humor in the situation (humor through tears):

> A man rushes breathlessly into his house and without a word to anyone crawls under the bed and pulls down the blanket.
>
> "All my nightmares on your head. Are you out of your mind? What are you doing?" asks his wife, puzzled and alarmed.
>
> "The 'catchers' are in town," whispers the husband from his hiding place.
>
> "But they are after the children, not you, schlemiel."
>
> "I thought they might be looking for a general."

One could still meet the cantonists, or *Nikolaevskie soldaty* [the soldiers of Tsar Nicholas (Pavlovich) I], as they were more commonly known in the first quarter of this century. Their Yiddish speech had a Russian accent and they frequently introduced Russian words. They seemed to have a certain inward look, as if contemplating the long road they had traveled.

Witnessing this scourge of God visited on so many families, my grandmother was frantic and racked her brain for some way, any way, of saving her son. She was finally given advice that was fantastic but foolproof. The advice was to become a Turkish subject. By distributing graft generously she somehow got to the Turkish consular authorities and obtained a Turkish passport. How she accomplished this feat I do not know. The passport may have been a forgery. In any case, she now had a new name and a "document" to keep the recruit catchers away.

Alas, all her efforts and aggravation proved to be a waste of time. Soon thereafter the dread law was abolished, Nicholas I died, and some years later a new law of universal conscription of four years service was promulgated. Grandmother did nothing to regain her old status.

Everything seemed to flow in an accustomed groove when disaster struck. Father had recently married and was about to settle down to an independent existence when the Russo–Turkish War of 1877–1878 broke out. An order was issued for the exchange of nationals of military age between the two countries. Grandmother and the entire family were desperate. The cure proved worse than the disease. It would have been sheer madness to send father to Turkey. He had never been there and did not know a word of Turkish. For some time he went into hiding, moving from place to place and suffering privation.

Finally the strain became unbearable. Father was a married man and the state of unsettled existence prevented him from making a decent living. A family council decided that it was best [that he] give himself up and risk the consequences. Father reported to the authorities and made a clean breast of it. He was placed under arrest and, after some time, [was put] on trial. Lawyers, graft, and appeals stripped the family of its last kopecks and put it in debt. The trial, postponed, renewed, dragged on, was transferred from a lower court to a higher, and finally reached Kiev.

At that time, [Lev] Kupernik, a converted Jew (the Jews were permitted to practice law within very restricted limits) though still young, was already gaining recognition as a brilliant barrister. Later he became one of the most celebrated jurists of Russia. He defended the victims of the Kishinev pogrom,[3] as well as other people who could not afford his fees. His death in 1905 was the occasion for a great antigovernment demonstration on the eve of the revolutionary events. This was, of course, much later. At the moment, grandmother was at the end of her means. She succeeded, however, in gaining an audience with Kupernik and got him interested in the case. After much manipulating and wirepulling, the case came up for trial. Kupernik made an eloquent plea for father, pointing to the anxiety of grandmother, the devotion of the young wife (this form of pleading reminds me somehow of Clarence Darrow), the severity of the now dead law, and ended with a fervent appeal for clemency. Clemency was granted in the form a two-year prison sentence, which was considered indeed merciful. Father won back his Russian citizenship and the disabilities that went with it, but the nickname "Turk" stuck with him to the end of his life. I suspect that the lightness of the sentence was due probably to the fact that the "document" was not a document, but a fake perpetrated on grandmother by an unscrupulous swindler.

In any case, father finally settled in the village of Ludvinovka for a long, hand-to-mouth existence. As is the custom among pious Jews, a succession of children began to arrive at regular intervals: three sons and three daughters, two years apart. Then eight lean years and I arrived, the last, the youngest, and the favorite child. Naturally father envisioned a bright future for me. He saw a happy augury in the fact that my name and patronymic, Lev Abramovich, were the same as those of Kupernik.

Ultimately my fate was to land on the banks of the Hudson rather than in the Bay of the Bosporus. To a product of the *shtetl,* Manhattan was a phenomenon as fantastic and improbable as Istanbul might have been.

2
HEDER, ELEMENTARY HEBREW SCHOOL

"Repeat after me: *Beréishis,* In the beginning, *boró,* created, *Elohím,* God, *es hashomáyim,* the heaven, *ve'es hoóretz,* and the earth."

Thus, the melamed started me on my first sentence in Genesis. Slowly he read each word in the "holy tongue" (Hebrew), then translated it into Yiddish. I dutifully followed him. To make sure my mind was on the lesson, he held my ear by two fingers, signifying by slight pressure whether I came along at a satisfactory pace. Whenever I was slow or hesitant, the pressure would increase. After we got through about half a page, I went to my seat where I did my best to memorize, by constant repetition, what I had just learned, while he took up another boy.

On his first lesson the child got off easy. When, however, he came back to be examined on his progress, he usually fared less well. The melamed still held him by the ear; but if he stammered or was not fast enough to give the right translation, his ear knew it immediately—it was pulled and twisted till the boy was ready to cry out in pain. Next he got a slap on the cheek, impartially left and right. Sometimes, at the end of a strenuous day, or when the melamed was particularly disgruntled, a pupil's face would be all aflame. For a change or variation the melamed would also pinch. And all this was accompanied by a string of epithets like "donkey," "snot-nose," "ignoramus," "lazy bones," and "peasant." When you really aroused his ire, he made you take off your pants, lie down flat on your belly in front of the class, and get a good whipping on your bare behind with a cat-o'-nine-tails, *kantshik* (the popular expression among the boys for *kantshik* was "pleated noodles," *geflokhne lokshn)*. The melamed was never worried about any complaints the boys might make at their homes. It was universally accepted that sparing the rod inevitably spoiled the child. In fact, if the child proved too difficult or obdurate, the parents supplemented the work of the melamed by using the rod at home.

To be sure there were a few—a very few—townspeople who no longer believed in this medieval method of learning by rote with the help of the *kantshik*. They were the few who subscribed to a newspaper, generally from Kiev, and so were informed about events in the state, the country, and even abroad and were, in turn, a source of information to the rest of the townsmen. They were the "enlightened" who believed in giving their children—even the girls—a general, as well as a Jewish, education. And they did not send their children to the kind of a heder in which I was enrolled. There were private teachers who could give instruction in Hebrew, Yiddish, and in other languages, as well as in mathematics, geography, etc. Of course, only the better-to-do could afford to engage them.

My father was certainly not among them. He believed that what was good for his parents and grandparents must be good for his children and grandchildren. But he had no intellectual authority or material means to compel obedience, and his children had left him one by one. What a tragedy this was for him. I was his last hope.

■

Incidentally, the first word of Genesis in its Hebrew form impinged on my attention quite suddenly in an unpredictable manner, in unexpected circumstances, a quarter of a century after I had first crammed it under the accompaniment of face-slapping. [When] I was in Berlin after the First World War, I bought a book entitled *Glossololiia, poema o zvuke* [Glossolalia, a poem about sound, 1922] by the well-known Russian author Andrei Belyi [pseudonym of Boris Nikolaevich Bugaev] and found it to be a very strange book indeed. It was both a poem in, and a poetic treatise of, sound (vowel and consonant) in its mystic and transcendental meaning. Without going into a lengthy explanation, I can best illustrate the author's approach by his analysis of the word *beréishis* (in the beginning):

> *Beréishis,* here are three letters: *bet, resh, shin. Bet* summoned in the heart of the sages the energy of action protected by a shield, energy of action in a shell . . . in nacreous flames. *Resh* summoned a great host of spirits, creative within the shell and casting speechless glances upon us. *Shin* unveiled torrents of surging forces striving outward. In the sound of *shin* there is challenge. Such is the picture which greeted the Jew with the germ of sound in the germinal book. The sounds in the Bible are a language apart; penetrate its soul and its meaning will be manifest. And the path to the understanding of the Bible will be made clear.

I surely did not study this in the heder!

There were about ten or twelve children (all boys, of course). They studied their lessons in full voice as they rocked back and forth, back and forth. At first I found it hard to concentrate in this perpetual din; after a while I learned to shut out the other voices and stick to my lesson by out-shouting everybody else. In later years I sometimes wondered why it was necessary to study aloud—this was the universal method. One of the reasons probably was the fact that the air in the room was foul, the windows were shut tight, and kitchen odors were wafting in, creating a well-nigh irresistible drowsiness. The melamed himself was sometimes overcome by sleep in spite of a frequent recourse to a pinch of snuff. He was inured to its effect; he no longer even sneezed. As soon as the pupils noticed him dozing off, their diligence slackened perceptibly. A few of them took to playing "buttons," of which their pockets had a great variety of sizes and colors, amid an assortment of glass, metal, and other objects. One of the prized of these objects was a piece of crystal which came from one of the better-to-do houses or from the chandelier at the synagogue. When you looked through one edge of its triangular shape, the world appeared in rainbow colors and you seemed to be walking on air into deep space. With half an eye on the melamed, the pupils spoke in whispers, even though they knew that the ensuing quiet would wake him up. It did and in a moment pandemonium reigned again.

I was no worse off than the other pupils. I got along and took the drill and the punishment in my stride. In one important respect, however, my case differed from the rest. At the end of the day all the other children went to their homes, [but] I had to stay behind because I was both a pupil and a boarder at the melamed's house. My father picked the melamed he could afford, one whose tuition rate was the lowest and whose scholarly qualifications were on the same level. Some of the parents of the wards entrusted to him knew more than the melamed. He was one of the characters all too common in small towns, [one] who could make a living at nothing else. Underpaid and harassed by his wife, he was held in very low esteem by the rest of the population. In colloquial Yiddish anyone not too bright yet priggish is called "melamed."

Such was my preceptor. During the day he imparted to me and the rest of the boys the meaning of the Torah with accompanying slaps and whippings distributed impartially. Although I accepted these punishments and outbursts as inevitable evils, I was hurt more mentally than physically. My father had never laid his hands on me, and somehow I felt, although I couldn't formulate it, a moral affront with each slap. I cringed when I saw that it was coming, not so much for the pain it would inflict—though that was real enough—as for the offense to my dignity.

During the day, I was under the melamed's surveillance. When everybody left, his wife took over. I swept the kitchen, rocked the baby, emptied the slop, and took a chicken to the *shoykhet* for ritual slaughter. I shuddered the first time I saw the *shoykhet* pick up the chicken, bend its neck backward, flick off some down, take the long sharp knife from his mouth, test its edge, then quick as lightning slit the chicken's throat, press a little blood from it, and throw the chicken on the ground where it leaped wildly up and down in all directions (its feet were tied), blood spurting like a fountain in need of repair.

My worst task was going down into the cellar. The cellar was a kind of refrigerating plant where things were kept fresh and cool: milk, borscht, cabbage, sour milk, potatoes, pickles, etc. I had come from the village with a firm and genuine belief in the existence of ghosts everywhere. And there was no likelier place and time for their mischief than [in] the cellar at night. As I came down the rickety ladder with a flickering candle, the spots of light in the impenetrable darkness; the queer, elongated, moving shadows; the scampering of a mouse; the leap of a frog; a gust of wind outside, assumed terrifying significance, threw me into agonies, and made me absolutely certain that I was in the presence of an evil spirit ready to grab me and choke me or, at the very least, break out in the bleating laughter of a goat. I snatched up the things I came for, slipped on the ladder before getting my bearings, clambered panting upward, and came into the light of the room breathless, to everybody's amusement. In my great terror I had forgotten something and had to go through the same agonies again, besides getting a whack for my pains.

Occasionally, though far too rarely, my father came to Guermanovka when he had accumulated enough grain from the peasants, which he brought to town for sale. He took me with him to the steam bath, which he loved and I hated. He would clamber up the steps [to] where the steam was so dense [that I] could not see him and so hot that when I tried to follow him I almost suffocated. He had a bundle of twigs with which he flagellated himself and grunted with pleasure. Then he would come down to take a dip in cold water that smelled of human perspiration and dirt.

I enjoyed much more going with him to the synagogue on Saturday, where I met my fellow pupils without being under the constraint of the *kantshik*. It was so pleasant to run around with the boys, to play pranks without being followed by the baleful eye of the melamed. I liked to listen to the cantor's singing. It is hard for me to know, even now, why I was so pleased to mingle with the congregation. In the intervals between prayers and the reading of the Torah (the services took all morning), somebody would always greet my father as a guest and pinch my cheeks by way of a compliment.

At the end of the service, we went to [the home of] a distant relative where my father stayed over the weekend and had a delicious meal. And what a meal it was! Cooking is not permitted to Jews on Saturdays. The meal is prepared on Friday and left in the oven to keep hot. Everything was so tasty, it melted in one's mouth: chicken noodle soup, chopped liver with onions and chicken fat, roast chicken, and compote of carrots or prunes. I was given a special treat—a gizzard and a little yellow ball, [the latter] a premature chicken egg before the albumen formed on it. And last, the crowning glory of a Sabbath meal, the *kugel* [pudding] made of noodles or potatoes filled with raisins and other goodies. My father would probably not have another meal like it for many months to come.

At the approach of evening, I would run outside to see whether the first three stars were in the sky, a sign that the Sabbath was over and that it was now permitted to light the lamp. *Havdalah,* signaling the conclusion of the Sabbath, is recited. The mistress of the house recites her own prayer in Yiddish—"God of Abraham, of Isaac, and of Jacob, the dear holy Sabbath is departing . . . "—and the work-a-day week was back again.

Sometimes father took me to the cemetery on the outskirts of Guermanovka. Mother lay buried there, and he came to ask her to intercede with the *beth din shel ma'aleh,* the heavenly court, for me, for the other children, and for himself as well as for his affairs, which, as usual, were going none too well. The cemetery fascinated and intrigued me; there were so many odd and strange things and sights. I knew that the dead arose at night to wander, to weep, and to visit relatives. How many stories were being told of calamities that befell the reckless who dared intrude on those nightly vigils of the dead? But in the daytime, with people around you, if you were careful not to wander off by yourself, you were fairly safe. I had no end of admiration for the caretaker who stayed there day and night unafraid. All around people were firmly convinced that their dear departed knew of their presence and heard them. People were bent over graves and were speaking in whispers as if the information they were imparting was confidential. Weeping was heard near fresh graves. Whenever a specially serious request to the dead was to be made, the assistance of the caretaker was solicited. He took you to the grave of a rabbi, a zaddik (there was always one in every cemetery). You put your request in writing which you put on the tombstone together with contributions to charity and to the caretaker.

The graves were crowded, many completely neglected and forgotten; some could not be found without the aid of the watchman. Tombstones leaned in all directions. Here and there stones carried crudely carved symbols: the Mosaic Tablets of the Law; two outspread hands indicating priestly descent; the Lion of Judah; etc. No doubt in this and other cemeteries many an example of true folk art was neglected and lost. Subsequently I tried to draw these images [with] my red and blue pencil [a color at each end], but I did not think I could ever match the skill of the anonymous carvers. Many years later a group of artists and writers traveled through the Jewish Pale copying and recording folk art in word and image. They succeeded in collecting only a small part of the available material.

At early dawn on Monday father left hastily. I was very sorry to see him go. I did not relish the new slappings to come. Then, too, father's departure reminded me of the village, the trees, the grass, the fresh air. Guermanovka, like hundreds of other *shtetlach* [Jewish villages], was a product of ingrown isolationism. Hardly a plot of grass or a well-kept tree—except around the few better-to-do households—the house slop thrown straight into the street, piles of dirt and refuse lying around, scrawny cats climbing over them, and goats eating everything. From time to time a stray pig would wander in from the surrounding peasant households and help with the sanitation of the street. Many of the kids in the street had running noses and scabby heads. After a rain the mud was knee deep and mixed with scattered and smelly garbage. Signs of abject poverty everywhere: broken windows stuffed with rags and roofs in disrepair. To be sure, all those unpleasant features were not of the Jews' own choosing but [were the result] of numberless economic and legal disabilities imposed on them by constantly multiplying Tsarist decrees.

I was too young to know the historic and social conditions. I only knew the contrast which could be discovered with a little effort, even in the *shtetl*. If you walked from the center of the Jewish section in any direction, you came upon the peasant settlements, which surrounded it almost like a ring. And there you found greenery everywhere. Of course, the finest gardens and orchards were found around the wealthier peasants' houses. But even the hovels of the poorest peasants had at least some flax or sunflower and perhaps a willow or a cherry tree. But I was afraid to walk there: first, because of the dogs—even if they did not bite you, they barked at you—and second, because of the kids, who, if they did not beat you up, called you names.

Father came to town rarely, but I had a sister [Pessie] who worked in Guermanovka as a seamstress whom I saw more often, though not often enough. She worked long hours and the melamed did not encourage long absences. My sister was a husky, good-looking girl of 13. She was already experienced enough as a seamstress to earn a small salary and she already had a "labor history" behind her. When she was 11 years old, it was decided in family council that she was old enough to begin preparing for a future career. The two older brothers lived in Kiev: one was a tinsmith and the other a bookkeeper. They brought her to Kiev and apprenticed her to a seamstress who undertook, for a certain sum, to teach her the profession. There was not much else they could offer her. Father was himself destitute, always on the verge of starvation; the brothers were just [barely] earning their own livelihood.

There were very few careers open to a girl from a home like ours. Most girls from poor homes hired themselves out as domestics. But the term "domestic" had a bad ring. Work in general was not looked upon with any respect in the *shtetl*. As for the labor of a domestic—that was held in utter contempt not only by the rich but even by the indigent. It was just one rung above beggary. The assimilated, Russified, wealthy Jews, who strove hard to keep up with the Russian Joneses, could say nothing more opprobrious about Yiddish than that it was the language of the kitchen maids.

And so my sister was apprenticed to a seamstress. The agreement was that my sister would stay for three years with the seamstress, by the end of which she should presumably have learned the profession. For this service, including room and board, the seamstress was to be paid 60 rubles. Before the expiration of six months my sister was forced to leave. She had been kept busy but not with learning to sew.

The workshop and residence were on the fifth floor in one of the poorer districts of Kiev. She was busy practically all the time doing household chores. In the kitchen she peeled potatoes, rolled dough, swept the rooms, helped to prepare lunch for the other girls, served at table, and washed the dishes. She ran out for groceries, needles, threads, and buttons. There was no elevator, so she had to run up and down the five flights of stairs two, three, five, eight times a day. She wore out three pair of shoes during her stay there.

And there wasn't much rest at night either. She slept on an old creaky sofa. As soon as she lay down, the battle began: An invisible army of bed bugs went at her in full battalion strength. All resistance was futile. The more she killed, the faster they seemed to come. The odor of their cadavers was nauseating and overwhelming. Fatigue of the day won out and she at last fell into a fitful sleep. Before long, however, she was awakened once more and the battle resumed.

She gave up and sought relief in the kitchen. She cleared the kitchen table, lay down on it, and tried to sleep. Alas she was no more successful in the kitchen than in the living room. There were other enemies here—cockroaches, which were tolerable (at least they did not bite), and rats. The rats were hurrying and scurrying on the floors, on the shelves; and in their desperate search for food, they also ran across the table. Thus between the table and the sofa, there was little rest. Finally, after six months of sleepless nights and physical exhaustion, she gave up.

My brother took her away and sent her nearer to home, to Guermanovka, which was several versts from our village of Ludvinovka. There she was again apprenticed to a tailor, a man this time, for a year, with a definite stipulation that he would teach her the trade. She learned rapidly so that the following year she could already earn a little.

The new place was an improvement, although far from ideal. She stayed at the tailor's house, but at least she worked at the trade and was making fast progress. There were no regular working hours; they varied according to the season. In the summer work started at dawn, about 4:00 or 5:00, just as the light was beginning to penetrate the windows, and continued, with short interruptions for meals, until 9:00 at night. In the winter work started at 7:00 in the morning and lasted until midnight. On Thursdays everybody worked all night, because on Fridays work ceased in the afternoon to allow everybody to wash up, dress up, and make ready to meet *Malkah Shabbos,* the Queen of the Sabbath.[1]

■

When it is remembered that such working conditions and worse were common throughout the thousands of *shtetlach* of the Pale [of Settlement], it will be understood why the young men and women constituted fertile ground for revolutionary propaganda and activity. The imprecations of the elders no longer had any effect. Rebellion spread like wild fire among the young. They organized, first against their employers, then extended their field of activity to include the state apparatus that allowed the pervasive exploitation to exist. When persuasion and argument were of little avail and the employers called in the police to quell the disturbances, they resorted in retaliation to sabotage, destruction of property, and sometimes physical violence. The ghetto was slowly, painfully being broken up.

This was also true of the peasantry. The *mir,* the village commune, was also dissolving. The preachments by the clergy against "agitators," "Godless free-thinkers" and threats of hell-fire and brimstone fell on an increasing number of deaf ears. Following the ferment in cities like Kiev and Odessa, the peasants began to take the law into their own hands; they took to robbing estates, breaking up and burning landowners' property, and sometimes assaulting the owners themselves.

Guermanovka was a typical *shtetl,* like hundreds and hundreds of other *shtetlach* large and small. The odd 3,500 of a mixed population was almost evenly divided between the Jews in the center and Ukrainians at the periphery—a "wheel within a wheel." The majority of the Jews lived in a compact mass in the center of town. A row of stores on each side of a long street was the business section where dry goods, groceries, and nails were sold, and grain, chickens, and eggs were bought from the peasants, generally on market day. Curiously, the government institutions—post office, jail, courthouse, and police station—as well as the drug store and a doctor's office, were all in the Jewish section of town.

Although Jewish Guermanovka was breaking up, it still retained many of its former characteristics of a nearly self-contained community, with its rabbi, *shoykhet,* synagogue, ritual bath, and a whole string of institutions that took care of the indigent—the poor bride who needed a dowry, the old men and women, the needy, and the sick. There were few dogs but many cats and the ubiquitous goats.

For some strange reason Jewish artists and writers regarded the goat as a "Jewish" animal. No artist's picture of a small town was complete without a goat somewhere in sight. If one wanted to make fun of a Jewish beard, it was likened to a goat's *(tsigene berdl).* To designate a small amount of money or income, one said it was just goat's droppings *(tsigene bobkes).* Perhaps it all goes back to scriptural authority. There is, for example, the "Song of the Kid" ([*Khad Gadya,* One kid] in the Haggadah used in the Passover service.[2] Then, of course, the famous scapegoat of the Bible. A well known Russian writer, not a Jew himself but bearing the odd name [Nikolai] Evreinov *(evrei* is the Russian word for "Jew"), wrote an entire book on the origin of tragedy (*tragoedia*—goat song), in which the Biblical ceremony of *Se'ir l'Azazel* (scapegoat) is very ingeniously shown to have played a predominant part.

My occasional meetings with my sister were a great relief from the daily drill in the heder, but they were far too few. Sometimes we would just walk the streets and around the church, and she would talk to me about the importance of learning and the universal respect in which it was held. She almost made me reconcile myself to the boredom of the heder. At other times she took me to a distant relative who owned a grocery and where my father stayed when in town. There I was always given some kind of a treat—an apple, cherries, a sweet drink, a piece of candy, and—the ultimate—a fig.

One evening I met my sister and we went to visit this relative. I was not feeling too well but the prospect of getting away from heder for a little tempted me. When we got there and I was offered the usual treats, I could not take them and complained of a headache. I insisted on going back to the heder, but they would not hear of it. I stayed with my relative overnight and felt worse the next day.

It happened to be market day. My sister ran to see whether she could find a peasant, either from our village or from one nearby, who would be willing, for a small fee, to take me home to father. She found one from the village of Rosalievka only a few versts from us. As I was clearly not able to take care of myself, she went along with me. She paid the peasant to take us to our home, to which he agreed; but when he got to his village, he refused to go any farther. We then had to walk the remaining few miles. I could not budge, so my sister had to carry me on her back. Although she was a strong girl, I proved to be a considerable burden; she had to make frequent stops. In the meantime it was getting dark and we were pretty scared. However, we got home somehow and I was put to bed immediately. I did not get up for over three months.

What was my sickness? I do not know to this day. It may have been pneumonia or bronchitis, according to symptoms later described to me. We had no doctor. I was cured by some home remedies. When I could, I ate what everybody else did: soup—that was what I liked best—bread, and herring. Once a *fel'dsher* (a kind of male nurse) was brought from town to have a look at me; but mostly nature simply took her course. Somehow I survived.

That winter an exciting event took place in Ludvinovka. Two Jewish merchants were driving from the town of Belaia Tserkov' and had to pass by way of Ludvinovka. They were returning from a business trip and carried money with them. A few local boys somehow got wind of it or perhaps they just chanced it. They ambushed the merchants near the village, beat them up, and robbed them. More dead than alive, the merchants escaped and hid in the house of our next door neighbor. As just a wall separated us from our neighbors and there was a hole in it, we heard all the details of the attack and passed a sleepless night. We were all in terror lest the boys descend on us and give us the same treatment. Fortunately, nothing like that happened. The next day the merchants left for home, where they took the case to court. Our neighbor acted as a witness and helped recognize [identify] the boys. They threatened to kill him, and—who knows—they might have, but the neighbor and his family moved hastily to another town, from which, after a short stay, they emigrated to America.

I did not return to the heder in Guermanovka but spent a quiet and pleasant summer in the village. It was probably the balmy air more than anything else that led to my complete recuperation. Now that the neighbor's children were gone, I played alone much of the time. I went with my father to the mill, crawled under it—how many times!—and clattered to the top to examine the mill stones. From time to time I even broke my father's injunction against playing with the peasant boys. As always I filled pages with my red and blue pencil.

My education in the next four or five years was rather planless and unsystematic. I spent another year at a new heder, then came home and went to village Russian school, then still [to] another heder in the town where an older sister lived. (I shall speak later about the village school.)

My sister Frieda had recently married and had gone to live in the *shtetl* Obukhov. Her marriage was arranged by a *shadkhan,* a marriage broker. Neither the bride nor the groom saw each other while the negotiations were in the preliminary stages. After the *shadkhan* reported to each of the two families about the physical, mental, and moral characteristics of the prospective partners (due allowance for exaggeration made by each side); after he reported to the bridegroom's family on the bride's dowry and to the bride's family on the bridegroom's means of livelihood, back and forth bargaining went on for months until some agreement was reached. A meeting between bride and groom was then arranged. Tea was served and cake and conversation. Sometimes such first meetings are also the last. More often there is give and take; the contractual details are agreed upon, and the date and place of the wedding are set. This was the case with my sister with whom I came to live in Obukhov to continue my studies. (I am sure that my uninvited presence in my brother-in-law's home was not in the marriage contract; whether he liked it [or not], I never found out.)

Obukhov was, for me, a great improvement over Guermanovka. I ate better. I spent only part time with the
melamed. I had more time to play with the boys of my age.
The town was bigger and gayer. Obukhov was an enlarged,
improved version of Guermanovka.

All the townships within the Pale of Settlement (where
Jews were permitted to live; residence was forbidden to them
in three quarters of the country) had many features in common despite some variations. Thus, half of Obukhov was in
the private (seignorial) domain. It belonged to Prince Konstantin A. Gorchakov, a leftover from the Pre-Emancipation
era. The Prince himself and his progeny seldom came there.
Their property was administered by a staff of employees who
saw to it that the rents and profits reached the Prince's family
wherever they happened to be at the moment—Moscow, St.
Petersburg, Paris. The Prince's mansion, just at the outskirts
of Obukhov, was an imposing complex of buildings with
what seemed to be a countless number of windows—a
palace, hunting lodge, horses' stables, and granaries all sunk in
magnificent orchards and forests. It made a most powerful
impression as one caught a glimpse of it from miles around. It
looked mysterious, like those fabulous castles one reads about
in fairy tales.

Obukhov had a population of some 8,000, including
tailors, shoemakers, coopers, wheelwrights, blacksmiths, and
potters. Many windmills dotted the landscape all around, and
a few water mills, which I saw for the first time. Obukhov
even had some fairly large enterprises, like a brewery and a
brick yard. And there were several elementary Russian and
Jewish schools, a *moshav zekenim* (house for the old), and a
hekdesh (hostel for people in the deepest misery and degra-
dation).

As in every *shtetl,* the Jewish section was in the center, the
other peasant population all around it, each living practially a
life of its own. The mingling of the two populations came
during the biweekly fairs and especially during the annual fair
in the fall. The town's stores, again as in other *shtetlach,* were
built in two rows facing each other. When there was little

business the women took time out to visit each other, brag about the accomplishments of their boys, and gossip about those not present; the men talked business or politics, treated each other to a pinch of snuff, and complained about things in general and their own troubles in particular. Some of the more liberal Jews received newspapers from the big cities, even from St. Petersburg. The arrival of a newspaper was an event which always elicited a variety of opinions and called forth heated discussions.

I was once again placed in a heder whose melamed was somewhat more of a scholar and a little more lenient with his charges. Again one studied by rote. You memorized the lesson by dint of endless repetition. Everybody studied aloud in sing-song, rocking and swaying, and trying to outshout everyone else. Any slip of memory or deviation from good behavior met immediate retribution by way of a slap in the face or the *kantshik*. There was even punishment for asking the wrong questions. The Bible, as is well known, speaks frequently and rather brutally about sexual practices in and out of wedlock. While the melamed translated everything into Yiddish, the embarrassing words and expressions remained untranslated. Sometimes a young pupil, unless enlightened by older pupils as to the meaning of such words, puzzled and impatient, would finally burst out: "Well, what does *zeinah*[3] (harlot) mean?" The answer to which was a resounding slap in the face and the admonition: "You'll find out when you grow up, you *smorkach* (snot nose)." He did, long before that.

Because of my greater leisure, more relaxed mood, and greater comfort, I enjoyed my stay in Obukhov. My favorite holidays were the three most secular ones. *Hamisha Asar B'Shevat,* the 15th day of *Shevat* (around January or February), was the holiday of trees and fruits. On this day, when pious Jews looked with nostalgia to the distant past when trees were planted in ancient Palestine, children were given the fruits of old Palestine: figs, dates, St. John's bread [fruit of the carob tree][4] oranges, nuts. Once a year it was an act pleasing to God to relish those delicacies; and it was only once a year that most parents could afford to treat their children to some of these things. The rarest treat was the oranges; a slice tasted heavenly.

Another minor holiday that I liked was *Lag B'Omer,* which came in spring, midway between Passover and the Feast of Weeks. It celebrates the victories of Bar Kokhba[5] and the staying of the plague by Akiva.[6] For this, all the boys played warriors, doing their best to emulate the heroic exploits of Bar Kokhba's army. We made wooden swords from planks snatched from wherever we could find them, or wheedled from our elders. We got hold of broken hoops and made bows and arrows. We made helmets and shields from anything handy. I used my red and blue pencil to decorate every available space on our weapons. All in all, we thought we made an impressive army. If the weather was good, as it usually was at that time of year, we went to the outskirts of the woods where we staged elaborate battles, recalled the ancient wars, and shouted till we were hoarse.

But the favorite of these secular, or semisecular, holidays was Purim. Purim celebrates the mythical story told in the Book of Esther about the good King Ahashverosh and his beautiful wife Esther who, together with her pious uncle Mordecai, foiled Haman's plot to exterminate the Jews. ("Haman" is a name the Jews use for their worst enemies, who they hope will meet with the same fate.) On the day of Purim the megillah (scroll of Esther) is read in the synagogue. Every boy (and some adults too) is equipped with a *grager* (rattle), which he spins, making a racket every time the name of Haman is mentioned. Then there is the beautiful custom of *shalach manos* (exchange of gifts) in the form of pastries of all kinds: *hamantaschen,* triangular pies[7] filled with sweet poppy seed; honey cakes; diamond-shaped cookies; and as many other goodies as the ingenuity of the housewife can fashion. An assortment of sweets is exchanged among friends. Children who carry [deliver] them are given coins and a taste of the pastries.

It is the custom, too, to enact the story of Esther by homegrown actors who perform, in the slap-stick style, a kind of Jewish *Commedia dell'Arte.* The audience and the actors are boisterous; the villain is booed; and the hero is applauded. Quite frequently, the actors, under the guise of playing history, indulge in broad satire of local people and situations. Purim is the day to let yourself go, to make merry, and even to drink until you cannot tell the difference between "cursed be Haman" and "blessed be Mordecai" (theoretically, that is, because such a state of inebriation was very rare and frowned on. That, they would say, is for the peasants).

I would have been ashamed to admit it, but an altogether different "holiday" also delighted me: the annual fair in the fall. For many days before the roads leading to Obukhov were cluttered with pedestrians and all kinds of vehicles. Oxen ambled along slowly, taking days to reach the fair. Faster came horses drawing ramshackle contraptions. The more prosperous, like the landowners and their managers, came in shining carriages. The biggest mob at the fair was concentrated at the center, on the open space around the row of stores. The horses were unharnessed, and the goods laid out on the ground (there was no pavement). Those who came late had to find places in the outlying streets and alleys. The peasants brought to market pumpkins, melons, cucumbers, cantaloupes, cabbages, apples, pears, peaches, and plums piled mountain high; strawberries (cultivated and wild), raspberries, and gooseberries, all in a magnificently colorful display that simply begged to be handled. The prices seemed to be irresistibly low. The cheapest fruit was mulberry, which one could get the tubful for a few kopecks. For sale also were geese, chickens, pigs, sheep, heifers, horses, and cows. All these animals produced the characteristic background accompaniment of the fair: The horses neighed; the cows mooed; the chickens cackled; the pigs squealed; the sheep bleated; and the human voices nearly drowned out everything else. Grain was perhaps the most popular and the most bargained-over item in the market. Buyers and sellers accused each other of fraud. The buyers accused the peasants [of] adding sand to the grain to make it weigh more; the sellers accused the buyers of short-weighing. Ultimately, a bargain was struck, and everybody was congratulated all around.

A special spot was assigned for trading and selling horses. The prospective buyer gave the horse the "once over"—felt its flanks, forced its mouth open and looked at its teeth, and leaped on its back and took a brisk run around the market. Then he offered half of what was asked. That was the start of a good bargaining session—one ruble up, one down. And every time they slapped each other's palm as the buyer offered his "last price." After several "last" offers, the buyer would seek his luck elsewhere. He might come back, and the bargaining start over again. Ultimately, a deal was concluded and the two retired for a drink to clinch it.

The hardest bargainers were the Gypsies, who were held in rather low esteem. They were at every fair with their families. The older women told your fortune. The younger ones sang and danced. Even the youngest tried to help. You saw a tot, of perhaps four or five, with a tambourine in one hand gliding along and shaking her shoulders in helpless imitation of the older dancers.

The most absurd rumors and notions were circulated among the populace. It was commonly believed that Gypsies kidnapped little children, then crippled them and trained them as little beggars. Children were warned to stay away from them. A current jingle went like this: *"My tsigane dobry liudi / Shcho pobachim te ne bude"* (We Gypsies are nice people / Whatever we look at disappears). Still another story went like this: Somebody asks: What happens to all the horses? Cattle are slaughtered for meat, but where do the horses disappear? Answer: the Gypsies steal them. Curiously, an altogether different view of them was held by the intellectuals, who considered them a highly romantic race. That is how they are depicted in [Aleksandr] Pushkin's *The Gypsies* and in some popular songs.

No fair was complete without beggars, singers, and musicians. The most characteristic Ukrainian national instrument was the bandura or lira, a box-like contraption with a handle at one end which is turned slowly while the left hand manipulates the strings. The bandura was usually played by a blind musician who sat on the ground accompanying his own plaintive singing. The songs were usually of ancient legends, the exploits of great Ukrainian heroes, etc. The tone of the instrument, regardless of what was being played, like the Scottish bagpipe, always seemed to produce a mood of monotony and mournfulness. There was always a crowd around the musician, listening to his lamentations. From time to time, a passerby gave him a piece of bread, or fruit, or, more rarely, a coin, which he at once put into a bag hanging at his side.

Among the Jewish stores a blind musician was led by a young boy. He played the ocarina, which emitted sounds as plaintive as the bandura. He sang topical ballads and songs about contemporary events, usually a tragic occurrence in some corner of Russia. Fragments of those songs still linger in memory. For example:

> Not far from Odessa
> There lives a family of very refined people
> *(Fun Odess gor nit vayt*
> *Voynt a semaystvi fun gants eydele layt.)*

Or:

> Bitter tears, woe is me, press upon my heart
> My great anguish, my great suffering do torment me
> *(Bitere trern, oy vey is tsu mir, legen af maynem hartsen*
> *Tsores mayne, groyse layden, tuen mir zeyer shmertsen.)*

I can even remember part of the melody, which is as sad as the words.

In the meantime, the peasants, having sold some of their goods, were now crowding the stands and stores, buying the things they needed for their homes and farms: boots (one pair for several members of the same family), wheels, rakes, shovels, and scythes. Young women sought out ribbons, kerchiefs, beads, etc.

One stand, which attracted more gawkers than buyers, was a booth selling chromos. These reproductions hung all over the front of the booth, and there was enough variety to please every taste. First, there were Biblical themes: the Assumption of the Virgin, the Resurrection, the Crucifixion, the Flight from Egypt, the Entry into Jerusalem. Then came the numerous miracle-working saints: St. Nicholas, St. Basil, St. Lavrus, and St. George. Famous generals and their victorious campaigns: [Mikhail] Kutuzov and the Burning of Moscow, the bedraggled and miserable looking army with Napoleon at its head; and [Aleksandr] Suvorov and his army crossing the Alps. Semilegendary national heroes: Il'ia Muromets, Nikita Kozhemiaka, and Dobrynia Nikitich (whose history was not familiar to me but whose intrepid deeds were plain to be seen). Fairy tales, like the Fire Bird, the Humped Horse, the Snow Maiden, and the Sleeping Princess. The seasons, each portrayed with its specific work and play: planting, harvesting, bathing, etc. I hung around [this display] far too long, and the man in the booth began to eye me with suspicion. I could not buy any of the pictures, not only because they were beyond my means, [but because] everybody would have laughed at me had I brought them home. Several times afterward I tried to reproduce the pictures from memory, but I don't think I was very successful.

The Saturday following the fair was celebrated in a more festive spirit than usual, [because] the fair proved to be profitable to many people. On Saturday men and women went to the synagogue for the morning prayer, which lasted till about noon. When they returned [home], not having eaten breakfast (at least they were not supposed to), they were famished and sat down to the best and biggest meal of the week with a gargantuan appetite. The meal had been prepared the day before and kept hot in the oven. Having stuffed themselves on all the filling dishes, full of starch and fat, the older people became irresistibly drowsy and went to sleep. There is a story to the effect that Jews believe they will rise after death because if they can wake up after a Saturday meal, nothing can keep them down.

The children went outdoors to play games. One curious game was to see who could string together the largest number of nonsense syllables. It went like this: "brendya, brendya" and, puffing out your cheeks, "pfutya, pfutya brissa," which came out in such combinations as:

Brendya, brendya, putya brissa

Putya brissa

Putya, putya, putya brissa

Putya putya putya bra

Bra, bra, putya bra.

Etc., endlessly. In Biblical times this would have been "speaking with tongues." (Many years later, when I was in Paris, I found phonetic poetry widely in vogue. Then my childhood game inspired me to publish a manifesto and almost found a new school of poetry [see Chapter 9].)

Toward twilight all the young, dressed in their Saturday best, went for a promenade and a little flirtation. A little distance from the row of stores rose a big town church on an open square. On Sunday, [the square] was crowded with Christian worshipers. On Saturday, however, the square was vacant, and the young Jews of both sexes took advantage of it. Strolling leisurely around the church, then back of the closed and silent stores, and once more around the church—repeating the same tour over and over again—the boys and girls each walked in a separate column. Modesty, at least in public, was a categorical imperative; nevertheless, there was a good deal of flirting back and forth. The girls nudged each other and giggled and parried an occasional remark from the boys. Of course everybody knew everybody else but the daily combativeness over trifles was absent. There was a mood of friendliness, of a secret yearning.

In the pathos of distance, I cannot help recalling another scene of men and women strolling back and forth in opposite directions. It was in the 1920s on Kurfürstendamm, Berlin. To put it crudely, in Obukhov as in Berlin it was sex seeking sex; but what a world of difference! In Obukhov, it was the secret search for intimate companionship; in Berlin, it was the open stalking of prey.

During my stay in Obukhov, I witnessed, for the first time, a public manifestation of Hasidism. A zaddik, the head of a Hasidic sect, came to town for a weekend. This was an event of extraordinary importance, for it seldom happened.

Hasidism, in its history, doctrine, and practices, has been described exhaustively in many books ([Simon] Dubnov and [Martin] Buber, among others). It arose in the eighteenth century at a time of great distress among the Polish and Ukrainian Jews, and was, in many respects, a reaction against it.[8] The Baal Shem Tov (Master of the Good Name)[9] and his first followers were simple, modest men who sought solace in neighborliness, cheerfulness, singing, dancing, and simple piety unmarred by casuistic, scholastic exegesis of the holy texts. Hasidism was essentially a movement of the poor and unscholarly. It therefore found fertile soil and spread rapidly despite strict criticism from the rabidly pious as well as the "enlightened."

The Baal Shem Tov died without leaving any written records. His legacy could, therefore, be given—and, in fact, was [given]—free interpretation. Soon the movement became institutionalized and appropriated by some leaders, now called zaddikim (the pious, virtuous). They established courts *(hoyf)* with an elaborate ceremonial, with an officialdom of factotums *(gabayim),* beadles, hangers-on, and sycophants. In time, the office of zaddik became hereditary. With little or no objection from the zaddikim, their followers [believed them to have] magical powers of healing, with the ability of leaping over distances merely by taking thought, etc.[10] A constant pilgrimage from near and far sought admission to the court. But you could not simply gain admission by knocking on the door. You had to go through the major domo, buy a *kvitl* (pass),[11] and wait your turn. You stated your case: the career of your son, the marriage of your daughter, a sick child, trouble in business, a barren wife. To each of your requests the zaddik had a word of advice and hope. Then you made [a] place for the next applicant or suppliant.

Generally the zaddik stayed in his own bailiwick; but occasionally, after much urging and a promise of generous returns, he would venture out to one or another town, usually for a weekend. There was a furious battle of wits and pocket-books as to who would have the honor of housing the zaddik, the victory most often going to the biggest contributors. The zaddik led the services and graced the banqueting done in his honor. The zaddik was always surrounded by a shouting and gesticulating crowd, singing, laughing, and trying to catch every phrase falling from his holy lips, phases which they were to repeat for years to come. The commotion was most marked during mealtime, because the zaddik distributed morsels of food to those nearest him. Many more would be happy with *shiraim* (leftovers). Even crumbs were swallowed as ambrosia of the gods. The biggest affair took place on Saturday night when the Queen of Sabbath[12] escorted *(melavveh malkah)*. Conversation, eating, singing, and dancing lasted till midnight and continued in the street. In their ecstatic transport, with hands uplifted and caftans flying in the air, the Hasidim must have looked very odd indeed to the stray peasants who witnessed the scene.

My father came from Ludvinovka especially for the occasion. He went through the usual procedure; price of admission and pass. We threaded our way past a mob of Hasidim, hangers-on, and beggars and were ushered into his holy presence. The zaddik made a few perfunctory remarks to father, patted me on the cheek, and prophesied a bright career for me as a learned sage in Israel. [With that,] the interview was over.

In all this, the women took no part at all. They were happy to prepare the food, to make perhaps the best meal in their [lives,] but kept out of sight for fear lest their appearance tempt the pious minds into sinful channels. They were glad when the binge was over and their husbands, sons, and sons-in-law were once more their own.

A considerable proportion of the *shtetl's* population was highly critical of the weekend affair. Many were caustic about the pious frauds (God's *ganovim*). Obukhov, like so many other towns, was shedding its medieval customs. Young people now studied not only Hebrew but worldly subjects as well: Russian, German, French, and arithmetic. There were young people, boys and girls, preparing themselves for the *gimnaziia* (high school) and even for the university. The Marxist [saying,] "religion is the opiate of the people" was already current. But, the Hasidim dismissed all critics as *apikorsim*, heretics and free-thinkers.

■

After my stay in Obukhov for over a year, my father thought that my elementary education was at an end. It was not, but he was not scholar enough to realize it. He was sure that with my "good head" I would make up in the yeshiva (higher Hebrew religious school) for whatever I may have missed in the heder. He was anxious to start me on a religious career before my brothers in Kiev snatched me away and turned me into a wordling like themselves. He wanted to see at least one of his offsprings devoted to a life of piety and be a solace to him in his old age. In this, alas, he eventually failed. But he made a brave try.

3
THE VILLAGE SCHOOL

When I recuperated from my long illness, I was still weak, and my father decided to keep me home a little longer. Not to encourage too much idleness, he placed me in the village Russian school. However, he was not sure I would be accepted. Several years previously, the oldest daughter of our next door neighbor Isaak had entered the village school. Just as she was well on the way to mastering the alphabet, her presence in the school came to the attention of a priest who lived in a nearby township. (He used to visit Ludvinovka on the more important holidays and on special occasions; the less important religious needs were taken care of by the deacon.) When he discovered that a Jewish girl was permitted to attend a "Christian" school, he was furious and thundered imprecations from the pulpit. Actually, he had no jurisdiction over the school; the school was built by the zemstvos (a partially elected organization from the gentry given responsibility of supervising the schools and roads) and was supported in part by the village commune. There was no law forbidding Jews to attend the school. Nevertheless, the girl was immediately thrown out. Her father then hired the same teacher to give the girl private lessons. Again, the priest learned of this (undoubtedly there were peasants congenially minded who made sure the priest would be notified), and he was so infuriated that this time he did not rest until the teacher, too, was expelled.

The priest was one of those characters not uncommon in Tsarist Russia, [one] who inflamed the peasants against the

Jews and the soldiers against the peasants. Informer, anti-Semite, and obscurantist, he spread his influence among many families in his district.

One more characteristic incident. The wife of Isaak was in an advanced state of pregnancy. There were, of course, no midwives in the village; women in labor used to hire a *babka* [old woman] to help deliver the child. The *babka* was an all-around specialist. She cured various illnesses by incantations, herbs, and love potions. I witnessed her incantations at night in a darkened room with a single sputtering candle; it was spooky. This *babka* helped Isaak's wife with the delivery of the baby, and everything went off without trouble. Enter our old friend the priest. He gave the *babka* such a dressing down, she swore never to have anything to do with Jews.

Isaak was a stubborn man. Having failed twice, he did not give up. He went to a neighboring town and came back with a young Jewish boy who, in return for board and a small salary, undertook to instruct all Isaak's children in Jewish and Russian. Now, residence in the village was forbidden to Jews except those who had lived there many years previously. So one day the authorities got wind of the young man's presence in the village. He was arrested and sent home *po etapu,* on foot, accompanied by two guards who took him to the next stop where they handed him over to other guards, etc., until he was brought to his own town. And that was the end of the girl's education.

■

I met her many years later in the United States. She worked hard and earned little ($7 a week and less in a New York sweatshop) but she was determined, whatever the cost, that her children were not to go through life without an education. She bore six sons; they all received college degrees.

■

Priests, as Sholom Aleichem [pseudonym of Shalom Rabi-nowitz] might say, may be likened to carpenters. Carpenters live, live and then die. So do priests. In due time, the priest went to meet his maker. The village landowner, Kozar, built a church for the village (and the good of his soul), [and the church,] like the school, was to be maintained by the community. A new priest and a new teacher were engaged. There was no objection to my joining the school. I enrolled.

The school, which stood next to the church, was a one-room affair, with a lobby where you wiped your boots before entering. The room had no wooden floor, just bare ground cleanly swept. The three grades were separated along the three walls of the room. In the center of the fourth wall facing the door sat the teacher, with a blackboard on one side, keeping a sharp eye on the noisy pupils. All the grades studied simultaneously and in full voice. The tools of learning were: ruled paper for spelling, squared (or graph) paper for arithmetic, and a slate, which was in the greatest use.

You began by learning the alphabet in its Slavonic nomenclature: *Az* (a), *buki* (b) down to *fita* and *izhitsa*. You had to memorize the alphabet so thoroughly that you could recite it backward and forward in one breath.

Then came spelling and reading. The whole first grade shouted after the teacher "OOO SSS AAA OSA, OOO SSS AAA OSA," etc. for each new word. The pupils were all Ukrainian; the textbooks were all in Russian. Ukrainian textbooks and even the Bible were forbidden in Ukrainian. Of course, among themselves the pupils always spoke Ukrainian. The only use they had for the Russian language was subsequently when they entered the army, but they retained very little of it on their return.

Besides Russian, the pupils also learned a little Church Slavonic, the language of prayer, the Bible, and the chroniclers. I did not have to study the prayers; but hearing them so often, I learned them anyway. The most common were the Lord's Prayer and a prayer for the Tsar (". . . grant our Emperor Nikolai Aleksandrovich [Tsar Nicholas II] victory over his enemies"). After struggling through the three grades, the pupil had a knowledge of the prayers, a little arithmetic, and a smattering of Russian. The length of the grade depended on the ability of the pupil, and the length of the school term depended on the weather. It was generally short. As soon as work in the field was possible, even the youngest were called upon to help their parents.

The teacher looked like a citified peasant. He dressed somewhat more neatly than the peasants. His boots were polished. His beard was trimmed to a point ("Van Dyke," it was called). His speech was a mixture of Russian and Ukrainian. It was obvious that he could, if necessary, speak fluent Russian, but he seemed anxious to make himself understood by the pupils. Perhaps he was even a liberal. I saw him once or twice reading a Russian newspaper, a rare thing for that part of the country. He showed no sign of anti-Semitism, which was even more rare. Though strict with the pupils, he was never brutal. The lesser form of punishment was to be made to stand in the corner; the more severe was to use a ruler over the pupil's palm. The worst, of course—and that happened very rarely—was to hand over the pupil to his father. Incidentally, the classes were never as unruly as I was to see some classes later in America. The boys were wild but only outside the classroom.

Occasionally, an inspector was sent by the zemstvos to visit the school, offer recommendations for improvement, and report back to the organization in the city. He would talk to the teacher and call up a few pupils for questioning. One such inspector came during my first year in school. We all sat in silence as we looked with great curiosity at the well-dressed man from the big city. He chatted for a while with the teacher, asking and answering questions. Then he looked around the class and rested his gaze on me. I was the youngest boy in the class and the only Jew. He motioned to me to come over. As I was hesitant and looked frightened, he said, "Don't be afraid little boy. I would like to tell you something you will like." I came over.

"Do you do what your father tells you?"

"Yes."

"That's fine. Now suppose your father gave you a ruble and asked you to buy fifty kopecks worth of flour, twenty kopecks worth of sugar, and ten kopecks worth of salt, how much change would you get?"

"Twenty kopecks."

"There is a smart boy. Here is twenty kopecks, buy yourself some candy or anything else you like."

He took out two ten-kopeck coins and handed them to me. I was still hesitant, thinking he might be playing a joke on me. The teacher had a broad smile on his face and motioned me to take the money. I was overwhelmed. I never had that much money in my life. I ran home to tell father the good news. He advised me to invest the entire capital in candy and distribute it the next day to the school. I must have bought out my father's entire stock. The next day I did as father told me. School work was interrupted for a while, and everybody had a grand time.

Whenever a pupil was transferred from one grade to the next, there was a school celebration. The teacher was given a gift, which was most usually a big loaf of black bread baked by the pupil's mother. The bread was wrapped in a kerchief purchased at the last town fair or from an itinerant peddler. For the class, the mother cooked an enormous pot of kasha, a kind of thick barley gruel.[1] The celebrant brought the pot to school steaming hot. One arm around the pot, he held a big spoon in his right hand. He scooped out a big chunk of the gruel and slapped it down on the desk in front of each pupil. The pupils took to eating it with their bare fingers. They burned their fingers and their palates but they swallowed the food with noise and gusto. When the feast was finished, the empty pot was taken into the yard and placed at one end. The pupils were then blindfolded in turn, and each tried to hit the pot and break it with a stick. When it was finally broken, there was a deafening roar and everybody filed back into class.

At the end of the term, I went back to the heder, but a year later I was again in the village school, this time to graduate. All the boys who had finished the three grades were loaded into wagons and taken to the district town, Vasil'evka, where they were joined by pupils from other villages. We all gathered in a big room, each school being assigned to a separate section. In a prominent place on the wall hung a big portrait of the Tsar bedecked with medals and decorations.

There were also pictures of famous generals. Icons with metal cutouts and flower decorations were in one corner of the room.

"Class arise."

The *popechitel'*, the patron [inspector] of the zemstvo schools, entered.

"*Zdravstvuite*," [Hello] he greeted.

Everybody replied in one voice, "*Zdravstvuite.*"

He sat down at the table next to a government official and the teachers and shook hands all around. The priest of the local church entered. He turned toward the icon and led the assembly in a prayer.

The examination started. The deacon of the church stood up in the room at a point of vantage and kept an eye on the behavior of the pupils. There were questions in geography, arithmetic, and elementary grammar. The struggle of some boys with the Russian language caused some fleeting smiles at the table. The priest examined the boys on religion (*zakon Bozhii,* literally the Law of God). I was, of course, exempt from the subject.

Intermission came, and we all ate the lunches we brought with us. The afternoon session was devoted to reading and recitation. Three pupils from our school acted out [Ivan Andreevich] Krylov's version of "The Ant and the Grasshopper." I was the Ant; the others were the Grasshopper and the Reader. When all examinations were over, the entire assembly went to church for a special service. I stayed outside the church.

Toward evening we again climbed into our wagons and started for home. The wagon creaked, and the dust [rose] up in clouds, but the kids—examination and school behind them—sang and joked. For once the teacher did not insist on strict discipline. It was pitch dark when we reached Ludvinovka, hungry and exhausted but happy.

4

THE VILLAGE
OF LUDVINOVKA

I lay in bed. Everybody had gone to sleep, although it was still quite early, 9:00 perhaps, I could not tell. We had no clock. Our days were regulated by sunrise and sunset, as were the lives of the peasants in Ludvinovka, the village where I was born. Outside our window on the village green, boys and girls gathered for a little fun, flirtation, and singing. Singing, that is what I was waiting for, the endless flow of song, one after the other, one more enchanting than the other, sad, gay, and comic. The Ukrainians are marvelous singers; they pour out their whole life and soul in song. Their voices are untrained, artless, but full of warm feeling. They sing for pure enjoyment, for the enjoyment of passing a few pleasant moments with their fellow villagers.

The moon was out, bathing everything in an unreal haze. On the roof across the street, a stork stood on one leg, motionless, as if he too were listening (maybe he was). I listened, absorbed in this stolen and forbidden pleasure. For father, these songs were alien, pagan, and profane—unfit pabulum for a right-thinking Jew. Although I was inclined to agree with him, the pull of the songs was irresistible. And so, little by little I learned to know all of them by heart: the song about the bitter lot of the peasant; the song about the mighty river Dnieper; [the song] about the lover who left and did not return; [the song] about the orphan deprived of love and warmth; [the song] about the pancakes which failed to rise; [the song about] the peasant's envy of his neighbor's wife and house; [the song about] the adventurous career of [Ustim]

Karmeliuk, *"harnii khlopets"* (handsome fellow), the Ukrainian Robin Hood, breaker of hearts and protector of the weak;
[the song] about the young and merry widow and the hired
hand; and, of course, [the song] about the inevitable passage
of time. [The last went thus:]

> Young years
>
> My young years
>
> Has the ocean swallowed you?
>
> Have the flames consumed you?
>
> Let us harness the fleetest horses
>
> And race in pursuit of our youth
>
> In vain *(ne vernemos')* we will never come back.

Somehow the sleeping village, the moon and the stars, the
stork on the roof, and the wonderful singing, put me into a
semiconscious state that held me spellbound till I fell asleep.
(Years later when I [went] to Kiev someone discovered my
familiarity with Ukrainian songs. I became a popular figure at
parties where I had to go through my entire repertory.)

Next morning I was awakened before dawn by the lowing
of cattle, the bleating of sheep, and the shouts of people on
the very spot where the previous night the voices of the
singers lulled me to sleep. From all parts of the village cows
and sheep driven by women or young boys in clouds of dust
converged on the village green where a shepherd, his helper,
and his dog were waiting for them. When all the beasts were
assembled, the women returned to their daily chores, the shepherd opened the village gate and drove the herd through it. His
helper closed the gate and ran to catch up with the herd.

The shepherd and his helper had been chosen by the entire community *(mir)* in late winter, when the cows and sheep
were still either in the barns or the houses. Usually the same
people were chosen several years in a row. Nevertheless, the
bargain had to be struck anew, and the ceremony performed
annually. When the conditions were agreed upon, the agreement was sealed with a drink *(mogorich)*. The first drive out to
pasture took place in the spring, with the blessing of the vil-

lage priest, who conducted special services. The church banners were brought out; the bells rang; the priest swung the censer; and, as the cattle passed by the church mooing and baaing, the priest sprinkled holy water on them; and the shepherd's season was on. The shepherd's stock in trade was a good dog, a strong stick, a long whip of strong flax which he could make crackle like an electric discharge, and a homemade reed pipe.

◼

The village green was a kind of local St. Peter's Square. Here were concentrated the most important structures, and here also were performed some of the most important affairs, functions, and events of the community. Here stood the well which supplied water for drinking and cooking and near which local gossip was exchanged. Here young recruits for the army gathered once a year with their families for a last farewell before being shipped off to far places for military service. When they returned four years later, they were equipped with a few dozen Russian words with which they crippled their Ukrainian speech and with stories of adventure in various brothels. Sometimes they also brought with them a venereal disease.

Not far from the well rose the tallest structure in the village, the church built of wood and painted in bright white and green. It was a gift from the landowner, Kozar. Adjoining the church was the cemetery and nearby the house and garden of the priest. Close to this house was the one-room village school, used irregularly during the winter season. Religious processions, holiday festivals, weddings, and funerals all passed by here on the way to the church. In the spring also the village came here to bid farewell to a few older people going off on a long pilgrimage to the holy places, mostly to Kiev. They took with them a bag of dried bread *(sukhari)* and walked on foot to their destination, begging on the way for weeks or months. They visited the shrines, kissed the holy relics or the coffin of some holy monk or martyr in the underground caves, contributed their mite from the alms they had collected, and returned home the way they had come (if they did not die on the journey) to tell of the wonder-working relics they had seen "with their own eyes."

To me, the most wonderful event to take place on the village green was the occasional visit of an itinerant peddlar who came to tempt the villagers with the products from the "big city." He arrived in a rickety wagon drawn by a scrawny horse. He unhitched the horse, tethered it, and gave it some food. Then he slowly unpacked his load, while women and children ran from all directions to attend the show. By the time the crowd gathered, there was already on exhibition many colored ribbons, cheap beads, brass rings, bright kerchiefs, needles, and combs. The peddlar was not anxious to be paid in cash—very little was available anyhow—by his prospective customers. He preferred commodity exchange. He accepted old rags, grain, chickens, and goose feathers. Best of all, he liked hog bristle; he was even willing to pay for it in cash.

The women and, even more, the unmarried girls, loved to preen themselves in the little cheap mirrors as they tied colored ribbons into their tresses, hung glass beads around their necks, or tied kerchiefs on their heads. Sly and suggestive jokes were passed around by the married women at the expense of the [unmarried] girls; [this] made [the girls] blush. Finally the purchases were made; the women got their finery; the children got their cookies or toys; and the peddler got his goose feathers, his flax, and hog bristles. He folded up his packs and stepped into one of the Jewish houses, which faced the village green, "for a Jewish meal." If it was late in the day, he would stay overnight, making sure that all his goods were stacked safely in the house.

And what a welcomed guest he was! He brought news from the "big world" outside: what new laws had been passed, good or bad; and local gossip from neighboring townships—who was born, who died, who got married and to whom, and what Jewish girl ran off with what Christian boy. More than that—he brought news from abroad: about some new calamity that had struck Jews in some foreign country and about the spread of Zionism. He brought books for prayer and books to entertain, novels and stories by Sholom Aleichem, Mendele Mocher Sforim, and others.

I had special reason for looking forward to his visits. He sometimes brought me a pencil, which was my delight in childhood. It was octagonal in shape, red at one end and blue at the other. With these two colors, I used to draw all kinds of things. I copied a whole deck of cards, which I used to play with the neighbors' children (the only game we knew was called *durak,* fool). I drew rabbits, lions, horses, houses, and people. Many years later, I met our former neighbor's oldest daughter in America. She reminded me of how angry I had made her when I drew her with a long nose. She did have a long nose, but I hadn't as yet learned the unwritten law about doing women's portraits.

In physical appearance, the village was a mass of dilapidated shacks thrown up without any apparent order or plan. If, however, you could see it from a bird's-eye view, you would discover a definite design. Like a medieval cathedral, Ludvinovka was clustered around the shape of a cross: One arm of the cross was formed by a dusty road running straight through the village and beyond till it was lost on the horizon; the other arm of the cross, cutting the road at right angles, was a tiny stream. The stream was too shallow for fishing and nowhere deep enough to cover a human figure, but there was nevertheless bathing in the summer, skating in the winter, and a place for washing the laundry of the entire village. A rickety bridge, made up from a few planks, spanned the stream where it met the road. The bridge broke down frequently; but as the stream was ankle deep at that point, man or beast passed it without trouble. It was, in fact, safer that way than going over the bridge.

After a rain, the road became a mire into which the wagons sank and had to be pulled out or pushed from behind. In dry weather the road was of the finest dust, which rose in clouds every time wheels past over it, especially when the wind blew. When the wind blew hard, the sand rose in a tall column; a sudden gust would shape it into a funnel; and then, according to local superstition, it was inhabited by a spirit. If you threw a sharp knife into the center of the funnel, you would hit the heart of the spirit and draw blood.

If you followed in a southerly direction from Kiev, you would pass many towns and villages until you finally arrived at Ludvinovka's south gate. Whether you were on foot, on horseback, or in a wagon, you had to stop, open the gate, close it behind you, and you were in the village proper. To the left of the road was the group of buildings, institutions, and sites already described: church, school, well, etc. On the right of the road was a double house with two separate entrances. Over each door was an identical sign saying "grocery" *(Bakaleinaia lavka)*. The occupants were two Jewish families (of which ours was one). The groceries brought no livelihood to either family, but they were a source of constant feuding. Unlike the other houses in the village, the double house had no fence, garden, or barn; it just stood naked in the sun—like an orphan, my father used to say.

Right across from the double house spread out in a continuous row were the village *khaty* (huts) and barns with their backs to the stream, all straw-roofed. When the houses were new, the roofs gleamed bright and golden in the sun. After a few months, the sun and the rain bleached the straw to a mouse gray. The very old roofs had gaping holes in them; their formerly straight and regular edges became ragged and scraggy like an old broom; and a thick accumulation of bronze-like green lichens was scattered in spots. Art students on vacation loved to seek out such houses as subjects of true Ukrainian exotica. Here and there a big stork's nest was elaborately put together on the roof, and a stork stood on one leg without motion, a perpetual wonder to the children. No one molested the stork because that led to sure misfortune. Around the houses grew willows, cherry trees, and occasionally an apple or plum tree; [and each house had] a small garden of vegetables, sunflowers, flax, potatoes, onions, garlic, pumpkins, and cucumbers.

Within perhaps five or ten minutes along the road, you passed the bulk of the houses, crossed the shaky bridge, and were on the opposite side of the stream. Turning sharply to the right, you saw a magnificent forest and orchard. It was the property of the large landowner, Kozar. His estate consisted of several large barns and storage houses, and a pretentious mansion with a high roof and gables. Fierce dogs and an equally fierce watchman kept you at a safe distance. But if you should penetrate behind the buildings, you would enter a shady orchard with the finest apple, pear, cherry, plum, and other fruit trees. Once a year I had the privilege of visiting the mansion, when my father went there to pay his annual rent and bring his annual presents.

Coming back to the dusty road, opposite to the land-owner's estate you saw the last building in the village, a small, solidly constructed *monopol'ka,* a government-owned liquor store. Formerly liquor was sold in private inns *(korchmi),* where peasants gathered to have a bite, to take a drink of wine, tea, or vodka, to gossip, and sometimes to fight. Travelers stopped for a meal and an overnight rest. The government, always in need of ready cash, took over the sole right of selling vodka and found the business quite profitable. The peasant women swore and cursed the *monopol'ka,* because many husbands spent their last kopecks—money needed for the barest necessities—and because it was practically a tradition for the men to come home drunk and beat up their wives and children. There were times when a grown-up son took the part of the mother; then there was a battle, with fists, boards, boots, and anything else [that was] handy. Indeed, in one case, the older man was so badly beaten [that] he died shortly after that.

No one lived in the *monopol'ka.* It was open only on certain days, and government clerks sat behind a bar as in a bank. The purchase had to be taken out immediately. The peasant took the bottle in one hand; vigorously banged the bottom in the palm of his other hand; and as the cork broke the seal and popped high in the air, he put the bottle to his mouth and never removed it till the liquor disappeared completely into his gullet. If he had the wherewithal, he went in for another tasting. Occasionally, when he had a drop too much, he fell flat on the ground, where he lay till he sobered up.

I came to the *monopol'ka* when no one was around to pick up the red sealing wax that fell from the bottles. I melted the wax and fashioned all kinds of things from it: animals, heads, fruit, etc.

Past the liquor store there was another gate, an exact replica of the one on the other end of the village. You had to open it and close it and the village was behind you.

Just outside the gate on a little hillock stood three windmills. The one in the center belonged to my father; [it was] built on land rented from the landowner, Kozar. The mill was busiest in autumn after the harvest. Father was at the mill whenever the wind was strong enough to turn the wings and there was grain enough to grind. Payment was in kind. The peasant brought a number of sacks of grain to be ground into flour, for which father received a certain share for his labor. When enough of the grain was accumulated, he took it to the grain merchants in town to sell.

The work around the mill was strenuous. In the morning father adjusted the mill according to the wind. The body of the mill rested on an underpinning from which a long round shaft protruded for several yards; [this] fitted into a wheel placed vertically on the ground. A strong rope connected the shaft to a pulley. As you strained every muscle to wind the rope around the pulley, the entire unwieldy hulk of the mill moved slowly around (the Russian windmills were primitive affairs compared with Dutch and American models) until the desirable position of the wings was attained so that they could receive the full impact of the wind. It was back-breaking toil, more properly done by beast than by man. (Ultimately, father undermined his health and had to quit. Not, however, before he had developed a hernia, which kept him miserable for the rest of his life. Operation? Whoever heard of such a thing? That was for the rich.)

In addition, each wing had to be adjusted, not only in the direction of the wind but according to its force and velocity. Each wing had a removable section, which could be taken out to break the impact of a strong wind and prevent the whole mill from toppling over. More rarely the upper and nether mill stones had to be sharpened. The lower stone, always stationary, remained in place while the upper stone had to be lifted to an almost vertical position. By a slow process of chipping the stones with hammer and chisel, raising clouds of dust that filled the lungs, the surface was roughened and made ready for crushing and grinding the grain.

I loved to play around the mill. I crawled underneath to examine the underpinning, or I sat on the first floor and watched the flour as it fell from a tiny chute into a sack, or [I] climbed to the top floor where the grain was fed to the stones that shook the entire structure. The noise made by the stones inside and the wings outside was deafening. I sometimes felt as if the whole building was coming apart.

Occasionally, the peasants brought their children with them. While the grownups talked business, we went outside and played "riding the wings." This was a dangerous game which could be played only when the wind was mild. It consisted in catching the corner of the wing when it came close to the ground, then being carried up for some distance, and jumping. The fun was to see who could go the highest before releasing the wing. Once down, you had to jump immediately to one side to avoid being hit by the next wing coming right behind. (Cases were known of serious injury to man and beast when they strayed too close to a moving wing. But this did not deter us any more than accidents deter American boys from stealing rides on trolleys or trucks.)

Most fascinating of all to me was a visit to the mill at night. Generally, there wasn't enough work even in daytime. However, during the busy season in the fall, father had to work late at night, and he did not care to have me around then. I used to beg and plead until he finally relented and took me with him after dinner. We usually spent the evening on the first floor under the light of a small kerosene lamp. The scene was perfectly Rembrandtesque, though, of course, I did not know it.

■

Association of ideas are formed in strange ways. As a student, I became acquainted with Rembrandt through reproductions; later, in my travels I saw him in the original at Amsterdam, Leningrad, Paris, and elsewhere. He has always been one of my very favorite artists. Whether that scene in my father's mill prepared me for Rembrandt or whether my subsequent acquaintance with him made me idealize that scene in retrospect (perhaps Rembrandt himself got his first glimpse of "Rembrandt" chiaroscuro in his father's mill at night), I still have a vivid memory of it.

I can still see the eyes, nose, cheekbones, and beard of father (who incidentally resembled some of Rembrandt's subjects) illuminated by the flickering light, casting a weaving shadow behind him, crossing the sacks of flour and boxes, and forming queer shapes. Like a projector, the lamplight picked out from the background a protuberance, a board, an edge, or corner of some object and left the rest in a penumbra or in total darkness. The sky outside, made deeper by the light inside, seemed impenetrable. I was sure that ghosts and goblins hovered outside and mingled their voices with the creaking of the axles, the swish of the wings as they cut the air, the rasping and grinding of the stone as it turned endlessly over the stationary stone underneath, and the "putt," "putt," "putt" of the little chute as the flour came out in spurts. The entire structure rocked like a cradle, and it finally put me to sleep. I woke up on father's shoulder out in the cool air as he carried me home. When I woke up the next morning, father was already gone.

■

The mill was one source of our income; the grocery was another. We straddled the village as it were: At one end was our mill; at the other was our house and grocery. The land on which each stood was rented from Kozar. We occupied one half the double house (the other half, including the grocery, was an exact replica). Any visitor to the village could not help noticing the double house because of its peculiar location. It was at the very edge of the village (and, thus, quite convenient for any night raiders from our or any other village), opposite and facing the rest of the houses, which all seemed to cluster in a solid row. Unlike every other house, even the poorest, ours, as previously remarked, had no fence around it, no gardens, no flowers, no trees, no animals—a kind of miniature ghetto.

Our grocery was open at irregular hours. In fact, one could hardly speak of it as being open at all. Whenever a peasant needed something, which was seldom, he knocked on the door, and we went to greet him and, hopefully, to sell something. But, in fact, we had little to sell, and there wasn't much he wanted to buy.

The needs of the peasant were few, and he satisfied most of them in his own homestead. He grew his own vegetables; baked his own bread; raised his own hogs, chickens, or cows, which he himself slaughtered for food; built his own house, such as it was; spun his own linen; and made his own clothes. Once in years he bought a sheepskin coat or pair of boots, which were worn by practically every member of the family, even if the fit was not ideal. But he went for those things [to] the next town fair, where he took his grain or vegetables for sale.

We did not keep such items in our store. We carried the more ordinary articles of daily use: needles, thread, nails, salt, and kerosene. Like the other articles, kerosene was not in frequent demand. Few peasants owned lamps. They rose early and went to sleep early. Sometimes they used candles. In addition to kerosene, we also carried wicks and lamp chimneys. We sold *bubliki,* a sort of cruller, though not sweet, kept for weeks until it was hard as rock; one solid block of cone-shaped sugar from which you hacked a small piece as you needed it, which was seldom; and flint steel and wick to light a homemade cigarette or a homemade pipe filled with strong and cheap tobacco *(makhorka)*. (From a small book of tissue paper, you pulled out one sheet, put *makhorka* into it, rolled it, and ran your tongue over the edge to seal it. Then you stroked the steel against the flint from which the flying sparks ignited the wick (after several trials), which then lighted the cigarette, and you were ready to enjoy a good strong smoke.) We also carried a small amount of gum turpentine "for medicinal purposes." Any stomach trouble, particularly in children suffering from "worms," was supposed to be cured by eating a piece of sugar dipped in turpentine.

Kerosene had occasionally a special use for the boys. They would take a mouthful of kerosene, roll a piece of wrapping paper, light it, and spray it with the kerosene. The paper would burst into a big flame, to everybody's glee. The taste of the kerosene in their mouths did not seem to bother them at all.

On Saturday nights our house was turned into a kind of village café where the boys came for a bit of temperate entertainment. They sat around the table and ordered a samovar of tea. *Bubliki* and candy were a special treat. The boys joked, horse-played, told local gossip, and, sometimes perhaps, an off-color story, especially if a former soldier was present. Occasionally, sometime around 1905, a subversive idea was thrown in, as if by accident, by someone who had been to the big city. To make things more lively, contests were staged to see who could eat the fastest a *bubliki* hung from the ceiling or who could drink the most glasses of tea. One samovar was emptied and another filled, as glass after glass disappeared in the ample stomachs of the contestants. They drank ten, twenty, and more glasses, sweating profusely (there is a Russian saying that you order tea with a towel) and going outside to relieve themselves until the stench filtered into the house, giving rise to [not-so-funny] jokes.

■

The population of Ludvinovka was roughly 900 souls, or about 150 families. The land was distributed about equally between the landowner, Kozar, and the rest of the population. There was a further division in the bulk of the population between two or three better-to-do peasants *(kulaki)* and the rest. The two Jewish families were not permitted to own land.

The peasant's meager income came practically entirely from the cultivation of the land, some of which he owned and much of which he rented from Kozar on a sharecropper basis. The main staple was grain: wheat, rye, oats, buckwheat. I was always envious of the peasant boys running through their parents' fields—the wheat swaying in the wind, the surface changing light constantly, and the blue cornflowers peeping out here and there. An especially pleasant sight was buckwheat in bloom, all white and showing patches of earth in spots. The peasants also cultivated sugar beet, flax, and melons. They grew vegetables around the house: potatoes, beans, peas, sunflowers, and carrots. The sunflower was found around every peasant's house. Its dried seeds were cracked by the girls with as much relish and frequency as chewing gum is rolled over the tongue by their American counterparts.

Held by the village in common was some pasture land, and a small granary (called *magazin)* kept some grain for an emergency sowing in case of a bad harvest. All peasants were still paying *vykup,* installment payment on the land granted them after emancipation. When the peasants were freed in 1861, they were, of course, landless. Some land was given them by their former owners upon advanced payment by the government. The former serfs, now "free" peasants, had to pay back this money [in] annual installments. Fifty years later they were still paying it. The poorer peasants were perennially indigent, for, in addition to their *vykup,* they had other debts, both public and private. To pay these debts and taxes, the parents and children went to the city and hired themselves out at ridiculously low remuneration.

When several peasants were in long arrears, the government would send in a commission of uniformed armed guards and local officials who were fairly well informed as to who had what and how much. These commissioners went from house to house, barn to barn, opened trunks, turned things in the house upside down, collected all they could, and sold [the confiscated items]. Such expeditions were seldom over without a fight, and the peasants always had the worst of it. They had to swallow their hurt and insults.

Everything seemed to have gone back to normal, but only on the surface. Underneath a storm of anger and indignation was always brewing, [ready] to break out with hurricane force at the first opportunity. This is what happened during the days of social ferment in the years 1904–1905. While landowners fled to the cities, peasants set fire to their property, broke into their granaries, and forcibly expropriated their land. Then came reaction and the *karatel'nye otriady,* punitive squads, which descended on the villages. Cossacks and soldiers wrought havoc on the peasants' property and punished the peasants with savage cruelty: beating, flogging, exile, imprisonment, and even murder were visited upon the villages. Almost always these squads were assisted by the better-to-do and more conservative local peasants, who were even more cruel than the strangers.

Graphic descriptions of these events and characters are found in the works of Russian novelists. The following is a brief summary of one small scene from the novel *Fata morgana* by [Mikhail] Kotsiubinskii (he was a Ukrainian himself and must have written from personal knowledge):

> When the news of the famous October 17th Manifesto reaches a certain village, some young peasants assume quite wrongly that it was a signal for the distribution of the land to the poor. A few of them gather in a house to work out plans for the distribution of the land equitably. The richer peasants stay in the background and keep their guns and axes in readiness. Within a day or two, rumor is heard that a punitive expedition is on the way. The *kulaki* then decide to take justice in their own hands, before the expedition reaches the village. Thus when one of the young planners, Maksimka, arrives to tell of those plans, he is felled by a severe blow; a shot follows; and when he tries to rise from the mud into which he fell, a blow from an axe finishes him. Then a second young peasant comes. He is at once sentenced to be shot. His uncle undertakes to do the job.
>
> Prokop, the boy, accepts the sentence with a peasant's fatalism. He calls his wife, tells her to sell the horse, to pay their debts.
>
> "Greet my mother, ask her forgiveness, and you too forgive me."
>
> He removes his overcoat so that it will not be spoiled by bullets.
>
> His uncle is ready.
>
> "Take courage my son. . . . God will reward you . . . make the sign of the cross."
>
> Prokop obeys.

"Say good-bye, son."

"Forgive me, friends, maybe I have done harm to someone. Good-bye."

"God will forgive. You forgive us."

Uncle Panas: "Where shall I shoot?"

"Shoot in the mouth."

Panas shoots. Others help him finish the job.

The soil, land, was an overriding passion with the peasant, above even his attachment to family. He never hesitated to risk his life in defense of the soil. Doctrinal differences among the various political schools with regard to the land interested him but little. In a novel *Forests Aflame* [*Les razgoralsia (And the Forest Burned),* 1906] by [Stepan] Skitalets [pseudonym of Stepan Gavrilovich Petrov], one of the more intelligent peasants, Miron, says:

> It is not for us to decide among them (political ideas—L. L.).
> We peasants know only one thing. . . . You give us the land,
> and then we begin to analyze the fine points of your doctrines.
> . . . And, if the land is not given, we will take it ourselves. . . .

In the many struggles about the ownership of the land, both sides fought with unparalleled cruelty and no holds barred. In 1917 this struggle or war broke out with renewed fury. There is no doubt that the Bolshevik slogans encouraging the expropriation of the land by the landless gained them great support in the countryside. Kozar was killed in one of those fights.

The most feared and hated man in Ludvinovka was undoubtedly the landowner, Kozar, on whom [depended] in one way or another the livelihood of a large portion of the village population. *Pomeshchik,* landowner, in Russian history denotes a special way of life, an aspect of civilization in the Pre-

Emancipation era: regal splendor, a court with its own theatre, musicians, and artists. (Moscow has an excellent example of such a theatre in Ostankino of the old Sheremetev family.) The relation between peasant and landowner had, of course, changed radically since Emancipation, but these landed gentry still sought to give their families a higher education, still lived ostentatiously and, in many cases, preferred life abroad or in the large cities of the country. They handed over their affairs to a factotum, who collected the rent for them, which they could spend [on] gambling and high living.

Kozar was a perfect caricature of this. He was illiterate and ruthless in his dealings with the peasants. He lived in an old mansion built by the previous occupant, in all likelihood some Polish *pan* [landlord]. The land around Ludvinovka was an old battle ground between Poles and Ukrainians. The Poles had been driven out. Small settlements and individual families remained scattered here and there, adhering fiercely to their language and traditions. During the many conflicts, the Poles' estates sometimes fell into possession of a shrewd *kulak* [wealthy peasant]. Such was probably the provenance of Kozar's property, or perhaps he purchased it as a big bargain from a bankrupt absentee squire. Whatever the case, the mansion was obviously too big and too luxurious for him. He had no children. He occupied only a couple of the rooms; the rest were used for storage. Some rooms were never entered and were reputed to be haunted by evil spirits and the souls of former occupants. A big courtyard surrounded the mansion and was filled with cows, horses, sheep, pigs, chicken, and geese. [In] back of the house was a magnificent orchard of apple, pear, plum, cherry, and other trees, a perpetual temptation to the village boys.

Kozar was ruthless with anyone in his debt, and many villagers were. Our neighbor, Isaak, once got into an argument with Kozar. When Isaak and his family were on a visit with friends in the next town, Kozar broke into the house, threw everything into the street—chairs, bedding, dishes—and let them lie there or be carried away.

Kozar's wife was his perfect match. Illiterate like him and unprepossessing in appearance, [she had] a plain face of which the most prominent feature was a bulbous pug nose. That, in fact, was what she was called behind her back—*kurnosa,* pug nose. She herself would joke about it and say, "When God was distributing luck, I was around and got my share; when it came to good looks, I was asleep and missed my chance."

■

There was one very old peasant who used to mumble, grumble, and talk to himself but was treated with respect by the entire village. His name was Kurnis. He was the sole survivor from the *panshchina,* serfdom. Like the Civil War veterans in the United States, he brought the past into the present. He was never tired of telling tall tales about his years of serfdom: how children and adults used to start work, winter and summer, long before sunrise and continued till long after sunset; what severe punishments were meted out to them for the slightest infractions; and how the serfs were forced to whip one another. One of his frequent tales (he was becoming forgetful) was how he was tied to a horse's tail—for some minor misbehavior—bound and dragged over the ground for all to see till he was bruised black and blue and a trail of blood was behind him. When untied, he was half alive and unconscious.

Despite the hard conditions under which the peasant lived, his life was not unrelieved misery. Quite the contrary. The peasant loved life. He loved weddings, christenings, and holiday festivities. In the winter, the peasants would arrange occasionally a *vecherinka* [evening party] for young folk, a night gathering where boys and girls would gather for talk, singing, and treats of homemade baking—[all,] of course, under chaperonage. Matches were made at these gatherings or engagements started. Sexual morals in the village were strictly puritanical. Deviations probably occurred in secret; but, if discovered, they meant social ruin for life (opinion was more indulgent with men). After such a discovery, the gate to the parents' house was painted with tar at night to notify the community of the girl's disgrace. And the father would beat her to an inch of her life. If an indiscretion went undiscovered until marriage, it was supposed to become evident on the wedding night and [almost] in open view of the community. For on the wedding night, after a lot of merry-making, singing, dancing, and drinking, the bride and groom were pushed into a barn, onto a prepared bedding of hay, where a test was made of the girl's virginity, while the bride's mother anxiously awaited the verdict, and the guests cracked jokes. The couple returned, and if everything had gone well, the merry-making resumed with a fresh spurt.

The peasants liked to embellish objects of daily use: sleighs, pots, cradles, and harnesses. Flowers were everywhere, both cultivated and wild. In the spring, the fragrance of lilac was in the air. In late summer, sunflowers were in every corner of the village. The sunflowers were both decorative as flowers and practical as food (seeds). Girls picked cornflowers and other flowers of the field, which they tied into their tresses to crown their heads. They gathered flowers to decorate the icon in one corner of the house. I liked best of all the velvety red poppy blossom. I drew it many times. When the poppy seeds grew ripe, I would crack the pod open and pop the seed right into [my] mouth.

We bought quantities of poppy seed, chiefly for Purim, the holiday that celebrates the events told in the Book of Esther. All Jewish families made sweet poppy seed brittle— *hamantaschen,*[1] the three-cornered pies filled with honey and poppy seed—as well as other sweets and cookies. We ate them, sparingly to be sure, to celebrate the triumph over Haman, the deadly enemy of the Jewish people, and of other big and little Hamans. Our own Haman, Kozar, loved these Purim sweetmeats; so, like it or not, we had to eat less ourselves so that we could bring him a goodly portion.

■

For many years of my adult life, I resided in one of the largest, perhaps the largest, city in the world; my childhood was spent in one of the smallest villages in the world. And yet, the miniature Ludvinovka did not leave me entirely unprepared for the giant New York. I am astonished to see, in retrospect, the many points that both places had in common in customs, beliefs, prejudices, and institutions—just a difference in scale and complexity.

Ludvinovka, like New York, had its rich (Kozar), its poor (the bulk of the village), and its middle-class (the *kulaki*). Property differences were sharp and clear; antagonisms were bitter and brutal. And where there were property differences, there was commerce. The peddlar came bringing goods from the city; the peasant took grain and vegetables to the city. A kind of primitive industry was represented by the windmills and a thrashing machine operated by a horse wearing blinders trudging endlessly around a treadle (like the donkey in [Lucius] Apuleius' *Golden Ass*). The school and the church were the educational institutions, inadequate but half a loaf [better than nothing].

■

Religion permeated the peasant's life from birth to death, although this did not prevent him from a belief in ghosts and witches. He thought the departed dead took an interest in his affairs, could visit him at night, and proffer advice. Those were the good souls. Naturally, there were the bad ones, too, and they were more numerous. The peasant had a highly complex demonology. The house had its house spirit *(domovoi),* the forest its forest spirit *(leshii),* the pond its water spirit *(vodianoi),* etc. A clever goblin could cohabit with a woman and produce a monstrosity. [Goblins] could take the form of sheep, goats, and roosters to mislead you and harm you. The cursed souls of the unbaptized, the witches, and the infidels were forever on a hunt to trap the unwary.

One of the most striking of universal phenomena on this tiny territory was the national question. In Ludvinovka and surrounding townships, four distinct nationalities were overtly or covertly warring among themselves. In Vasil'evka, a small settlement of Poles considered themselves the aristocrats of the territory, perhaps with good reason. They all had a good education; they had their own church and clubs, defiantly spoke Polish, and had contempt for the rest of the population. Then there were the Russians, few in number but in a position of power. They [controlled] the government; even the Poles had to pay taxes to them and be hailed before their courts. They ruled the country with an iron hand. The Ukrainians formed the bulk of the population, but they had to serve in the Russian army and learn, when they had a chance, the Russian language. They could not even print the Bible in Ukrainian. Lastly, the Jews. On the surface, their relations with the other three groups were normal, even friendly, but there always seemed to be an undercurrent of mistrust on [all] sides. And, in time of crisis—for example, during the peasants' uprisings against the landowners—the Jews had to run to the big cities to find some protection, although they did not always get it. At this point, it should be emphasized that these national hostilities were artificially created. Divide and conquer. There were always some, though not too many, who saw through the prejudices and fought against them. I am simply describing the national relations as I saw them, remembering clearly the reservations just made.

The Ukrainian would say occcasionally without apparent ill will: "The Jew neither sows nor reaps but he always has money," or "We love each other like brothers, but in business we deal with each other like Jews," and other such pleasantries without realizing that in Ludvinovka the Jews were the poorest of the poor.

The kids would sing jingles like the following:

Zhid, Zhid parkhovik

Zahubiv cherevik

A ia shov

Tai znaishov

Tai nasrav

Tai pishov

(Sheenie, sheenie, scabby sheenie[2]

Lost his shoe

I passed by

I found it

I sh–t into it

And was on my way)

Such jingles—and there were quite a few like it—didn't make much sense, but they hit the mark.

Even when the peasant meant to pay a compliment, it came out left-handed. Thus I grew up with the peasants; so naturally I spoke like them. They would pay me the following compliment: *"Zhidok, a balakaie iak cholovik"*—"A sheenie boy but talks like a human"—i.e., a Ukrainian.

The Jews tried to pay back in kind, at least verbally. Through no fault of their own, the peasants were 80–90 percent illiterate; the Jews, on the other hand, were literate in approximately the same measure, for the purpose of prayer in any case. Hence, when a Jew wanted to call another Jew an ignoramus, he would say obliquely "peasant." By the same token, he could pay a left-handed compliment to a peasant by saying that there was a Jewish head on him.

Jewish children, like the peasants, had their own jingles. For example:

Vakhalaklakes

Goyim makes

Yidden brokhes

Goyim kadokhes

(Vakhalaklakes

Sores [plagues] to the goyim

Blessings to the Jews

Chills [fever with chills and sweating] to the goyim)

The word *"vakhalaklakes"* is used here purely for its clearly articulated syllabication—*"Va-kha-lak-lakes";* its meaning has no relation whatever to the rest of the jingle. Why it was chosen would make an interesting inquiry for the student of folk-

lore. The word is found in Psalm 35 and means "slippery."[3]
Sholom Aleichem has an interesting and amusing story woven around *vakhalaklakes.*

Around 1905 there began to appear in small towns and
villages young men and women, in the guise of teachers,
midwives, etc., underground specialists trying, among other
things, to break down national prejudices. The task was hard,
but slow progress was being made, as I can testify from my
own experience.

■

Among the most remarkable phenomena linking the village
to the metropolis was art. The word "art" is part of the language of the Ukrainian intelligentsia; the peasant just used the
word *"harno,"* pretty. Art was, nevertheless, all around him. In
fact, next to labor and religion, art was the most pervasive activity in the life of the village. In this tiny community art was
perhaps more closely woven with daily tasks than was the case
in far larger social centers. The peasant decorated with gay
colors and with carvings sleighs, horses' harnesses, wives'
spinning wheels, and babies' cribs; he made beautiful toys,
whistles, and shepherd's pipes. His wife embroidered his shirts
and hers, as well as blouses, skirts, towels, and kerchiefs. Before Easter everybody, especially the women, took a hand in
the coloring of Easter eggs, covering them with a great variety of designs.

Perhaps nowhere was this spontaneous, unconscious use of
art as intimately interwoven with the life of the community as
in the Church. It was as if some expert, secret master organized painting, music, and architecture into a powerful synthesis that cast a spell over the congregation. I mentioned
before that the peasant's life was inescapably bound up with
the Church. His own birth and marriage; the birth, baptism,
and marriage of his children; the death of any member of the
family; celebration of holidays; the blessing of the harvest;
even the setting up of a new beehive, had to get a priest's
blessing. In consequence, the influence of the Church was
well nigh overwhelming. In times of crises the priests were

always ready to preach a sermon against the "free-thinkers" *(vol'nodumtsy)*, "rebels," "agitators," and "enemies of Tsar and country."

Compared with the cathedrals in cities like Kiev or Moscow, the village church may have appeared insignificant. For the village it was most impressive. This "frozen music" rose high into the air. Its white walls, green roofs, and tall belfry were in such great contrast with the small, grey, sprawling and often dilapidated *khaty* [huts] that it looked indeed like the abode of a superior being. Perhaps the architecture was a mixture of many styles (although some villages had excellent examples of original wooden architecture); to the peasant it looked like a sanctuary to be approached with reverence and awe. When, in response to the pealing of the church bells, the people poured into the church, that impression was multiplied manifold. All senses were assailed by a coordinated play of all the arts. The awesome images of the saints, the apostles, and the trinity painted by some itinerant *bogomaz* (painter of potboiling holy images), were seen in the crepuscular candle-light; the solemn voices of the choir—priest, deacon, teacher, and a group of local boys—held the congregation spellbound, while the floating odor of incense and the flickering lights of the candles kept it in a semihypnotic state. Here was a dramatic performance that really carried an emotional impact scarcely matched on any theatrical stage.

■

[On] the morning of New Year's Day, young village boys would come to our house with fistfuls of grain, which they proceeded to scatter to every corner of the house while singing the *koliady* [holiday songs] at the same time that [they] wished us *"zhito, pshenitsa i vsiakaia pashnitsa,"* a harvest of "rye, wheat, and other crops." We gave them some small coins; and then we wished one another a Happy New Year, and they departed. The boys did not realize the subtle irony in wishing us a "good harvest." We did not have any land to plant rye and wheat on. We were "outsiders." We constituted a miniature ghetto with all its legal and physical disabilities.

There was the village population on one side, with all (more or less) the appurtenances for a normal, integrated life on the land. And there was our house on the opposite side, set down plunk in the middle of a vacant lot exposed to the elements, just dust and a patch of grass here and there. We ate our own kind of food; we gave our children our own kind of education; and we celebrated our own holidays.

The house we occupied was rented from Kozar. Our neighbor and we, each, had a grocery, a tiny cubby hole at each end of the house. To supplement our meager incomes our neighbor rented a melon patch while we rented a windmill. Our livelihoods came obviously from dealing with the peasants, but this was restricted to the barest possible minimum.

Socially we might as well have been on a distant planet. Father was unhappy in this environment. Fanatically religious as he was, he would have preferred to go to daily prayer in a synagogue, listen to the singing of a cantor or the sermon of an itinerant preacher. He felt he was in exile *(golus),* but he was sustained by the firm faith in a happier hereafter. Not so the children; not for them the consolation of a hereafter. They left home as soon as they were able, lured by the vision of a freer, richer life elsewhere. Two of my brothers and a sister were in Kiev; two other sisters left home to get married (they got married by the intermediary of a *shadchan,* a marriage broker).

■

Like the other houses in the village, ours had a straw roof and an earthen floor inside. In the winter the windows were permanently frozen, and the accumulated snow on the window panes was decorated with fantastic flower-like designs, which I tried to copy.

The one place in the house where everybody liked to gather was around the oven, which was in a corner occupying about a third of the kitchen. The oven was a structure that rose from floor to ceiling in three sections, vertically one above the other. The lowest section was a square opening extending to the back wall; it was a storage place for vegetables, potatoes, onions, beets, pumpkins, and mainly straw for fuel. The next section above it was a step back in front and on the side. It had a semicircular opening like a barrel cut in half. This was where all the cooking and baking were done, and it was also the central heating plant. The fuel was straw. Because it was so rapidly consumed, it had to be fed to the stove continuously. Above that and reaching [to] the ceiling was a platform roomy enough to sit or lie [on]. It was the warmest spot in the house and was used mostly by older people and children.

The second half of the house, which was occupied by our neighbor, was exactly like ours but in reverse, that is, the two ovens were back to back. To enter our neighbor's house, we had to go outside. However, there was a hole in the wall connecting the two platforms above the oven, a short cut for the children to crawl from one [house] to the other. It was also a handy transfer spot when one family had to borrow something from the other. Its constant use was as a means of eavesdropping on conversations, not intended, or deliberately intended, to be heard; the two families quarreled from time to time, and they could always bolster an argument by citing something overheard.

The furniture of the house was of the simplest [kind]: a bed, a table, two benches, a couple of chairs, a cupboard, and a few boards attached at one end to the oven and at the other to the wall opposite and serving as additional sleeping space. The walls were bare except for two pictures. A *mizrach* hung on the East wall *(mizrach* means "East") indicating the direction of Jerusalem toward which the Jews turn in prayer. There was, in fact, an imaginary view of Jerusalem in the center of the *mizrach;* [this picture was] flanked by two equally imaginary lions. The other picture was of three heads: the Biblical Moses, Moses Maimonedes, and Moses Montefiore. An inscription read: "From Moses to Moses, there was no one like Moses."

When a piece of bread fell on the floor—even a crumb— it was to be picked up and kissed. Bread was precious. We did not starve, but food was not too plentiful. Our diet was perhaps adequate but somewhat monotonous: black bread, herring, potatoes, kasha, and borscht of beets or cabbage. A hard crust of bread rubbed with garlic was a between-meal snack [along with] tea with sugar, not mixed in the glass but held in the mouth to make it last longer. Meat was seldom on the table. When father had a chance to go to town, he would come back with a kosher chicken (slaughtered according to ritual). We then had a real feast in honor of Queen Sabbath: white bread (challah), chicken soup with noodles, chicken, and carrot or prune compote.

In the summer, when vegetables and berries were ripe, we had cucumbers, and we made the favorite jelly of raspberry. "Pray God we may not need it" always accompanied the making of jelly. Somehow jelly was supposed to be very good for the sick and convalescent. I was always present when the jelly was being made. When the foam reached the top of the vessel, it was skimmed off and given to me to taste. It was heavenly.

Like jelly, many household objects and foods were supposed to have medicinal value. In the winter, when headaches were frequent because of the overheated atmosphere in the house and the hermetically sealed windows and doors, a potato was sliced and the slices placed around the head to draw out the pain. For a bleeding finger, spider webs were collected from the corners, mixed with earth, and applied to the bleeding, etc.

A far more complicated folk medicine was practiced by the peasants. Practically every flower and plant was good for some disease: headache, toothache, and menstruation. Love potions were mixed for the lovelorn. Usually it was the women *babkas* who were the "medicine men." They knew the properties of herbs and roots and exactly what to apply to which disease.

Back to the oven. In the winter the top platform was the children's playground. Through the hole in the wall we climbed from one [house] to the other. We invented all kinds of games, including some not intended for the eyes of adults.

In the summer, it was, of course, the outdoors. I was alone a good deal of the time. Our neighbor's boy, though somewhat younger than I, was already away in a near town in a heder. My father did not favor my playing with the girls (I did not always obey his wish) and still less the peasants' children. So, I used to walk around in search of adventure by myself. I went to father's mill, but it was closed most of the summer (the busy time was in fall). I wandered around it and crawled underneath but got bored in the end. I went to the river. The tadpoles were just beginning to breed. The water was black with the myriad of black dots. I dug a small pit on the bank, which immediately filled with water by seepage. Then I scooped up a handful of tadpoles and put them into the pit. Daily I returned to see how they developed—a head, then two legs, then four legs, then lost their tails and leaped about in the grass.

I watched ants. Once I came across them clustered in a busy mass, moving restlessly like quick silver. They were dragging a tiny dead bird, evidently just hatched because it had no feathers yet. It must have fallen out of the nest. The ants swarmed around it, pulling it this way and that. They ran to the side, to the front, tried to straighten its course, and inched forward at the tiniest pace. Their action was so thoroughly reminiscent of human efforts to move a heavy load, I was fascinated. But I had to leave; and when I returned, there was no trace of the bird or ants.

■

Strange how associations of ideas or just ordinary memory will play tricks in unexpected ways. The scene of the ants' frenzied commotion came to me—of all places—in Egypt. I was visiting the Aswan Dam while it was still in the process of construction. It was 9:00 or 10:00 at night. The search lights cast an eerie, luminous haze over the extraordinary spectacle. In the human vortex on the bottom of the yawning abyss, one could not distinguish individual human beings but only masses of changing shape and as frenziedly agitated as the ants many times multiplied.

Stranger still—the other comparison I thought of almost at the same time was Dante's *Inferno*.

∎

Sometimes I would walk out [in the] early morning and find
a brilliantly sparkling spider web and a dewy bush. I walked
on to the river, sat on the bank, and just did nothing. On the
opposite bank, willows bent over the water, their leaves stir-
ring almost invisibly in the faint breeze. Dragon flies flitted
over the surface of the stream in front of me. Tiny fish rose to
the top in a mass, dipped down rapidly, swept forward in a
semicircle, like a flock of birds in the sky. I watched and
watched and finally dozed off, until I was awakened by a
woman who came down to wash her laundry. She rinsed the
towels in the stream, then put them on a wooden plank and
hammered the dirt out of them with a wooden mallet.

Once I decided to become a planter. Not far from our
house I found a patch of tall weeds inside of which I cleared
a spot where I planted a cucumber. Secretly I weeded and
watered the plant and was thrilled to see it grew beyond the
cleared spot into the thick weeds.

Once in my ramblings, I came upon a swarm of bees in a
black squirming mass settled on the trunk of a tree. Unthink-
ing, I picked up a twig and hit the mass square in the center.
In a flash, I did not know what hit me. It seemed as if every
one of the bees was after me. I ran as fast as my legs could
carry me, but I couldn't outrun the bees. They alighted on
my head and kept sending sharp arrows into it. I cried out in
pain and flailed my hands wildly about my head. When I finally got home, my head and arms were full of bumps. They
[those who tended me] mixed sugar and water and smeared
this sticky mixture [on] the affected areas. This made me extremely uncomfortable. And I wasn't allowed to scratch myself. I kept shy of bees forever after.

5
THE YESHIVA

Armed with the prophetic blessing of the zaddik, my father took me to the yeshiva in Vasil'kov. Situated on the river Stugna, a branch of the Dnieper, Vasil'kov was, and still is, an important city, a county *(uezd)* seat, administratively next in importance to Kiev itself. Although some 30 versts from Kiev the two cities had a common history. At one time all of Vasil'kov belonged to the *Kievo-pecherskaia lavra* [Kiev Monastery of the Caves], the most famous of Russian monasteries. A railroad connected the two cities, though the Vasil'kov station was eight versts from the city proper. This circumstance gave employment to some drivers who owned phaetons, horse-drawn cabs, that ferried passengers from the station for whom they fought like tigers. You could not drive a phaeton unless you had strong fists and a sharp tongue.

The population of close to 20,000 was about half Jewish. The city had several elementary Russian schools, and one junior high school *(dvukhklassnaia,* two classes above the elementary grades), several churches, a regular fire brigade, and a fire watchtower on top of which firemen stood watch 24 hours a day. Besides the weekly fairs, there was a big annual fair which drew crowds from far away, even beyond the county. In addition to the government and police institutions, the city could boast a regiment of dragoons. Among the industries and businesses were lumber yards, leather factories, brick yards, pottery establishments, breweries, seltzer works, and a steam flour mill besides the many water and windmills. Along the main streets were many handsome buildings, two and three stories high. One three-story building was topped by a tower almost as high as the entire building. The tower was gaily decorated with colored triangles.

The Jewish sector, as usual in the center of town, was correspondingly complex. Besides the many institutions that characterized every large Jewish community—homes for the aged, orphanages, charities for the indigent, and heders—it could also take pride in things other Jewish communities lacked. Thus, at one time Vasil'kov was the seat of the celebrated Zaddik of Talna, whose influence among the Hasidim was enormous. He presided at his "court," was held in great reverence, and was supported in grand style. People from everywhere came to him for solace and advice. Then, of course, Vasil'kov had a yeshiva, the object of our journey, also widely known and highly regarded.

Father could not afford my maintenance, and so I became a ward of the city. Before leaving me in the care of my custodians, father and I had a very serious conference.

"You are now joining the ranks of the chosen from among the Jews," said my father. "Never forget this and make yourself worthy of your task and the good name of your family. Remember, you do not come from a family of shoemakers; you come from a family of scholars who were as pious as they were learned."

"You do not come from a family of shoemakers." Father worked harder than any shoemaker and earned less. One daughter was working away from home as a seamstress; a son worked as a locksmith in Kiev; and I was a ward of charity. Yet, he entertained the customary disdain for work of the hands and had the fanatical belief that only in piety and learning lay the salvation of Israel. As he and others told me, he came from a family of scholars. Untoward circumstances had prevented him from reaching the goal; now his son would achieve where he himself had failed. It was not very long before this ideal lost its glamour for me, but for the moment, I fully agreed with father.

I lived *af tag,* day to day. I ate and slept each day with a different family by rotation. Monday I stayed with one family, Tuesday with another, Wednesday with a third, and so on through the week. The following Monday I would be back with the family I started with, and the circuit would be repeated. What kind of families were they? Workers mostly and small merchants—not rich at all. The rich presumably supported charity in other ways, or perhaps I did not represent a desirable boarder. I have no clear memory of my benefactors. I saw them only at mealtimes. They did not take any special interest in me. I was shy, and they probably felt they were doing their duty by God and their conscience. I do remember, however, one woman who bandaged my finger when I cut it at one meal. The same woman also occasionally washed my head. I used to go to the public bathhouse, but the wearing of old clothes, the unsanitary conditions of the yeshiva, and the general neglect of personal cleanliness (which was definitely not next to godliness) brought on the Pharaoh's Third Plague in almost Biblical proportions.[1]

The yeshiva introduced me to the Talmud, and it was a painful introduction. The students ranged in age from under ten (I was about nine) to young manhood. They all seemed to be ahead of me. They all had a more systematic preparation, having started, many of them, at the age of three or four. Our studies consisted of a rapid weekly review of a section of the Pentateuch; the rest of the time, it was the Talmud. Hour after hour we sang out the text, swayed rhythmically back and forth as we delved into the involved reasoning and hairsplitting argumentation. I was reading familiar words but found it difficult to know what they were saying. However, as my father had said, my "good head"—i.e., my retentive memory—and endless repetition helped me retain the words in proper sequence, though in only a slightly intelligible connection.

My incomprehension worried me. Why was I such a "peasant"? I was absolutely certain that what we were studying was divinely inspired. I vividly recalled the scenes I had been witnessing in the synagogue—of the pious Jews arguing fervently and with passion the fine points of Talmudic lore for hours on end. Would illumination ever come to me? My hope was strengthened as I watched the older students, some of whom surely must have been initiated into the mysteries of what they were learning. They swayed back and forth and from side to side as well, and they sang out the words as in a daze or in a trance. Were they "God-intoxicated," or was it just the foul air of the room?

The studies went on from early morning till late at night. A few flickering, sputtering, smoking kerosene lamps provided the illumination. It did not take long before my eyes became sore and inflamed. I woke up in the morning with my eyes pasted together, but the recuperative power of childhood is marvelous. I went to school and got through the daily routine as usual. Late at night we all scattered to our homes through the pitch darkness.

■

I shivered with fright because my head was still as full of witches and ghosts and *nit gute* (evil [not good] spirits) as when I left the village. In fact, it was enriched by many additions picked up along the way in a kind of extracurricular education. Those beliefs were to me not superstitions; they were confirmed by many "eye witness" accounts. Here, for example: I am passing by the synagogue and the following is a "true" story of what happened in it only the other day:

> A local woman woke up one morning toward dawn.
> Time for the morning prayers, she said to herself. She dressed and went out. Not a soul in the street. Too early, perhaps. However, as she approached the synagogue, she noticed a light in the men's section, though the women's was still dark. Thank God, the men are already there. Inside the women's section, she discovered that she was the first arrival. Stumbling in the dark she came over to the little window in the wall that separated the men from the women and said: "Will you please give me a light."
> A hand pushed through the window carrying a lighted candle. It did not stop but kept moving, propelled by an enormously long arm that stretched all the way across the room to the opposite wall. Nobody was visible on the other side of the window. Horrified and speechless at this extraordinary sight, the woman could only stare with open mouth.

"You aren't frightened are you?" boomed a funereal voice coming from somewhere and nowhere and everywhere at the same time. A gigantic tongue came slithering through the window like an eel or a snake crowding the room with loops and bows and convolutions. With a thunderous laugh that reverberated throughout the synagogue, it clasped the woman in its coils. She was found unconscious the next morning.

But look, here is a goat crossing the path, undoubtedly a *gilgul,* a changeling that loves to appear in the shape of a goat.[2] In a moment it (he/she) might break out in demonical laughter and melt into thin air. And over there . . . but I am already at my door. I rush into the room, say my night prayer, leap into bed, and in a minute am dead to the world.

■

A yeshiva *bokher* (young man) was recognized by certain external "trademarks." He wore a long caftan, grew long *peyos* (earlocks), and wore a tallith katan (a small praying scarf).[3] In front of each ear, you let your hair grow long, sometimes twisted into a corkscrew, which flaps in the wind as you walk. One day I suffered a near tragedy. I was getting a haircut when the barber thought he would have a little fun at my expense. (Life in a provincial city is dull, and I was defenseless.) When he got through, I saw him wink at his partner and, quick as a flash, half my earlocks were gone under his shears. Fortunately only half, but still I felt naked. I shed bitter tears, fearing that the wrath of God was going to descend upon me.

Underneath my coat, next to my shirt, I wore the tallith katan, a rectangular piece of cloth with a hole in the middle, which slipped over the head like a Mexican serape. Its edges stuck out in full view. Dangling from each corner of the scarf (two in front, two in back) was a long fringe, whose strands were strongly wound and tied at the top. These fringes had a talismanic power against many evils, but they were wholly [ineffective] against vermin. In fact, they offered about the best breeding place for them; the nit nests were so artfully hidden in the many windings and knots [that] no amount of washing was able to remove them entirely.

■

I missed my red and blue pencil, which had given me so much pleasure back in Ludvinovka in the drawing of birds, flowers, etc. That was not to be thought of now. It was alright to play with pencils in "babyhood." I was now engaged in a serious mission and had to leave childish things behind me. However, I secretly enjoyed looking at pictures, if not making them. There were new pictures [in Vasil'kov] that I had not seen before. I admired the store signs and none more than those over bakeries: resplendent horns of plenty from which fell, in a generous cascade—cakes, challahs, and cookies *(bubliki)* of all kinds. I looked with envy at the walls and the vault of the synagogue where birds, flowers, vines, leaves, and scroll were skillfully combined in colorful arabesques.

Only once did I make a drawing in ink. As is well-known, many Jewish holidays and prayers harken back to life and customs in ancient Palestine. Thus prayers are still read requesting rain and dew *(tal u-motor)*. I made a little drawing in the fall announcing the prayer. No one needed to be reminded of it, but no one objected to the drawing. It was done, after all, for a good purpose, though I actually did it for my own pleasure. I embellished the borders with scrolls and flowers.

But there may have been still another reason, of which I was not aware of at the time. To the ghetto Jew rain is only an inconvenience—slush in the street and a leaking ceiling in the house. Dew is just a minor nuisance, if the Jew ever becomes aware of it at all. *Tal u-motor* is but a pathetic, historic memory. To me, on the other hand, looking back to the village of my birth, rain and dew meant the rainbow in the sky, the echo of a distant thunder, rivulets through the grass, and clean, wet, glistening trees. Dew was even nicer than the rain. You walked out early in the morning to find a pearly carpet sparkling in the morning sun. You sloshed your bare feet over it—what a delicious coolness—and made a path of green velvet. Somewhere on a bush a magnificently contrived spider web hung as if floating in the air, lustrous with a million minuscule lights. Birds spoke to each other in the trees, and sheaves of slanting light streamed down through the foliage.

Gradually, as the weeks and months went by, my incomprehension [of my studies] began to melt. I was catching up with
the rest of the clan. But, just as I sighted land, disaster struck.
My brother in Kiev learned where I was and under what
conditions. He asked one of my aunts from Kiev to take a trip
to Vasil'kov to investigate. A cab brought her from the railroad straight to the yeshiva. When I was pointed out to her (I
had never met her before), she shuddered. Pale with red eyes,
dressed in ill-fitting hand-me-downs, I looked like an orphan
in a Talmud Torah (school for the indigent). She reported her
findings to my brother, who came down on the first train
out. Without as much as a "by your leave" to anyone, he
took me out of the yeshiva and to Kiev.

My own feelings in the matter were mixed. I was glad to
go because I knew that I would eat better, dress better, would
not have to go out alone at night. On the other hand, Kiev
was, as I knew from conversation with other boys, a den of
iniquity, where Jewish men walked around bare-headed, married women did not wear wigs, and Jewish children did not
speak Jewish but only Russian. But then again, did not Daniel
come out of the lion's den unharmed? Thus were the *yetzer tov*
(the urge to do good) and the *yetzer ha-ra* (the urge to do evil)
engaged in a tug of war—as [is] our profound belief [that]
they always were—for the human soul. Perhaps, if I had my
choice, I might have stayed in spite of everything. But I had
no choice. I followed my brother to Kiev with my inner conflict unresolved. Father's triumph had been short-lived.

6

KIEV ART SCHOOL

The trip from Vasil'kov to Kiev was so full of surprises, so full of unexpected sights and sounds, so wholly absorbing that I forgot for the moment all my doubts and fears.

First, we hired the best phaeton available. My brother evidently wanted to start me off right. Until then I had ridden only in peasant wagons, crude affairs knocked together from unfinished boards and logs, shaped like a trough, [with] straw covering the bottom to ease the ride. Into [the wagon] were piled sacks of potatoes, flour, pumpkins, and people. It rested on hard wheels and was pulled by two, more often by one, nag. The roads were, of course, unpaved; and when you rode, the wagon shook [so hard it made] your bones rattle and your guts shake. The dust rose in clouds filling your nose, ears, and eyes.

Now we sat in a comfortable seat; the driver was perched high in front. The horses moved at a fast trot; the carriage rocked gently on its springs as the wheels rolled along a paved road. I had seen such carriages occasionally driving through town, but I always imagined they were only for the rich. And here I was carried in one of them myself. Gradually, as we left the center of town, the houses became smaller and smaller, and we were out in the open field. Before I had a chance to examine the suburbs, we arrived at the station.

At the station, we found a large crowd inside and out: some people seeing relatives off, others expecting relatives to arrive, merchants, traveling salesmen, and police. We stepped into the buffet and had a glass of tea. A piercing whistle rent the air, and an enormous, odd-looking monster lumbered in. Mentally I compared it with the biggest and strangest thing I read about, the Leviathan. It huffed and puffed; the wheels screeched over the tracks; steam hissed below; and thick clouds of smoke belched above. Suddenly, it gave up its breath and stopped. People began climbing in and out of the doors.

I had never seen a train before. When we took our seats, I bombarded my brother with questions. He tried to explain to me the workings of the train, but I don't think he had sufficient knowledge of it himself. He said, as so many parents say to their children, "When you go to school and learn more of science, you'll understand all about it." My attention was already on something else. I was looking through the window. Houses, trees, and telegraph poles flew past before you had time to look at them properly. Sometimes it seemed as if the train was stationary, and everything else was moving. I was turning my head trying to follow the vanishing objects. Before I was aware of it, we arrived at the Kiev station.

We descended, and I saw more of the same kind of monsters, but now they did not look so menacing. An enormous crowd, moving in all directions without any apparent destination, swallowed us. My brother took me by the hand and guided me carefully through the mob until we came to a trolley. The trolley took us straight to the aunt who had visited me in Vasil'kov. [My] brother gave her some instructions, assured me that everything would be well, and left.

My aunt was a widow with three daughters, one a year younger than I, the next a year older than I, and the third of marriageable age. In fact, she [the third] was engaged to my eldest brother, a bookkeeper. The aunt lived on Kurenevka [Street], at the outskirts of Kiev where she owned a grocery.

Only certain categories of Jews enjoyed the right of domicile in Kiev: workers in a number of trades, students attending an institution, cantonists (veterans of the army of Nicholas I), First and Second Guild Merchants, and women hired out as domestics. Young women students not attending schools but preparing themselves for examinations often took advantage of this practice [of hiring out as domestic help].

Failing [to attain a job as a domestic], they could always purchase a Yellow Passport (license to engage in prostitution)—and some did. Thus only a limited number of Jews could settle in Kiev legally; yet, there were always several times the legal number. How did they manage it? Chiefly by the unwritten "Law of Greasing Official Palms." But there were also legal ways. My aunt illustrated [one] of the ways. She owned the grocery, but nominally she was only a clerk and heir to a cantonist to whom she paid a monthly fee for the service. At the same time, the police, too, were not neglected. The grocery prospered.

She accepted me as part of the family. First, she got me a new suit of clothes, which, for once, was a good fit. Formerly, my suits were usually bought "with an eye to the future,"—i.e., a couple of sizes too large so that I would grow into them. By the time I did, they were reduced to little more than rags. Next, she threw all my old clothes into the garbage, including the prayer scarf. My hair was cut to the skull, which she doused and scrubbed thoroughly with kerosene. It felt so pleasant to wear clean clothes and not to have to scratch oneself.

My brother engaged a teacher to give me instruction in the Russian language, arithmetic, and geography. He was an extern, one who studied privately—outside the regular school system—in preparation for the college entrance examinations. Among the many disabilities to which Jews were subject under Tsarism, one of the worst was the restriction on education. Within the Pale of Settlement (the territory on which the Jews were permitted to reside), the secondary and higher institutions of learning admitted (at least in theory) 10 percent Jews. In practice, this made it difficult, often prohibitive, for the poor to gain admission. The rich could hire a tutor to prepare their sons and daughters for the entrance examinations, which had to be passed with the highest marks in every subject, and also to help them with their studies at school. Not infrequently bribes to school administrators were helpful.

The thirst for knowledge among the less prosperous Jews was phenomenal. No sacrifice was too great to give the sons and daughters a good education. The "people of the book" transferred [their] zeal from holy lore to secular knowledge. And the poor students found a way around the restrictions. They studied at home with private teachers. At the end of several years they took the college entrance examinations. The few lucky ones were admitted; the others, with the help of some wealthy patron or relatives, went abroad to complete their studies. And thus, there were regular colonies of those students in France, Italy, Belgium, and especially Switzerland. They were a wonderful group of young men and women, unquenchingly thirsty for knowledge, enlightenment, and justice. One found them in every social movement and party: Social Democrat, socialist, revolutionary, Zionist, Bundist, etc.

Such were the externs, one of whom was my teacher. I made rapid progress, especially in the Russian language. (My aunt's daughters spoke only Russian, as did their friends.)

I was learning rapidly, but everything was bewildering. I had come from the tiny village of Ludvinovka (500 souls) to Guermanovka (3,500), to Vasil'kov (20,000), and now to the mother of Russian cities, Kiev (250,000). The continuity of my progress was only apparent. Actually, Kiev meant a sudden, violent break with my past. I was lifted out of one environment and set down into another, terrifyingly different. Previously, I had known the peasant and the ghetto. To be sure, I was aware of the outside world of policemen, merchants, and soldiers. But that did not concern me. My road was clear and my destination certain. Now it was precisely this outside world, vastly enlarged, into which I plunged without sails or a rudder. I was forced to make adjustments to a world I had been taught to ignore or even to despise.

Sights and sounds, one stranger than another, crowded upon me: rows of graceful poplars along the hill-and-dale configuration of the city; the vast expanse of the Dnieper River flowing below the Hill of St. Vladimir; beautiful parks and great historic monuments; a seemingly countless number of churches, whose resplendent domes dominated the streets; fashionable Kreshchatik [Street] and the magnificent displays of gold and diamonds at Marshak's; and gastronomic opulence at Pashkov Brothers—imported wines and sweets and

exotic fruits like bananas and pineapples that I had never before seen. And the people! People moving in all directions, in
endless and inexhaustible waves. Uniforms everywhere: soldiers, officers, policemen, Cossacks, and—perhaps the most
colorful groups of all—students. You knew what school a girl
attended by the design and color of her uniform: blue, white,
green, and brown, etc. Male students were more easily recognizable by the color of the stripes on their suits and the emblem on their hats.

■

Kiev was the "mother of Russian cities," according to Prince
Oleg,[1] the cradle of the Russian Orthodox Church, the birth
place of the Russian Empire, a city of holy relics, churches,
and monasteries, none more holy than the [Kievan] Monastery of the Caves *(Kievo-pecherskaia lavra)*. Pilgrims came here
in a steady procession from all parts of the vast empire,
dressed in the oddest attire, depending on the section of the
country they came from, making a striking contrast to the
Kievites. Many of them had walked for months in order to
reach the *lavra,* to kneel in the churches, beg forgiveness, seek
a cure, visit the catacombs, kiss the sarcophagus of some
saintly monk, and leave their kopecks, which they had
begged on their way.

■

I revisited Kiev several years ago. After the destruction of
much of the city by the Teutonic fury of the Nazis, Kiev was
rebuilt almost beyond recognition. Many spots of the city that
I had known so well were gone: the Duma (town hall) in
front of which I stood on the fateful October 17, 1905, in the
midst of a jubilant people; and the Karaite *kenassa* [house of
worship], which I had sketched as a student. My two sisters
and their families, my aunts, and other relatives were lying in
Babi Yar (perhaps buried half alive).[2] But the catacombs were
still there, and the pilgrims, perhaps in smaller numbers, were
very much in evidence. I bought a candle and went down

into the caves. There were the same narrow cubicles [with] sarcophagi in them which many pilgrims bent down to kiss. There were the underground chapels and people shuffling along like shadows, holding flickering candles, and singing hymns. Suddenly I was startled by a familiar melody. It was the hymn to the health of the Tsar that I first learned in the village school; the hymn included the lines "Victory to our Emperor Nikolai Aleksandrovich [Tsar Nicholas II]." Incredible. I came closer to the singers and listened more carefully. Yes, the melody and the words were the same with a very important exception: Victory was now asked for the Church instead of for the Emperor—"victory for our holy Church" *(E pur si muove)*. The monastery was restored to its former state. One tower, however, was left standing in ruin to remind the world of Nazi atrocities. A sign hung in full view giving the address of the nearest atheist center.

■

Another point of central interest was the statue of St. Vladimir. Erected in 1853, it stood on top of a high and steep hill overlooking the spot were Vladimir is supposed to have led (or driven) his subjects to baptism.[3] [The figure] holds a tall cross which is lighted by electricity at night and can be seen on the opposite side of the river.

Kiev was a city of many and frequent church processions, celebrating some holiday (Easter, for example), blessing a departing army, pleading for victory in war, and sometimes even joining a pogrom mob ("love thy neighbor"). The two most important ones were on July 15, the Day of Prince Vladimir, and January 6, the Day of the Epiphany. On July 15, every church in the city sent out a procession with banners, icons, and choirs. As the church bells pealed everywhere, the many separate processions merged below the statue of Vladimir, at the baptismal well to celebrate the conversion of Kiev to Greek Orthodoxy.

Perhaps the most impressive spectacle of all was the procession on January 6. It took place on the frozen Dnieper in order to sanctify its water. As the city shook with bells resounding in every section, the marching masses proceeded at a slow pace. The highest dignitaries of the church and the city government led the procession. What resplendent vestments! Satin, velvet, brocade, damask, lavishly embroidered in gold and silver thread and encrusted with pearls and other stones. Countless banners, richly decorated, rose above the marchers. Throughout the long lines, people carried crosses, icons, and portraits of the Tsar. The choir sang hymns, and the censers sprayed holy incense. Many people carried vessels of all descriptions in which to bring home the sanctified water of the Dnieper. (Years later I watched Hindus at Benares taking with them holy water from the Ganges after they had bathed in it.) The vast throng, outlined sharply on the white glistening ice, looked from a distance like some fabled creature gliding slowly forward, its outward shape constantly shifting and changing color.

But I am getting too far ahead. I was learning to know Kiev and, in time, came to have a deep admiration of its many beautiful sites and rich historic associations. Even now after I have seen many capitals of the world, I still regard it as a city not to be missed by any world traveler.

■

I was making steady progress, but the process of learning was perhaps no harder than the process of unlearning certain habits, beliefs, and practices formerly acquired. I arrived from my "previous existence" with a set of convictions I was taught to regard as immutable, absolute convictions whose violators were visited upon by inexorable retribution. My father, with whom I carried on a regular correspondence, never failed to remind me that I was a member of the "chosen people." But my new environment subtly, imperceptibly, even pleasantly, tended to undermine those convictions, tended to show them as harmful, unnecessary, and obscurantist.

It was a difficult, sometimes painful transition. I gave up slowly, stubbornly, step by step; each step, however, making the next step easier. To begin with, I was thrown into the company of women. Except for my early childhood, my playmates had always been boys. For a yeshiva *bokher*, to play with girls would have been both incongruous and a sin. Wasn't I offering in my morning prayers thanks to God "that Thou hast not made me into a woman?" I was very shy at first, and when the little girls gathered at my aunt's, I sulked in a corner. However, in a matter of weeks, I was out in the street chattering Russian with the neighborhood boys and girls.

It is required of every pious Jew that he wear his hat at all times. I did at the beginning. This made me conspicuous, especially when other men were present who, of course, removed their hats on entering the house. One of my cousins who was a frequent visitor at my aunt's house used to grab the hat from my head and throw it angrily on the floor. I was hurt and, though I was ashamed to cry, my eyes would fill with tears. Soon, whenever I expected him, I would remove my hat and put it on again as soon as he left. It did not take long before I was bareheaded like the rest with no urging from anybody. (My cousin later emigrated to Australia where he married and became a faithful member of a synagogue.)

It took even longer for me to ride the trolley on a Saturday, something strictly forbidden by orthodox custom. Normally, when I went to see my brother midweek, I took the trolley; but when we had an appointment on Saturday, I walked the long and hilly distance both ways, even if I came home pooped. One day I made the fatal step, with a lot of trepidation to be sure, but I made it. Thereafter, it was easy.

I went through a similar evolution (or revolution) with food. I no longer looked for the kosher sign when we stepped into a restaurant.

It was decided to place me in an art school. Why an art school? My flirtation with pen and pencil had reached Kiev before my arrival. I also continued to sketch during the months of my preliminary preparations. Everybody was thereupon convinced that a born artist was in their midst. An artist's career looked glamorous (none of my family ever met an artist), as it generally does to people who know artists from books and opera. My aunt's two younger daughters were themselves studying music and looking toward musical careers. But the consideration that probably outweighed all others was the greater accessibility to the art school as compared with other secondary schools. By some quirk of official illogic, the quota system (10 percent or less for Jews) did not apply to art schools. Yet it was in the full sense a secondary school both in art (preparation for the Art Academy in St. Petersburg) and general education (college preparatory). While the study of art was obligatory, the classes in general education were not. You could take art alone or together with education; you could not take education alone. And, although you might have completed your general education with the highest marks, you were not automatically admitted to college.

I passed the examination in education; in art a talk with an instructor was enough. My brother fitted me out with a brand new shiny uniform embroidered all over with blue stripes, the official color of the art school. With his own hands he made me a metal case for my pencils, pen points, and charcoal erasers. I was launched.

The system of art education in the Kiev Art School differed considerably from that which I came to know later in Western Europe and the United States. It was a melting pot containing ingredients from distant lands and times, a carry-over from the Royal French Academy, something from the old Russian Imperial Academy, and even a pinch of [Baccio] Bandinelli.[4] There were three faculties: painting, sculpture, and architecture (this had been a feature of [Ivan] Shuvalov's Art Academy of the Three Distinguished Arts established by Queen [Empress] Elizabeth in 1758).

The method of art instruction was exaggeratedly academic and rigidly departmentalized. You began with [Paul] Cézanne's favorite figures (though the teachers had never heard the name [of Cézanne]): the cube, the cone, and the cylinder. They were made of wood. You drew them separately, then in various combinations. First you drew them in line; later you learned how to shade them. The teacher was a woman who had her own peculiar notions of how to impart knowledge to her charges. She placed the cylinder on the table against the background of a white wall so that the light from a window on the left illumined one side of the cylinder and threw a shadow from it on the right. A bright line was formed where the edge of the cylinder met the shadow. For some reason, that bright line displeased the teacher.

"Do you see the bright line on the cylinder?"

I agreed.

"Well, it's not really there, as you can prove by moving the table some distance from the wall so that no shadow falls on it." Suiting action to the word, the teacher moved the table; and sure enough, the bright line disappeared.

"You see, the white line only *seems* to be there. Consequently, when you put the shading in, grade it from light to dark but disregard the line."

I disagreed; but at that time, I still believed that teachers knew best.

After this lesson in chiaroscuro came the lesson in perspective. A cube was placed where the cylinder had been.

"As you know, the three planes of the cube that we see are equal. The lines that connect them are also equal. And yet the vertical line closest *seems* longer than the ones more distant. Similarly, of the four horizontal lines which bound the top plane, the two nearest you *seem* longer. And that is how you must draw them."

It was somehow confusing, but teacher knew best.

There was an examination every six months. If you had mastered the first lessons and were at home among geometric toys, you were transferred to the next class, the Ornament Class. At first you were given casts, like fleurs-de-lis, egg-and-darts, and acanthus leaves. By degrees you passed to something more elaborate, like Renaissance and Rococo ornament. This was one of the most difficult classes in the school. You were not promoted to the next class until you could draw and shade with the most photographic exactitude every leaf, scroll, and convolution. Incidentally, this minutest verisimilitude was required in every class including the highest. You were not considered incompetent if it took you as long to graduate from the art classes as it took [you] to graduate from general education—seven years.

Next came the Mask Class. Casts from the front part of a head [were studied] to familiarize the student with the facial features of the head. You drew the mask in profile, three quarters, or *en face* [from the front] as it hung on the wall; again, to study foreshortening, you drew it as it lay flat on the table.

The next, more advanced class [Head Class], substituted full-size plaster casts of the head: Caesar, Blind Homer, Alexander the Great, Diana, and others. You were now ready for the living model, not the full figure, but only the head. The models chosen were "types": the bearded peasant, the ice cream vendor with padded head gear and ice cream pail on top, and the pilgrim with a sack on his back.

After months of drawing the head, you went back to the cast in the Figure Class, where you painfully learned to draw the figures of Apollo Belvedere, Hercules, the Discus Thrower, and other classical plaster casts.

Last and highest was the Life Class. Unlike the other classes, which met in large square rooms, the Life Class met in a room shaped like an amphitheatre or like an operation room in a school of medicine. Circular rows or seats receded toward the wall, one above the other; facing them was a dais for the model, a little higher than the lowest row. Seats were chosen by lot. Number one entered the room to pick his seat; others followed in rapid succession; and pretty soon there was a general scramble up and down the rows, the last as likely to find a good seat as the first. The teacher was present to pose the model.

The process of drawing the model was slow, elaborate, and according to a regular routine. You made a preliminary "blocked in" sketch in charcoal. You shaded the main areas. Then you corrected the sketch with the teacher's approval. Now over the charcoal sketch you made a precise outline in carbon pencil. You brushed off the charcoal with a chamois cloth, which left the carbon outline exposed. Slowly, meticulously, you began shading the drawing in carbon pencil, every detail rendered with the utmost precision. Each step had to be approved by the teacher, who came to class once or twice a week. There was, of course, a monitor to keep order in the room in the teacher's absence. It took from three weeks to a month to finish the drawing (in Western Europe and the United States a week is more than enough). When completed, you sprayed the drawing with fixative and showed it to the teacher for final approval.

There were periodic memory exercises in all the classes. There were composition assignments. I remember one that caused a lot of hilarity. The Head Class was given the poem "Tsar Saltan" by Pushkin to read and [from which to] pick any incident for illustration. It is briefly the story of a king who marries one of three sisters. Naturally, the other two sisters are jealous and watch their opportunity for foul play. While the King is away on an expedition and the Queen gives birth to his first son, the sisters are busy plotting. They intercept letters. By various intrigues and manipulations, they convince the Senate that the Queen and her son must be imprisoned in a large barrel and floated out to sea to starve and drown. Of course, the plot is foiled and "they lived happily ever after." When the compositions were brought to class for inspection, more than half of them showed no King or Queen or Senate. As if by prearrangement, about half the students chose the same incident—the barrel floating on the waves.

Painting began with the Head Class: still life at first, then heads, and finally figures. Anatomy was a required subject for the Life Class. The more advanced students had to do actual dissecting, not in school, however, but in a special institution called the Anatomical Museum. A physician was in charge. The bodies of indigents and criminals were used for the purpose of study.

The students formed a conglomerate body probably not paralleled in any other Russian school. Youngsters in their teens, men past middle-age—bearded and serious—well-to-do city slickers in uniforms of the finest materials with trousers tight to the bursting point (the style of the period), and country bumpkins who had walked from their village like their neighbors who had come on a pilgrimage to the holy monasteries. Sometimes they [the students from the country] received a package of food from home. In the summer, they would be back in the village to help their families with work in the fields. There were bohemian-looking students, hair in "artistic disorder," jacket thrown carelessly over the shoulders like a cloak; and university part-time students who attended their own institutions [as well as] the art school. Sometimes, when the teacher was absent, arguments floated in the air—political, literary, and aesthetic. The most common language was Russian; but once in a while one could hear a couple of Ukrainians exchanging ideas in their mother-tongue or Jewish students swapping jokes in Yiddish. There was the regular assortment of political faiths; but they were not often aired aloud, because, while most of the students were liberal, radical exceptions were not uncommon.

During vacation the art students left Kiev for the most part. The better-to-do went to a dacha (summer resort); many went to the villages to help with labor on the farm; a few found work in the city. I usually went to visit my sisters, [each of whom] lived in a different town. As the new term opened, everybody brought sketches and stories of summer adventure and romance. A couple of students told of being arrested for sketching on suspicion of spying (it happened during the Russo–Japanese War). New faces made their appearance, and a few lucky ones had gone either to the Academy in St. Petersburg or abroad.

The school faculty of the art department was undistinguished. Only one of the teachers, a kind of visiting professor, N[ikolai] K[ornilovich] Pimonenko, had a local and even something of a national reputation. The Ukrainians considered him a national artist because his paintings depicted Ukrainian life and customs: wedding ceremonies, work in the fields, and views of villages. One of his paintings, which we went to admire in the local museum, represented people returning from church in the evening. The mixed orange and blue lights of the lanterns and the moon formed a pattern of contrasts on the snow and the people, which was pointed out to us again and again as a skillful accomplishment to emulate.

The Museum of Art and Antiquities, where this painting was housed and which to us was an extracurricular source of education, was situated at one of the most picturesque spots in the city, on Aleksandrovskaia Square at the confluence of several streets: On the left, it was flanked by Kreshchatik, the most fashionable street in Kiev; on the right, by the Royal

Garden and the Dnieper beyond; and straight ahead was the monument of Prince St. Vladimir surveying the city from the top of a hill. The Museum was eclectically classical in style, a broad stairway leading to the entrance, sculptured lions—one on each side—and a stately colonnade above. The collection inside was not particularly outstanding: a few foreign pictures, more representative Russian art, and, probably best of all, a collection of Ukrainian folk art. What we went to the museum for were mainly exhibitions that came occasionally from other centers.

The artists who drew the greatest attention were the "Wanderers" *[Peredvizhniki]*, rebels of another age. The Wanderers had their origin in the seventies [1870s] in the wake of a widespread movement (parallel with a similar movement in literature), which was both political and aesthetic. One of its members, [Ivan] Kramskoi called the movement "the second emancipation of the serfs." They condemned unreservedly the academicians for dealing almost exclusively with "refined" subjects drawn from Greek and Roman life and mythology. The Wanderers wanted to learn from the people—the people here and now—to learn from them, to teach them, and to come close to them. With this in view, they organized traveling exhibitions throughout the country, bringing to the people the kind of pictures that dealt with their own experiences.[5]

The most celebrated artist among the Wanderers, the "Samson of Russian Art," according to the noted critic [Vladimir] Stasov, was Il'ia Repin. I remember the veritable furor among students, teachers, writers, and critics that greeted his painting *The Temptation of Christ (Get Thee Behind Me, Satan)*. The huge canvas occupied an entire wall. On the crest of a rock rising out of a yawning abyss stands Christ—lean, ascetic, and firm. Behind him, Satan, like an inflated giant rubber doll, dark but for the leaping flames that crown his head and eyes that glow like embers with an inner fire. Satan's effeminate nudity is half hidden and enveloped by vapors which bathe the picture with a miasmatic exhalation. Discussions of the painting went on for weeks, months, and soon passed from the aesthetic to the religious and the social plane. The consensus, on the whole, was unfavorable to the artist.

There was one picture of his [Repin], however, that attained the popularity of Whistler's *Mother [Arrangement in Black and Gray No. 1: The Artist's Mother]* in the United States for reasons outside its pictorial value—appeal of youth, freedom, and hope. The title of the picture is *What Expanse (Kakoi prostor):* a university student and his girlfriend are walking hand-in-hand, laughing exuberantly as they plow through spring freshets, entirely oblivious of melting ice, the water that swishes up to their knees, and the mischievous wind that tugs at their clothes. People asked: Did the artist mean literally space, expanse, distance? Was it not rather symbolic of wide intellectual horizons? Is the water just plain water, or does it also perhaps suggest the stream of life, the dangers which youth faces with confidence? Is it just a scene of boy-meets-girl out for a stroll, or isn't it rather the rebel (student) and his comrade in battle as well as in love? In the main, the public took the picture both literally and symbolically—an embodiment of youthful aspiration, of courage, and of an inexpressible yearning for a better life. There were numerous reproductions of the picture. I took one with me to the United States where I kept it for some years until hard-boiled sophistication got the better of my sentiment.

To complement our visits to the museum, we went to the Cathedral of St. Vladimir ([built in the] mid-nineteenth century) to study mural paintings of celebrated contemporaries like [Viktor] Vasnetsov, [Mikhail] Nesterov, [Mikhail] Vrubel', and "our own" Pimonenko. We also paid our respects to the St. Sophia Cathedral, the most ancient and venerable church in Russia ([built in the] eleventh century), with its fine mosaics and frescoes. But somehow we missed its full importance. We felt it was the special preserve of historians and scholars.

In addition to those semiofficial channels, I had my own source of information about the newest trends in art: a student by the name of Grabovskii [who was] several years my senior. He was subsidized by a rich art patron who had a well-stocked library on the art of all countries and periods. Grabovskii avoided political discussions, held himself aloof from the other students, and affected superior airs. I was impressed by him and foresaw a great future for him. He introduced me to [Arnold] Boecklin [Böcklin], [Aubrey] Beardsley, and [Sir Edward] Burne-Jones. He liked to quote from Shakespeare, especially from *Hamlet,* in Russian, of course, and to propound such puzzlers as "Who would survive historically: [Anton] Chekhov or [Maxim] Gorky?" It was from him, too, that I first learned about the "World of Art" *[Mir iskusstva],* the movement that supplanted the Wanderers. The World of Art considered the Wanderers a mob of low-brows, vulgarians who dared [to] profane the temple of art with their "smelly boots." [They believed that] art was sacred, unconcerned with the brutish facts of daily living.[6] The doctrine did not appeal to me; but with the passage of years, as I became more familiar with the work of the group, I came to admire some individual writers and artists whom I felt were superior to the dogma they preached. The Revolution of 1905 ended my attendance at the art school, and I lost track of Grabovskii.

■

By one of those coincidences with which life abounds (if I may grow philosophical for a second), I met him [Grabovskii] in Liverpool on my way to America. We both settled in Newark, New Jersey. He continued to quote from *Hamlet* and to propound conundrums like: "If you had to chose between art and family, which would it be?" Although his spirit was somewhat dampened—he had to work in a factory—he continued to draw and paint, and encouraged me to do so. Then he met Professor [Boris] Schatz who came to America to collect funds for the Bezalel Art School, which he had established in Palestine (it is still in existence). Grabovskii decided to join him. Before that, however, he did something utterly typical of his self-confidence and self-importance.

The famous Russian basso, Fedor Shaliapin, was at that time singing at the Metropolitan Opera in New York,

Grabovskii decided he would get two tickets from Shaliapin himself. He took me with him to the Sherry-Netherlands Hotel, where Shaliapin was staying. From the lobby of the hotel he called Shaliapin, frankly told him of his impecunious state, asked for two tickets, and mentioned the name of his Kiev art patron with whom Shaliapin was presumably on familiar terms. Of course, he [Grabovskii] got nowhere, but he was not discomfited in the least. While the hotel attendants smiled sarcastically at our shabby outfits, which looked so incongruous in the surrounding glitter, Grabovskii strutted out laughing. We stepped into an ice cream parlor and had an ice cream cone.

Shortly thereafter, he left for Palestine and the Bezalel Art School. He did not last there very long. Evidently feeling he was not getting his due at the school (he held a very low opinion of Professor Schatz), he moved his quarters to Paris. I received one letter from Paris. He was not over-eating, said the letter, "but everyday I come to worship at the Louvre." I never heard from him again. I have never stopped wondering what might possibly have befallen this strange and gifted man who crossed my path, made his impression, and disappeared into the void.

■

Once I was on the way to an exhibition in company with several other art students. We met a group from Commercial High School going in the opposite direction. Words passed between the two groups, then jeers, and—before we knew it—to fisticuffs. I had never been in a fistfight before (or after); besides, I thought it was stupid for intelligent people to engage in such "barbaric" practices (I had greater respect for "intelligence" [in my youth] than in my maturer years). However, I was now among "Romans," so I put in my own few licks. In a few minutes the scuffle was over. We were shamed into separating by some passersby. The sequel was a little sadder for me than for my colleagues. A few days later I walked along the same route, blissfully unsuspecting evil from any quarter, when I was overtaken by several of my former adversaries from Commercial High. They were about to pass me when one of them recognized me. They roughed me up a little, but one of them, with a sense of knightly justice, reminded [the others] that I was one and they were many (maybe he held my views about fistfights), and so I got away with relatively little damage.

■

My aunt's daughters were passionately fond of dancing. They taught me to dance, and I used to occasionally accompany them to a dance hall or some charity affair. Curiously, the Russian dances had all (or almost all) foreign names: *pas d'Espagne, Krakowiak,* polka-mazurka, *Czardas, Lezginka, Vengerka* (Hungarian), *Valse,* etc. The Russian waltz was danced with a more rapid whirling action than the American. At first it made you dizzy; but with some practice, you could whirl endlessly like a dervish. I remember it used to be the favorite dance of sentimental high school girls fed on the romantic licorice of the poet [Semen] Nadson. Although used to the rapid tempo of the waltz, they would become flushed and half intoxicated with the endless whirl round and round. They would close their eyes and hold helplessly to the protecting arms or shoulder of the cavalier. Polka-mazurka, on the other hand, was the special quarry of the male. Fast steps, a dashing movement forward, stamping of the feet, a periodic leap into the air, and, at the psychological moment, the gentleman would kneel before the lady. An officer with spurs was the ideal performer.

For the first time in my life I attended the opera. My brother took me to several among which I liked especially [Charles Françoise Gounod's] *Faust* and [Petr Tchaikovsky's] *Evgenii onegin.* Socialist as he was, my brother drew my attention to Mephistopheles' song about the Golden Calf. (I recalled this a few years later when I read [Anatolii] Lunacharskii's Marxist analyst of Goethe's *Faust.*)[7]

■

And then I became an "actor" myself. I joined a children's theatre that attained some local fame. It was organized and trained by several people under the guidance of a professional actor, Ivan Lvovich Paliudin. Working with him was a younger sister, an attractive girl of about 18, and an older married sister whose only child, a little girl of about 10, was one of the players. This actor's family was quite remarkable and struck us with awe. They all seemed to have a university education and spoke fluent French and German, as did the little girl. Sometimes during rehearsals when something did not please him, Paliudin would address one of his sisters in an angry French or German. We did not understand what he was saying, but we pretty well guessed what he meant.

Our repertoire consisted of dramatizations of fairy tales like "The Sleeping Princess," "Snow White and the Seven Dwarfs," and a suite of international dances. Paliudin himself taught recitation, acting, and proper deportment on the stage. A ballet master led us through intricacies of various international dances: Spanish, Polish, Hungarian, and American. America was represented by a "Cake Walk," and it was one of the hits of the show: A boy was chosen with high cheek bones and a pug nose; when he [was] made up in black face, put on a top hat and carried a cane under his arm, he somehow represented the popular notion of a Negro (the majority of the audiences had never seen a Negro). The really biggest success was reserved for a young boy who danced the Ukrainian *Kamarinskaia*. His high leaps into the air and his corkscrew whirling always brought the house down. There was a Polish dance (I was in that one), the boys in red square hats and resplendent jackets and pants and the girls in costumes that matched. Another couple, beautifully attired, were the dancers of the Caucasian *Lezginka*. A tailor traveled with us. He made all the costumes to the specifications drawn by Paliudin and his sisters.

The children were 10 to 12 years old; they played the less important parts (for example, I played one of the dwarfs). For the main roles—there always was a prince and princess—the troupe had two youths, an adolescent boy of perhaps 15 or 16 and a girl of about the same age. They were, as I remember, particularly attractive: the boy tall, strong, and handsome; and the girl delicate and fragile, [who] to us looked as charming and forbidden as a real princess. The boy came from a moderately well-to-do family; he was a student of Commercial High and intended to make acting his career. The princess, on the other hand, came from a wealthy family to whom this activity was a pleasant distraction. She was always accompanied by her mother and wore the finest dresses we had ever seen. Of course, she also spoke fluently French and German, unlike the boy who spoke French only and not too well. On stage she played a princess with all the grace of manner and beauty of speech expected of a real princess.

Usually we rehearsed at a dance studio. Occasionally, we would have a rehearsal at the house of "The Princess." We looked forward to that, because after a short rehearsal, there was always a party with ice cream, cookies, and sweet drinks. Besides I liked to walk around in open-eyed wonder in those rooms, which seemed to me the acme of luxury.

Our group traveled to summer resorts around Kiev and to provincial cities like Belaia Tserkov'. In Kiev itself we played in a hall called Château de Fleur, a sort of vaudeville house for performances of all kinds, concerts, recitations, and dances. It was beautifully situated on a hill in Merchant's Park *(Kupecheskii sad)*, [which was] renamed Worker's Park after the Revolution.

Once I remember a Jewish comedian was standing on the podium telling Jewish stories in dialect, in what he thought were funny imitations of the way Jewish men and women talk and gesticulate. He was dressed in a caftan tied with a silk belt and wore white socks and flat shoes in imitation of a Hasid. An umbrella was tucked under his arm. In a thick "Jewish" accent he related the troubles a pious Jew has with several wives: one, a physical scarecrow; the next, an untidy slob; and the third, a gossiping hussy, etc.—and all this in exaggerated mimicry and wild gestures. Curiously, not only gentiles but also many Jews laughed uproariously. However, a couple of college students whistled in disapproval (in Russia actors dread whistling in the auditorium because it means condemnation of the performance). They were led out but they had their revenge. The comedian was performing some tricks with eggs. When he finished, he put the eggs in his pockets and walked out. A student approached him and began to praise his performance. Evidently pleased, he listened attentively. Two other students came alongside and at once slapped his pockets where the eggs were kept and disappeared amid the laughter of the crowd. In his rage and haste to clean up the mess, the comedian seemed to imitate his own gibberish on the stage.

One of the oddest performances that I had a chance to attend was a Yiddish play—odd not because of the play itself, [which] was an inconsequential farce—but because of the nonliterary factors surrounding the play. The circumstances under which such productions were made possible illustrates once again the handicaps with which Jews had to contend. Performances of plays in Yiddish were forbidden; but they took place, nevertheless, by the use of certain stratagem plus, of course, [by] the usual distribution of graft.

The Yiddish language, as is well known, derives from medieval German with an admixture of Hebrew and Slavic elements. In their wanderings the Jews adopted at various times the languages of the people among whom they found refuge: Aramic, Persian, and Spanish. At that very time I am speaking about, there was a small Jewish sect in Kiev called Karaites, who spoke a dialect of Tartar. In all instances, however, their script was Hebrew; the same alphabet served Hebrew, Tartar, Persian, or whatever.

Now, utilizing the fact that Yiddish sounded like German to the uninitiated, the producers of the Yiddish play simply applied for permission to stage a *German* play. If permission was granted, they printed posters in Russian and German announcing the production of a German play. Of course, no Jew was ever fooled by these posters, and perhaps not many of the Russian censors either; but the latter had, as it were, an escape clause—if caught red-handed, they could always claim ignorance of German. Such permissions were not granted very often; but when they were, the Jews had a good laugh both at the farce and the censors.

∎

Shortly after entering the art school, I moved in with my brother, who lived nearer the school than my aunt. My brother was a very busy man. He worked long hours; and, as I remarked before, he was a socialist, and [his] work for the "movement" took much of his free time. Nevertheless, he did not neglect my extracurricular education. He took me to various historic places in the city; and when he could not go with me, he directed my attention to various places worth visiting. And, unobtrusively but frequently, he directed our conversation into socialist channels. Thus, for example, as we walked along the harbor and the second-hand open-air market *(tolkuchka* or *tolchok),* he would point out the miserable conditions under which the population lived and worked. In the *tolchok* particularly, the streets were thronged by derelicts, drunks, beggars, and syphilitics. Just a few minutes away, on the hill was Kreshchatik [Street], with its magnificent stores and restaurants loaded with the finest imported goods, clothes, and jewelry. Occasionally we would step into the best dry goods store in Kiev owned by [Isaak] Shvartsman. He imported dry goods from several European countries; one could find there, for example, the finest English tweed. The store sold both retail for customers in Kiev and wholesale to many smaller towns. An older brother of mine worked there as a bookkeeper. (He was engaged to my aunt's oldest daughter. Just before he was to be married, he was called up for military service.)

∎

Russian *soldatchina* [military service] was a scourge feared and detested by most. I remember how the village mothers cried their eyes out when their sons were to depart for the army. Stupid disciplinary action for the slightest infraction of the rules: *mordobitie* (punching in the jaw) and flogging. The Russian author A[leksandr] Kuprin has a horrifying story, *The Duel,* which graphically depicts life in the Russian army, the depravity of the officers, and the brutalization of the rank-

and-file soldier, sometimes to the point of crippling for life. Conditions for the Jews were especially bad. Here is an abridged little scene from the novel. A sergeant is cramming into a private *slovesnost'* (literacy). Question:

> "What is your gun for?"
> "To defend the throne and country from inner and outer enemies."
> "Who are the internal enemies?" casting a glance at the Jewish soldier Markuson. The soldier does not know, [so] the sergeant helps him out.
> "The internal enemies are all those who are against the law, like the rebels *(buntovshchiki),* students, horse thieves, Jews, and Poles."

Little wonder Jews were less than anxious to join the Russian army. A friend of my oldest brother recommended certain pills that would weaken him and disqualify him from service long enough for him to get married. My older brother, the tinsmith, would have acted differently. He would have gone into the army where he would have continued his socialist activities. The bookkeeper [brother] was sympathetic [to the socialist cause], but not to the extent of actual participation. He took an overdose of the pills and died.

■

Shvartsman went down in the history of Russian culture indirectly through his son, known to the literary world as Leo Shestov. Young Shestov or Shvartsman got the best education available both in Russia and abroad. An admirer of [Søren] Kierkegaard, Leo Shestov evolved into a philosophic and religious thinker. His writings on [Leo] Tolstoy, [Friedrich] Nietzsche, and [Fyodor] Dostoevsky are rich in abstract subtleties and generalizations. As might have been expected, he was disdainful of the revolutionary movement. He died abroad.

Across the street from Shvartzman's emporium was the richest museum of sacred art and a higher school for the training of Greek Orthodox priests. Whenever I think of

Shestov, this seminary and the dry goods store hover some-where in the background.

■

My brother introduced me to his friends, who were, in most cases, like himself, in the socialist movement. I learned the revolutionary songs, like "You Fell as Victims in the Fatal Struggles," "Arise, You Prisoners of Starvation," and many more. [Once] I joined him in a forest behind Kiev at a secret gathering *(skhodka).* I read some illegal pamphlets. There was a propaganda picture circulated among workers called "The Pyramid," a kind of visual aid, a modern *biblia pauperum* printed in large numbers and distributed by underground channels. The top of the pyramid was crowned by a double-headed eagle symbolizing the Russian monarchy. Immedi-ately underneath were the Tsar and Tsarina and an inscrip-tion alongside: "We reign over you" *(tsarstvuem).* Underneath them, on a wider platform, the ministers and other high gov-ernment officials and the inscription "We govern you." Be-low that, on an even wider platform, the hierarchy of the Greek Orthodox Church and the text "We bamboozle you" *(morochim).* Going [further] down, the army brass in full re-galia commanding soldiers to fire: "We shoot you." Continu-ing downward in an ever-expanding area, the capitalists, bankers, industrialists, merchants, and their wives and sweet-hearts around a banquet table partaking of the most appetiz-ing food and wine: "We eat for you." Last of all, at the base of the pyramid, workers whole and lame, laboring, suffering, and dying but holding up the entire iniquitous superstruc-ture: "We support you."

Those friends of my brother were simple people, but they seemed, in my eyes, beings of a special breed. Their personal life and interests seemed to mean very little to them. They were ready, if called upon, to give up their comfort, their in-come, and their lives, if necessary, for their ideal of social jus-tice. But they had their moments of relaxation too.

My brother took me to a *vecherinka* (evening party). There was eating, drinking, and good-natured joking. After toasts for the liberation from the Tsarist yoke came the singing of songs in a manner to me utterly new and unforgettable. They filled a big bowl with what looked like salt, poured alcohol over it, put a match to it, then put all the other lights out. Under this eerie illumination, which picked out a face here, an arm there, a plate on the table, and cast the rest of the room in total darkness, song poured forth, first revolutionary and after that folk songs—Russian, Ukrainian, and Yiddish— adumbrations of deeply felt gaiety and sadness, sung without theatrics, in true folk flavor. For a brief moment, the cares of the country and the world were left in the shadows.

■

Unrest was spreading through the country. Strikes succeeded one another and were savagely suppressed by arrests and even by shootings. No school was untouched by the rising waves of revolutionary agitation. Political agitation penetrated to the classroom. Many students were impressed into the army as punishment for illegal activity. They continued their agitation in the army. Discussion reached a fever-pitch. Everybody talked politics, day and night. A revolutionary event, like the revolt of the cruiser *Potemkin* in Odessa, or a counterrevolutionary event, like the massacre of January 9 [1905] in St. Petersburg,[8] threw every socialist and liberal party [member] into a new and increased spirit of revolt. [An example:] a Jewish student of Kiev, Petia Dashevskii, shot [Pavolaki] Krushevan, the evil genius of the Kishinev pogrom [of April 6–7, 1903].

The critical situation in the country was aggravated by the disastrous losses suffered by the Russian army and navy in the war with Japan. At first, the Russian reactionary press was jubilant—the war would be an easy walk. There were many pictures showing the Russian Army riding roughshod over the *kikomoras* (monkeys) [with the caption]: *Shapkami zakidaem,* "We'll bury them under our hats." But corruption, inefficiency, bureaucracy, and plain treason kept losing battles and finally lost the war itself. Patriotic parades, of which there were many, did not help. The underground movement against the monarchy grew and spread in wider circles. There were national disturbances in the Caucasus, Ukraine, and Poland. The peasants in numerous villages sacked and the burned landowners' estates and were savagely dealt with. Schools were being closed. Forces were ripening for the outbreak of 1905.

"I want to tell you a story of my own uncle and my own aunt." That was the innocent beginning of a tale published by Sholom Aleichem in Yiddish in [1904], "Uncle Pinny and Aunt Raizi." The usually suspicious and rigidly vigilant Russian censor failed to grasp the significance of the simple story until after the Jewish population from one end of the Pale to the other rocked with laughter at the stupidity of the censor as well as the discomfiture of the Tsarist regime in the Russo–Japanese conflict. For that is what the story was about. Aunt Raizi (Russia) a hulking giant of a woman, crude, superstitious, inclined to hit the bottle, a bully [who] struck with terror her husband, Pinny (Japan), dark, diminutive, with excellent manners, though something of a braggart and not adverse to tampering with the truth. Pinny was in mortal terror at the sight of his powerful spouse, and this made him so miserable that he decided one day to seek the advice of his friend, the nouveau riche and sharp trader Yankel Dovid (Yankee Doodle). Yankel Dovid's advice was brief and to the point: Stand up and fight. Terrified at first of the very idea but finding no other way out, Pinny acted on Yankel Dovid's advice. The effect was miraculous. Aunt Raizi, black and blue from the chastisement administered by her husband, now, in her turn, sought the advice of Yankel Dovid. He was very sympathetic, but in secret he applauded and encouraged Uncle Pinny. When Aunt Raizi learned a lesson she would not soon forget, the honest broker Yankel Dovid arranged a peace between them.

The characters were, of course, stereotypes, but the details with which the story was embroidered and the rollicking good humor characteristic of Sholom Aleichem made the story an immediate popular success. The people and circles in which my brother moved read the story and enjoyed it; but there were a few who criticized it because it did not clearly draw the line between the Tsarist regime and the Russian people. As if in reply to such critics, Sholom Aleichem wrote the novel *The Storm* (also called *The Flood*) in 1907,[9] encompassing the events of "Bloody Sunday" [January 9, 1905], the granting of the constitution, and the pogroms.

Ultimately, the censors caught up with the events and proceeded to act, albeit belatedly. In a confidential report sent out by the Tsarist Ministry of Internal Affairs (uncovered in the archives after the Revolution; [see] *Sovietish Heimland* #3, 1969), [stated that] public safety forbade the reprinting of, among others, 1) "Uncle Pinny and Aunt Raizi" by Sholom Aleichem and 2) *The Poverty of Philosophy* by Karl Marx, etc. How proud and pleased Sholom Aleichem would have been had he known of the company he was made to keep by the censor!

My brother was deeply involved in all this social ferment. He had been arrested once and was now in even more serious trouble. He was implicated as a member of a punitive squad in a scuffle with strike-breakers and the police and had to go into hiding. His comrades decided that it might be advisable for him to leave the country "temporarily." They procured a forged passport for him, and he left for America. The "temporary" turned out to be permanent. He soon found work, did well, married, and raised a family of children and grandchildren. [For him,] the past [was] a closed and romantic book.

■

I moved to an uncle's [house] on Shuliavka [Street], at the opposite end of town [from] where my aunt lived. In my first two residences in Kiev the environment was almost completely Russian, and I underwent, in a sense, the process of Russification. My uncle, on the other hand, lived in close proximity with a fairly compact settlement of Jews. This, in fact, furnished him with his livelihood: he was a kosher butcher (meat prepared according to religious dietary law). A man of middle-age and of powerful physique, he liked to eat well and take an occasional drink. He and his wife had no children and made me feel at home. In my new environment I became subject, if not to new influences, at least new contacts.

For the first time I came face to face with something I had heard about but had never observed at first hand, the *oblavy*, raids on Jews. In order to check up on those Jews who had no legitimate right of residence in the city, the police would make periodic raids into Jewish homes, generally at night without previous announcement. There were Jews who, if they stayed in Kiev for any length of time, were left in peace by paying weekly assessments to the minions of the law, beginning with the corner policeman and ending with the district chief and not forgetting the janitor of the house. This, of course, did not stop the raids. In the middle of the night, say 2:00 or 3:00, you heard violent knocking on the door. If no "illegals" were present, you showed your documents, and the police proceeded to ransack the house: [they] looked under mattresses and beds, in the closets, trunks, and places where no human could possibly hide, just to be nasty. They left the house as after a pogrom. Sometimes the police exchanged greetings with old clients whom they had arrested once or twice before. If they found no "illegals" after looking into every nook and corner, they reluctantly left. On some people the raids had a frightful effect, perhaps disproportionate to the danger. Stories are told—perhaps apocryphal—of raids ending in tragedy. Thus, it is told that a young man, having no other place to hide, crept into an airtight trunk from which they took him out suffocated.

If the police found on these raids anyone without documents to prove his right of residency, he was taken to the police station. After either he or his friends greased the palm of the policeman or the captain, he was allowed to stay—until the next raid. Sometimes, however, the victim was too poor to pay or had no friends to pay his ransom; he was then sent back *po etapu,* by convoy [and accompanied by guards] on foot, wagon, [or] train to his town or village, regardless of how far it might be. It was a common sight to see a Jew walking in the middle, flanked by two fully armed guards marching him to the next village or town, where he was handed over to the local authorities who, in turn, sent him under guard to the next stop, and so on, until he reached his home. As likely as not, that same Jew would turn up in Kiev again after a month or so of absence. The danger from the police was great, but the need to earn a livelihood for wife and children greater.

■

I made the acquaintance of many new friends of liberal and socialist views of various shadings. There were several cross-breeds of socialist internationalists and Jewish nationalists: the Labor Zionists *(Poale Zion),* the socialists, the Territorialists, and the Workers' Union ([Jewish Socialist] Bund). I read Leon Pinsker's *Auto-Emancipation,* [Grigorii] Bogrov's *Memoirs of a Jew (Zapiski evreia),* and, more intensely, Yiddish literature.

I even began to notice things peripheral to my new interest.

Thus I had passed many times the *kenassa* of the Karaites, a building of modest proportions in Moorish style, without paying much attention to it. Now I became interested. The Karaites were a small Jewish sect that broke away from the mainstream of Jewish history [more than] 1,000 years ago; and since then, they continued to drift further and further from the compact mass of Russian Jewry. The Karaites, unlike the larger body of Jews, found the source of faith and the guide to life in the Bible alone. They rejected the vast prescriptions, commentaries, and commentaries upon commentaries in an endless accretion in Talmudic and Rabbinic law. Their conversational language was a dialect of Tartar, while the language of the mass of Jews in Russia was a dialect of old German [Yiddish]. The language of religion was the same for both, the "holy tongue," Hebrew, and the Karaites kept the Sabbath even more strictly than the other Jews. The Karaites intrigued me—Jews and yet not Jews. I went up a few times to the *kenassa* hoping to talk to a Karaite, but I could never pick up the courage either to go into the *kenassa* or to start a conversation, so I just made a sketch of the building.

There was one circumstance which, through no fault of the Karaites, alienated the other Jews. The Karaites were not subject to the disabilities that plagued the rest of the Jews. The Karaites were never referred to as Jews. They enjoyed (if that is the word) the status of equality before the law with

Russians. [This circumstance] is presumed to have come about this way. A Karaite scholar of the nineteenth century, A[braham] Firkovich, claimed to have discovered a document which proved that [the] settlement of Karaites (one of the lost Ten Tribes) in the Crimea antedated the birth of Christ and, hence, [they] could not have been implicated in his death.

The last information about the Karaites I came across was in *Babi Yar* by [Anatolii] Kuznetsov. It tells of the wholesale massacre of the Kiev Jews and their mass burial in the ravine called "Babi Yar." Kuznetsov mentions casually, in a short paragraph, how the Karaites gathered in their *kenassa* to pray all night, emerging the next morning to walk their last mile. Thus ended the life of the little community whose privileges did not prevent its members from sharing a common grave with my underprivileged sisters, uncles, and cousins.

This was a period when I was reading voraciously, though planlessly. For a few kopeks, you bought a pocket-size booklet in thin yellow covers published by the Universal Library. The Library included translations from apparently all languages. Some of the books were hard going, but I persisted. I read Knut Hamson years before he was translated into English, Selma Lagerlof, [Henrik] Ibsen, [Hugo von] Hofmannsthal, Multatuli, and Phibyshevsky ([the latter] still unknown in the United States). This was literature for the intelligentsia. There was also another kind known as *bul'varnyi roman,* the novel of the boulevard, i.e., trashy, published on newsprint in weekly installments, a kind of soap opera in pamphlet form. One title of such a novel was *Grafinia nishchaia* (The destitute countess). It went on and on; each week one found lines waiting at the newsstands in breathless expectation of the next *dusheshchipatel'nyi* (soul-seering) episode.

■

My main occupation [in Kiev] was, of course, attendance at the art school. I passed successfully the Ornament Class, the Mask Class, and was now in the Head Class. I was also beginning to paint in oils and watercolors and was looking forward to next summer's vacation to be able to paint freely outdoors.

7

1905
Rehearsal for 1917

It had to come. Rumbles of an approaching storm were growing louder and more menacing.

Humiliating defeat at the hands of the Japanese.

Workers' strikes in cities, paralyzing entire industries.

Peasant uprisings in the villages. Burning of estates; death of landowners.

Unrest and mutiny in the army and navy. Sailors seize the cruiser *Potemkin*.

Assassination of government officials.

Desperate measures. The government infiltrates workers' organizations; workers infiltrate government institutions.

"Bloody Sunday": Father [Grigorii] Gapon (government agent?) leads a mass of workers in peaceful petition to Tsar for relief of grievances. Mob massacred.

Minor nationalities—Poles, Ukrainians, and Caucasians—restless and rebellious.

Something had to give.

On the eve of October 17, 1905, the government issued a manifesto, which promised five great freedoms: freedom of the press, assembly, conscience, organization, and the inviolability of the individual. The manifesto proposed the election of a Duma, a parliament on the basis of universal suffrage, with the participation of all political parties. In a word, the manifesto envisaged a constitutional monarchy after the model of Great Britain. Reason enough for celebration.

On the morning of October 18, I started out early for the art school and found the streets everywhere buzzing with excitement. When I entered the school, the faculty was absent and the students had the school to themselves. We gathered first in the corridors and next in front of the school. Then, as if in answer to a hidden command, we formed ranks and walked off in marching order. A couple of red flags appeared from nowhere. In a few minutes we caught up with the students of Commercial High School nearby, who, like us, were marching with flags and songs toward the broad highway of Bibikovskii Boulevard. As we turned left on Bibikovskii, our procession was absorbed like a small rivulet in the mighty stream that flowed onward, swelling even bigger by the addition of surging crowds from side streets and alleys. Behind us were the railroad yards and the Polytechnical Institute (a university), two of the most active centers of revolt. Further along was the University of Nicholas I.

The weather was made to order—May Day in October—bright balmy, and invigorating. The streets were alive with color: flags; banners; flowers; students in uniforms—blue stripes (art), red stripes (commercial), yellow stripes *(real'noe* [modern, nonclassical secondary school]), white stripes *(gimnaziia)* [traditional secondary school]; red, white, and brown uniforms of high school girls; men and women in workers' clothes; and women in the latest fashions. Meetings were staged spontaneously on street corners, on the roofs of trolleys, and on balconies. Strangers kissed and congratulated each other. All traffic stopped as the crowds jammed the streets from sidewalk to sidewalk, all flowing toward the center, toward the main thoroughfare of the city, Kreshchatik, toward the City Hall (Duma). Those who did not march were on roofs, on balconies, even on telephone poles, waving red flags and cheering. There was lusty singing of forbidden revolutionary songs like the "International" and "You Fell Victims in the Fatal Conflict." A universal mood of gaiety and good humor prevailed. Someone stuck a red flag into the hand of the statue of Nicholas I.

I shared the general mood of exaltation, more, perhaps than many others. My brother's and his friends' prophecies were being fulfilled even sooner than anticipated. I was too young and too much absorbed in my own work to appreciate

the subtle differences among the various socialist parties. In
the crowd there were surely people to whom the event sig-
naled the first step on the road to total socialist triumph; to
others, this meant the emergence at last of Russia into the
European community as a constitutional monarchy; still others were simply swept by the current.

Something like this was expressed by the artist [Il'ia] Repin in his painting *October 17, 1905*. Under a recent cloud of
distrust and suspicion among liberal and socialists for his ob-
sequious work, *The [Ceremonial Meeting of the] Imperial State
Council* [1903], Repin was now back in the liberal camp. *October 17, 1905* is conceived in a romantic mood. It is a day of
universal jubilation (accent on universal). An orator waves a
broken chain as a symbol of liberation. Around him swarms the
variegated populace of a Russian city. Every section of society
seems to be represented. Students, male and female, sing
lustily; the unending stream includes workers, professionals,
soldiers, sailors, government employees, young and old, house-
wives, and society women. In the very front, there is a mod-
estly dressed woman and next to her a lady in the latest word
of fashion. People sing, gesticulate, and greet each other. The
sky is bright; red flags, varicolored attire, and flowers enhance
the festive air of the scene. It is the nation on parade.

To me, the event had a personal as well as social meaning.
Welcoming the broad implications outlined in the Manifesto
of October 17, I also naively expected to see the eradication
of those social and personal handicaps of which I myself had
knowledge and experience. I imagined how happy my
brother would be in far [off] America to read about the celebration and to know that his struggles had not been in vain.
He might even want to come back. Thinking thus, I was
forcibly propelled ever forward.

Because [the students from] our school started [out] early
and took a short route, we were able to reach a place near the
Duma (City Hall; not to be confused with "Duma," the national parliament envisioned in the manifesto). Even before
we reached the Duma, organized marching became impossible. It was each for himself. For blocks around, the distinction
between sidewalk and street disappeared. I slowly pressed for-

ward until I stood in front of the balcony where speaker succeeded speaker, where impassioned exultant and denuncia-
tory oratory flowed on and on, where resolutions were drawn
up and programs of action outlined. One of the resolutions
adopted was to free from the city jails the political prisoners
immediately. A delegation took off at once. After the expiration of a fairly long time, a group of political prisoners was
brought up, causing a great pitch of excitement. One of them
was the prominent attorney [Mark] Ratner, who stepped
onto the balcony and embraced the socialist Schlichter in full
view of the audience and to the accompaniment of a thunderous applause. He delivered a fiery speech, whose tenor
was like that of other speeches: Not enough. This is only a
beginning. Onward to greater triumphs!

The balcony where the speeches were given was above the
ground floor entrance. A metal wreath with a crown on top
and the letter "N" in the center decorated the balcony. At a
certain moment during the ceremonies, a speaker wanting to
emphasize a point or to provide a historical illustration, bent
the royal emblem to the apparent delight of the audience.
(On a subsequent visit to Kiev, perhaps twenty or more years
later, I stood in front of the Duma, gazing long at the old
structure, recalling and reliving the turbulent moments of
1905, as the crowds hurried by indifferently. The building
was practically the same, just a little shabbier with age. The
"N" on the balcony was, of course, missing. On the terrace
in front stood a bust of Karl Marx, with the inscription
"Workers of the World Unite.")

As the proceedings continued, with speaker after speaker
outlining the next steps, drawing up more resolutions, flaying
the autocracy, keeping the crowd in a high state of tension—
it was now early afternoon—suddenly a few stray shots rang
out, throwing the crowd into a commotion. A company of
dragoons had fired at the crowd prematurely. As was subsequently established, the government planned to turn the celebration across the country into a colossal January 9 [i.e.,
Bloody Sunday, 1905]. At the moment, however, this provocation was not suspected; it gave the speakers a chance to demand the punishment of the guilty (under the newly estab-

lished "freedoms"). The proceedings continued, although here and there people were beginning to depart.

Toward dusk shots rang out again, now on a more massive scale and [fired] point-blank into the mob. This time there was no mistaking it. The shooting was deliberate. Panic ensued. The crowd, which but a moment ago was so composed and reasonable, suddenly became an uncontrollable mob scattering precipitously in all directions. People were screaming, falling, rising again, and stepping over the wounded without a second look. No one paid any attention to the few level-headed [people] who vainly tried to slow down the stampede. Squeezed on all sides and propelled in the direction away from Kreshchatik (the street of the Duma), I found myself hugging the wall of the Museum of Art and Antiquities, [which] was situated at the confluence of two streets. The [museum's] imposing front faced Aleksandrovskaia Square, while the side walls were each on a different street. People were running past the museum, down the hill to Podol, where most of the Jewish population was concentrated. I stopped a young student and asked him whether he knew what was happening.

"The Black Hundreds[1] are armed to the teeth and on a rampage. Not a policeman in sight. Hoodlums are beating up everybody who looks suspicious to them. They run like crazy shouting 'Kill the Jews. Save Russia.'"

I recalled my thoughts of the morning—about how my brother in America would be happy at the good news—and laughed aloud. I immediately cut myself short. The young man looked at me suspiciously and ran off. What an ending for a day that began so gloriously.

I walked up the hill away from Podol, weaving in and out of streets, alleys, and bypaths in an enormous arc until, after hours of wandering, I finally reached the house of my uncle, where I lived. The next morning we still did not know what was afoot. The liberal papers suspended publication. Only the arch reactionary [newspaper], the *Kievlianin* (the Kievite), appeared and that was not much help. Obviously there was a pogrom. Will the chief of police or the governor do something to stop it?

I decided to go to school again, to investigate, and report my findings. I had to pass the Jewish market *(Evreiskii bazar)*, and there I came upon the pogrom in full fury. Men and women were looting, breaking into stores, robbing, and screaming. I made a hasty detour. I was now thoroughly frightened and did not know what to do next. I finally decided to continue on the way to the art school. When I got there, I found a number of students who had come there apparently, like myself, in search of information. The school was closed. We exchanged notes and I learned that the people released from prison the day before were being rearrested and that pogroms were [occurring] with savage violence in all districts inhabited by the Jews. After hanging around the school for a while, most of the students went home to their parents to share whatever was in store for them. I had no parents in the city. I lived with my uncle. There were no telephones by which I could reach him, and I was in terror of going back and meeting up with the raging hoodlums, especially as I was in a student's uniform.

While I was standing thus, thinking to myself and weighing the next move, one of the remaining students said: "Why don't you come and stay with me a couple of days till the thing blows over." He was a strappy Ukrainian, perhaps 18 years old, with the air of the village still about him, his Russian speech colored by Ukrainian accents. Of course, I readily accepted his invitation.

He occupied a small room in the basement with a single cot. The walls were covered with sketches of some Ukrainian scenes, and a number of copies of works of [Vasilii] Vereshchagin. (Strange the ways of memory. There are things and events of the period that I have completely forgotten, but those copies of Vereshchagin's battle scenes are so brilliantly clear in my mind, I can almost see them in front of me.) An easel was standing in the corner and a paint box exposing a palette recently used. I slept on the floor. That day I stayed indoors, but the uncertainty of the future, indeed, of the present, was nerve-wracking.

I decided to take a chance and go out the next day together with my friend. As he looked every inch a peasant, I

felt it was fairly safe if he came along. The experience, however, proved [to be] ghastly. We walked from district to district, and I marvelled at the methodical way in which the
hoodlums (were they really all hoodlums or were there some
among them who were collecting goods to replenish their
own establishments?) went about their business: The windows were being smashed, and the goods carried out and
loaded [into] *izvozchiki* (cabs)—[whose drivers] must have
done a landslide business that day—or [into] hand carts.
Some carried as much as they could in their arms or on their
backs. What could not be taken was destroyed on the spot.
Houses were equally vandalized. Furniture, glass, crockery,
kitchenware, and feathers were scattered about.

Somehow torn pillows and feathers floating in the air unhur-
riedly and settling leisurely on the ground have always been
regarded by the Jews as a typical outward sign of a pogrom.
Female members of traditionally oriented Jewish households
would gather together to pluck geese feathers, separate the
down from the rest, and turn them with loving care into
the softest pillows and bedding, which were put aside for the
happy day when one of the girls should become a bride.
Feather bedding was not something impersonal, like a mat-
tress; it was an indispensable item in every girl's dowry and
the pride of every Jewish home. Perhaps this was one of the
reasons why the *pogromshchiki* [perpetrators of the pogrom]
took special delight in disemboweling pillows and covering
the ground with them.

Banter passed back and forth in a kind of thieves' fellowship:
"Hey, there, Fedka, are you going to open a little business of
your own?" "Is that a wedding gift for your sweetie?" At one
place, we noticed a student shake his head in silent disapproval. A burly "patriot" went up to him and gave him a resounding slap in the face. "Get the hell away, you Jew-lover,

before I bash in your skull." A policeman was gravely promenading a few steps away.

My friend tried to dissipate my gloom, though with very
little success. We passed a restaurant, and he suggested we
drop in for a glass of tea and some diversion perhaps. It was
one of the cheaper eating places, dirty, crowded, smelling of
cabbage, onions, sausage, herring, and human sweat. A penetrating fog of smoke filled the room, thick enough to cut
with an axe. Conversation was loud and general, centering, of
course, around the events of the day. We took the first seats
available. A group of men slightly under the weather were listening in partial attention to one of their number, who held
forth in an oracular tone:

". . . and mark my words, gentlemen *(gospoda),* you haven't
seen anything yet. You have only seen the blossoms; the
berries are still to come. I have it on the most reliable authority that the government has passed a decree to wipe out every
damned last Jew in our fatherland, old and young, root and
branch, once and for all. Soon the police will begin a house
to house search. I said house to house, because if any Christian is dupe or criminal enough to harbor any Christ-killers,
he will share their fate. And listen carefully. . . ."

I sat petrified. I was very credulous at that age, listened to
the peroration and the haw-haws that accompanied it, and
believed every word of it. My stomach felt queasy, and I covered my mouth to hide the nervous twitching of my lips.
Fortunately, my friend had finished his tea and we left. When
we arrived at his basement, we found a mutual acquaintance
who came to talk things over. They took me in hand. They
tried to argue that the Tsar was, whatever his prejudices, sen-
sitive to world opinion. They pointed to the growing
strength of the socialist and the liberal parties, [which as]
much as they differed among themselves on other issues, were
solidly in opposition to anti-Semitism. They discounted the
importance or influence of such elements as the crowd in the
restaurant.

Then they switched the subject of the conversation, probably also for my benefit. They were both socialists and
Ukrainian nationalists, and now their subject was the national

Ukrainian poet and artist Taras Shevchenko and his friendship with American Negro actor Ira Aldridge.

■

Aldridge had toured Russia in the 1850s in a Shakespeare
repertoire. He made a tremendous impression on Russian intellectual circles. He became a close friend of Shevchenko,
who painted his portrait and presented it to him. This friendship of the two remarkable men, descendants of serf and slave,
each eminent in his field, made a wonderful romantic story.

Incidentally, there exists a drawing by Leonid Pasternak
(father of the poet Boris Pasternak) which represents an intimate scene of the two men in which Aldridge holds up his
portrait done by Shevchenko. In Shevchenko's *Diary,* published after the Revolution of 1917, [there is] this "American" thought:

> Great [Robert] Fulton! And great [James] Watt! Your
> young child growing by leaps and bounds will soon devour the
> knouts, the crowns, and will swallow the diplomats, the
> deputies for dessert . . . that which the encyclopedists started in
> France will be finished for the entire planet by your colossal
> child of genius. . . .

■

Once again I was relaxed somewhat by the conversation.
Surely, I thought, these two well-informed, intelligent men
were more trustworthy than the tavern riff-raff. And so, we
all went out for another walk. Soon we came upon something new in my experience and quite extraordinary. It was a
patriotic and religious procession wending its way to one of
the holiest shrines in Kiev—and perhaps in all of Russia—the
ancient Cathedral of Saint Sophia. The Russian flags, the
gilded icons, the portraits of the Tsar, military men, priests,
distinguished civilians, the singing of hymns, and all the rest
that made up the procession were in themselves nothing extraordinary. The odd feature was the tail of the procession, for
it consisted of the *pogromshchiki,* who were there with their

loot on their persons or in carriages. As if to symbolize the harmony between the two sections, some of the more devout "true Russians" spread shawls, rugs, and other colorful items under the feet of the holy procession. (Christ entering Jerusalem!)

On October 20, the *Kievlianin* announced that order was being restored in the city. Gradually the Jews began to emerge from the cellars, the attics, the stables, and the Christian households that had given them refuge. I left my companion and set out on the way to my uncle. However, before I got there, I met a friend who advised me against going home. He said that despite government assurances (the government thanked the population and the police for their good behavior in the face of "provocation"), no one was as yet sure of safety except in some specially organized centers such as hospitals, schools, theatres, etc.

The nearest place to where we were talking was the theatre Narodnyi dom (the People's House). When I arrived there, a police guard was standing outside. After what had happened, I did not have much faith in the police, but I had no choice. I entered, gave my name, told my story, and was assigned a cot in a big room with dozens of other people—husbands, wives, and children—not a few with bandages on arms, legs, and heads. The more serious cases were in hospitals. I joined a few boys my age, and we drifted from group to group and all around the room. There were a few circles engaged in serious, lively conversation. The discussions focused, naturally, on the recent events angled from a definite "line"—socialist, Zionist, Anarchist, etc.—[with] the speakers insisting that those events proved "once more" the correctness of their separate views.

"The Monarchy cannot be reformed; it must be destroyed."

"The enemy is the State, capitalist, Zionist, socialist, whatever."

"*Jewish* blood is the axle grease of the *Russian* Revolution."

In the heat of the argument, these young people forgot the tragedy of the moment. Not so the rest. The tragedy was still very much with them. They were now relating to one another the things that had happened to them and to their neighbors. Compared to their stories, my own experiences seemed hardly significant. [There were] tales of robbery, assault, murder, rape, vandalism, and torture. From their stories, a definite pattern emerged. Almost everywhere the hoodlums, the Black Hundreds, seemed to operate in an organized manner. Wherever the Jews put up a vigorous self-defense, the police suddenly made an appearance and helped the hoodlums. Wherever the Jews had the worst of it, the police were either absent or looked on passively. The mood of the people who told the stories as well as those who listened varied from gloom to utter despondency, hopelessness, and helplessness. They felt trapped. "What now," they seemed to say, and there was [no one] to answer.

In the meantime, while I was inside the shelter, provided with food and a bed, my relatives outside were wondering what had happened to me. My father had written from Vasil'kov, where he had settled during the uncertain days of riots and uprisings. He had left the village, where his life was even more precarious than in the city. When his letter of inquiry came, I wasn't there to answer it. My relatives made a search of the hospitals, scrutinized the lists of the dead and wounded, and even went down to the morgue. Ultimately, they found me in Narodnyi dom, and I went back to live with my uncle.

On the surface life returned to normal. Preparations began for the national elections to the Duma, as provided in the October Manifesto. There were, in fact, two separate elections. In view of the recent events, the left-wing parties—the Social Democrats in their two wings, the Bolsheviks and the Mensheviks; the Socialist Revolutionaries; and many liberals—considered the October Manifesto a fraud and refused to have anything to do with it. They, therefore, proceeded with an election for a Soviet of Workers Deputies. Especially active in this unofficial election were the workers from the large railroad repair shops, the mills, and the factories [, as well as] high school and university students. In fact, the largest election rallies were held within the precincts of the universities. (The university administration rule had broken down completely.) The Kiev Soviet was finally elected in late October and was in session from October 28 to November 6. (The elections to the First Duma came only in 1906.)

[In] Shuliavka, the district where I lived, the rule of the workers and students was so complete, it got the name of "Shuliavka Republic." The workers and students organized their own militia and dismissed the regular police force. It was truly a "rehearsal for 1917," but it was short-lived. The government army and police invaded Kiev in overwhelming numbers, and the suppression of the Soviet followers was bloody. Particularly fierce battles were fought out at the so-called *Evreiskii bazar* (Jewish market). It was an unequal battle, and the outcome was predictable. The workers put up a determined resistance but were constantly driven back and routed. Many were shot and many more were put in prison. The chairman of the Kiev Soviet, who was in prison for some time, succeeded in escaping to the United States, where he took up farming and disappeared completely from public view.

After the suppression of similar uprisings in other cities—the last one in Moscow in December of the same year—reaction was really riding high. A veritable crusade was unleashed against workers, students, soldiers, sailors, and anyone else in the slightest degree suspected of complicity in the events of 1905. The revolutionary movement continued, of course, but it went deeper underground.

The strength of the reaction was evident, among other things, in the subsequent trials over the Kiev pogrom. For two years (1907–1908), prominent lawyers, scholars, and liberals were collecting data and lining up witnesses. They had dates and names [of] persons involved and property destroyed, [which were all] carefully, scientifically, and factually analyzed. The evidence implicated not only the riff-raff but also members of the army and the government. All the accumulated evidence was of no avail. The police and the army were forbidden by the court to testify, and the lawyers for the defense simply used the courtroom as a platform for anti-Semitic propaganda. Enlightened public opinion might well be horrified at the grim comedy staged in court, official justice ground on to a complete whitewash. Flushed with an easy victory, the most frenzied lawyer of the defense, [Aleksei

Semenovich] Shmakov, demanded that the Jews be placed on the bench of the accused.

A. S. Shmakov, an indefatigable, virulent, and obtuse monarchist and anti-Semite, an "expert" on the "Jewish Question," published a book in the defense of the pogroms of 1905. To bolster his authority and establish his scholarly competence, Shmakov makes reference to Homer, Aristotle, Plutarch, [Johann Wolfgang von] Goethe, [Arthur] Schopenhauer, [Victor] Hugo, and [Otto] Weininger, to name but a few. He ranges over all ages and civilizations to establish the "guilt" of the Jews. Then the mountain gives birth to a mouse: Shmakov develops a series of "arguments" [the idiocy of which] would seem to be glaringly obvious but which apparently found an audience. The following are a few of them:

> Shmakov: The Jews were themselves to blame for the pogroms. On the eve of October 18 the Jewish *kahal* [community] distributed arms to all the Jews in preparation for a bloodbath, a massacre of the Christian population in Kiev. The pogroms were, thus, an act of self-defense and came just in the nick of time, thereby saving the Russians of Kiev from total annihilation.

> Shmakov: The Jews tied icons, crosses, and portraits of the Tsar to tails of dogs and pigs which they then let loose to roam over the city.

> Shmakov: The Jews raced through the streets of Kiev shouting: "We gave you a Jewish God; we will give you a Jewish Tsar."

And many more "arguments" of the same caliber made in the belief that any absurdity cooked up in his disordered brain was equivalent to proof. It made one despair of human intelligence. During the Beilis Trial in 1910, Shmakov had another opportunity to display his fertile imagination. This time, however, his luck failed him.[2]

Reaction was gradually recouping its losses. The Duma, the national parliament, was born sickly and going from crisis to crisis, each one making it more anemic than the last. Voting rights were being constantly restricted at the expense of the underprivileged. In 1906–1907, Kiev was host to a gathering of the most prominent guardians of autocracy and Greek Orthodoxy—[Nikolai] Dubrovin, Count [Ivan] Shakhnovskii, Archimandrite Vitalii, Prince [Nikolai] Golitsyn, and others. In the background of the deliberations was the idea of strengthening and perpetuating the triune principle of AUTOCRACY, ORTHODOXY, NATIONHOOD. It fell to [Vladimir] Gringmut to restate (once again) the doctrine of the Third Rome (Rome, Constantinople, and Moscow), which originated in the reign of Ivan III as formulated by the Monk Filofei: " . . . all Christian kingdoms are merged into thine alone. Two homes have fallen, but the third stands, and there shall be no other."

■

Alas, history played a trick (as is its habit) on the guardians of Holy Russia. The Third Rome went (like the Third Reich years later) into the ample archives of "Lost Causes." [The events of] 1917 scattered the recidivists of all colors to Prague and Paris, Berlin and Shanghai, New York and Detroit, to wait there confidently for the day of reckoning when they would return to greet the welcoming throngs, regain their "rightful" privileges, and settle accounts (with accrued interest) with all those responsible for their "temporary" discomfiture. But I am getting ahead of my story.

■

When my brother, [who was] installed more or less comfortably in America, received my letters and also read in the American newspapers about the events of 1905, about the demonstrations and the pogroms, he wrote asking me to quit school and prepare to leave Russia as soon as possible. He assured me that there were good art schools in America and that I would have no trouble continuing my studies. I could even take up the study of medicine, which was held in great esteem in America. I, therefore, did not return to the art school but stayed on with my relatives in Kiev for a few months before joining my father in Vasil'kov. I [visited] my aunt with whom I stayed on my arrival in Kiev. I was anxious to find out exactly how she fared during the pogroms. My aunt and her two daughters lived on Kurenevka at the very edge of the city. The pogroms reached them, but they got off with only a bad fright.

It came about in a very interesting and significant manner. A group of young boys, known in the neighborhood as a tough gang, used to drop into her grocery store from time to time for a handout of cigarettes, candy, or soda. Of course, she never thought of asking them for payment. A few months before the October Manifesto was issued, their behavior underwent a puzzling transformation. They stopped dropping in for their free treats. On the 18th of October, they went up town to participate in the demonstrations. When, on the next day, some Black Hundreds drifted down from the center of town to "have some fun," they were met by these local boys brandishing clubs and pistols as if they meant business. With no police around to help, the intruders made a hasty retreat and did not show up again.

■

This sort of "conversion" was not unique during the revolutionary upheaval. Social ferment at high tension becomes contagious. One could easily build a theory on it. I shall merely cite one more instance. In 1905, there existed a tug of war between the two leading trends in art, the Wanderers and the World of Art. The first and older of the two, active since the eighties [1880s], was—to use a modern term—"committed" to the belief that art both mirrors and molds society, that art is a factor for progress. The second, in existence only a few years, rejected this and preached the autonomy of art, the doctrine that aesthetic pleasure is the beginning and end of artistic activity.

Most unexpectedly, some of the best known members of the World of Art were swept off their feet (there were notable exceptions) by the events of 1905 and plunged into enthusiastic activity on behalf of the Revolution. They spoke at public meetings; they wrote articles; they were arrested; but, most important of all, they helped issue satirical journals, made drawings, cartoons, and caricatures. Their contribution was particularly valuable, because the World of Art excelled in graphic work. To this day the drawings by [Ivan] Bilibin, [Mstislav] Dobuzhinskii, Eugène [Evgenii Evgenevich] Lanceray, and others make a powerful impression, even if the events they refer to are not fully understood. Predictably, with the defeat of the Revolution, there were defections among the elite as well as the hoi-polloi.

■

After bidding farewell to my friends and relatives and listening to the usual pleas—"Don't forget to write"—I packed up and left for Vasil'kov.

8

RETURN OF THE PRODIGAL

Back in Vasil'kov

The Revolution of 1905 was smashed. The rebels who were not killed or imprisoned were driven deeper underground or went abroad determined to continue on their course after the "temporary interruption." The peasant uprisings were suppressed with savage cruelty. Anti-Semitism was more virulent then ever. Wide sections of society were in the grip of fear, despondency, cynicism, and sexomania.

I dropped out of the Kiev Art School and went to live with my father in Vasil'kov. My father moved to Vasil'kov because it was becoming unsafe for him to stay any longer in the village. In the bloody clashes between the landowners and the peasants, the looting and burning of estates, granaries, stables, and the raids of punitive squads—in all this ferment and charged atmosphere, the Jews made a handy target, especially after the Kishinev pogrom of 1903. The Jews in small settlements were trying to find some safer haven. The ideal place to go, of course, was America. Those who could, did; the others moved to larger centers where sharing danger and suffering was perhaps less fearsome. Father sold his mill and left Ludvinovka forever, probably without regret. He chose the city of Vasil'kov because he had some distant relatives there. In Vasil'kov he could fulfill his religious duties—attend the synagogue regularly, celebrate all the holidays with others of his faith—and live in what was to him a congenial milieu. He bought a little stand where he sold bread, sugar, salt, pickles, garlic, and sweet drinks. He eked out a miserable living but was more or less content. He had a rather hard time of it in the winter, because while the stand had a roof to protect the items on sale from rain or snow, it had no walls. You had to bundle up in as many coats and rags as you could carry on your body and keep a pot with burning coal handy to warm your hands.

Scarcely four years before, I had left, or was taken from, the yeshiva of Vasil'kov [and moved] to Kiev, where I prepared for the local art school. In the distant village of Ludvinovka, father was following his daily routine ignorant of what happened and happy in the innocent assumption that I was as ever laboring in the vineyard of the Lord. Soon enough he learned that I had been taken from the house of Jewish learning and piety to a city full of godless men and sinful temptations. He made his peace with what happened but it hurt. It hurt badly.

And now the prodigal returned. Father was obviously happy. If he could not treat me to a fatted calf, he did his best with a scrawny chicken. He was a man of firm convictions (mostly religious) and few words. But I sensed he was troubled, and surely there were many reasons why he might have been: poor health, economic insecurity, [his] children scattered in parts of Russia and America, and now I was only a visitor for a few short months to be gone, perhaps forever.

I tried to please him. I offered to help at his stand, but there was very little to do. I came frequently anyway, just to make conversation about America and about affairs of the moment. I went to prayer with him. In Kiev I had completely lost the habit of going to the synagogue except as an observer of the several lavishly appointed houses of prayer in different districts of the city. Now I picked up where I had left off. On Friday we went to the steam bath, according to the universal custom among Jews. On Saturday when we were together in the synagogue, father was visibly pleased and proud when members of the congregation pointed me out to one another as "Avrum's son," "the student from Kiev," or "the future artist." After prayer or during intermission, people came over to shake hands with the usual greeting "Sholem aleichem" [literally: Peace unto you; colloquial: Hello, how are you?] or engaged me in conversation "like a grown person" about life in the big city, the Revolution, and the pogroms. Father and I went to a local photographer and had our picture taken, father posing in a long caftan and yarmulke, and I in my school uniform, a dark suit with blue stripes [Figure 3].

I continued to wear my uniform during my stay in Vasil'kov, and this gave me something of a status. I made the acquaintance of many adolescents of both sexes and soon discovered that Vasil'kov was a "hot bed" of revolutionary activity, both legal and illegal. One of the more memorable of these acquaintances was a young girl of about 16, a graduate of a local high school that had only two of the seven classes in the full course of a *gimnaziia*.

She had an unquenchable thirst for knowledge and education, and she was violently in revolt against the forces that stood in the way of so many others striving toward the same goals. She was preparing herself as an extern and hoped some day to be able to take college entrance examinations, although the obstacles seemed insuperable.

Once in conversation she cited as an example of the "dark forces" (words from a revolutionary song) her former teacher of Russian literature. In teaching his subject, the teacher had the habit of deliberately pointing out to his students the passages that made derogatory reference to Jews. In classical Russian literature his choice was wide. For example, he made her read aloud in class the following section from [Nikolai Vasil'evich] Gogol's "Taras Bulba":

"Hang all the Jews" rang through the crowd . . . "Let's drown the rascals in the Dnieper."

Those words were like a spark in a powder magazine. The crowd rushed to the suburb with the intention of cutting the throats of all the Jews.

The poor sons of Israel, losing what little courage they had, hid in empty vodka barrels, in ovens, and even crept under the skirts of their wives, but the Cossacks fished them out from everywhere.

"Into the Dnieper with them. Let's drown the dirty rascals."

. . . the Cossacks seized the Jews by the arms and began flinging them into the river. Their pitiful cries rang out on all

> sides, but the Cossacks merely laughed at the sight of a pair of
> Jewish legs in shoes and stockings kicking in the air. . . .

When the girl read "crept under the skirts," the teacher leered significantly.

The girl was a few years older than I, more intelligent, better informed, and more self-reliant. Yet, because of my uniform, and chiefly because I went through the 1905 Revolution, she credited me with greater knowledge and more maturity of judgment than I possessed. She questioned me closely about the "October days," which I could answer as an eye witness. But when she passed over into the field of the theory among the several opposing parties, I was on less sure ground. I soon learned that she was in the underground, active in organizational and educational work. It was the custom in such organizations—even in prison—for the more informed and educated to give free instructions to the less educated in political economy, history of civilization, natural science, and literature. Once I mentioned cautiously the danger from undercover government agents.

"Oh," she replied defiantly, "I realize it only too well. But if you are afraid of drowning, you'll never go near the water. Yes, education is important; friendship is important; and personal safety is important. But they are only secondary to the fight, even at the risk of one's life, for the emancipation of man from tyranny and oppression."

Nowadays such sentiments seem almost trite, yet they were uttered with such conviction as to be anything but trite.

We talked about literature, Russian and foreign: Knut Hamson, Anatole France, Oscar Wilde, Arthur Schnitzler, Leonid Andreev, and [Maxim] Gorky. I remarked that elsewhere authors of world literature were so widely translated and so cheaply sold that young and old read them. I did too, [though] whether I understood them fully is highly doubtful. Once I expressed a preference for stories of [Anton] Chekhov as compared with Gorky. To this she took vehement exception: Gorky was her ideal author—a man of proletarian origin, of great gifts, and a revolutionary to be emulated.

At another time, she expressed her admiration for the career I had undertaken: the study of art. She knew something about Russian art but little more. Precisely for this reason, she placed the artist on a lofty pedestal from which his art shed its beneficent rays on the prosaic life of mankind. I am afraid my contribution to the conversation was not very enlightening.

■

Our talk brought to mind my association with an older student in the Kiev Art School, Grabovskii. While in the art school, all I wanted was to learn how to draw and paint, to master the craft in all its possibilities: perspective, anatomy, chiaroscuro, color values, etc. To Grabovskii, this was just the alphabet. He tried to propel me beyond that. He himself was subsidized by a wealthy patron who not only paid his tuition but also, through personal contact, tried to give him a broader orientation in art and its relation to other aspects of culture, literature, music, and architecture. All the members of the family were evidently highly cultured; they read the important art publications in Russian and other languages so that they were abreast of all the new developments in the art and literature of many countries. To all this, my friend had free access. By proxy I benefited from the same source.

In the art school, as I had occasion to note formerly, the great god and model to emulate was the famous artist Repin. He was the pinnacle, the acme toward which the students were urged to strive. Some even spoke of the three Rs: Rembrandt, Raphael, and Repin. An exhibition of any of his work was an event to celebrate. Repin was a member of the Wanderers, a school [of painters] with a social orientation, [who worked] in a technique of vigorous realism. At the turn of the century, a new trend, the World of Art, made its appearance, drawing to its ranks a number of prominent artists and writers. Its philosophy was in almost total opposition to that of the Wanderers; it preached the doctrine of art for its own sake. My friend, like his patron, was all for the World of Art. I began to hear a lot about [Arnold] Böcklin, [Aubrey]

Beardsley, [Sir Edmund] Burne-Jones, T[homas Theodor] Heine, and the Russians, [Aleksandr] Benois and [Konstantin] Somov. What struck me more than all this wide information was my friend's spirit of exaltation. He seemed to regard art more as a cult than a profession. His head was so high in the clouds, he became practically unsociable. I could not follow him that far, but—by way of imitation perhaps—I did begin to regard art as a high mission. The notion was vague but, I admit, it made me feel good.

■

While in Vasil'kov I went around sketching, which always attracted viewers who engaged in a lively exchange of opinions. Once, fascinated by a Christian cemetery with its variety of tombstones, crosses, weeds, and flowers, I spent a long time drawing in pencil and water color. When I brought it home, my father looked at it and his face changed. I immediately realized my thoughtlessness. Crosses in a pious Jewish home! Father said nothing. He just picked up the drawing and tore it to shreds.

In the yard where my father rented a tiny shack, there also lived the families of a tailor and a grocer. They had boys about my age with whom I used to go swimming and take long walks. Next door lived a mother with two daughters, 12 and 14 [years old], and a boy about 10. Her husband had left for America some years previously, with the usual promise that he would send for the family as soon as he earned enough money. However, while he sent her a few dollars now and then, he kept postponing the date of the family's departure to America. The woman was not well; the children were idle and neglected. The younger girl was a wildcat and ran around with all the neighborhood boys. They bragged of how she gave her favors to anyone for a *piatak* (five kopeks). Her mother gave her a beating once in awhile; but she [the mother] was too weak to follow her around, and the girl was too obstreperous to pay any attention to her mother.

Years later I met her [the daughter] in America in a photographer's studio where she had come after a night of carousing with several male and female companions. The females were dressed gaudily, all painted up, and loud in conversation. She was now a professional prostitute and lived outside her family. Her mother, tired of her husband's procrastinations, had collected enough money from the town's charities to take the family to the United States. She found her husband was married to another woman, younger than she. He wasn't exactly pleased to see his first wife but neither was he embarrassed. He struck a bargain: he would support both families but live with the younger woman. I once had an occasion to visit his house as he lay ill with some spinal trouble, lumbago perhaps. The pain seemed to come in waves. When the pain gripped him, he clenched his fists, his face became distorted, and he groaned aloud. Gradually the pain subsided; he wiped the profuse sweat from his face, breathed a sigh of relief, attempted to smile, and remarked: "God, if only I knew that there were women in the next world, I wouldn't mind dying."

■

After some months stay in Vasil'kov, I received a ticket for an ocean liner from my brother who urged me to hasten the trip [to America]. I prepared for the journey at once. I took along one extra suit, a few shirts, socks, a brand new set of phylacteries (a present from my father), and $25 in cash to present to the American authorities on arrival at Ellis Island. All this fitted in a small valise. Beside that, I also carried a sack filled with slices of dark bread dipped in beer and toasted. This was supposed to be the best food on a sea voyage; and as additional insurance against sea sickness, lemons and lemon drops. Of course, the boat ticket was for steerage.

Travel to America was a thoroughly organized business, operated by agents stationed all along the way, from the point of departure to the port where ocean liners sailed to the United States: Agents in the large cities who organized the traffic and expedited the passengers to the border; others at the border negotiated with the border authorities for illegal traffic (where necessary); still others beyond the border who were notified in advance [of] how many to expect and to what next stop to direct them. My brother had left the country illegally, [so] it was thought best that I do the same to avoid a possible detention at the border. Thus, wherever I stopped or changed trains, there was always an agent helping me to the next stop. New members were added to our group as we approached the Austrian border, which we were to cross.

At the border all the immigrants were crowded into an inn for a few hours. Toward midnight in a drizzling rain, we all set out with a couple of peasants at our head. It was totally dark and deathly still. Our steps in the grass and over the wet ground were audible only to ourselves. Undoubtedly the border guards were well paid so that there wasn't much danger; but our agents, in order to impress us, told us that the border guards were on the alert and looking for smugglers, that they sometimes stopped people and arrested them or even shot them. And since there were some people who for one reason or another did not want to fall into the hands of the authorities, their fear communicated itself to everybody and we all prayed and hoped that the ordeal would soon be over. Every once in a while some suspicious noise was heard, and everybody stopped with bated breath. Once or twice the guides told us to wait while one of them went on to reconnoître. Finally, we saw a house on the other side of the border. We quickened our pace and were soon on Austrian soil. There was a wild release of pent up feelings. People laughed and cried and congratulated one another. We went into an inn. Tea and bread were served. Early the next day, we were on the way to Brody, one of the most active centers for the transportation of immigrants.

Again the immigrants were passed from hand to hand. One guide shipped us to a city where another took us to an office, verified our documents, placed us in a miserable hotel, took care of our amusements, and passed us on to the next guide. Here and there, we picked up an immigrant who, for some reason or another, had been left behind; here and there, we lost one whose papers were not in order or who ran short of funds and had to wait for additional money from America. Where the need was small, we made a collection. Thus we bundled from Brody to Lemberg (now Lvov'). Though we stayed in Lemberg only one day, one of our company managed to find a house of prostitution, something he looked for whenever we came to a new city. We had a glimpse of Paris and of Antwerp. Antwerp impressed me enormously, by the busy traffic and the sturdy muscular draft horses, the like of which I had never seen. In comparison, the horses of Ludvinovka looked pitiful indeed. From Antwerp we crossed the channel to Liverpool. This short sea voyage made almost everybody sick and gave us a foretaste of the longer trip ahead. In Liverpool, I had my first taste of a banana. I remember having seen bananas in Kiev, in one of the "gastronomic" Pashkov Brothers' Stores, where they looked so forbidding, intended only for the tables of the rich. Here was my chance to emulate the rich. It was a disappointment. As soon as I took a bite, I had to spit it out; the cloying, sweet taste was very unappetizing. (It takes time to get used to even good things.) In Antwerp, I met a friend of mine from the Kiev Art School [who was] going to America but [in] a different boat. We promised to look each other up in America, and we did.

In Liverpool we boarded the small ocean liner, *Carmania,* I think it was called. I was in steerage "E" [and was] miserable and seasick most of the time. The bunks were hard and uncomfortable. Women groaned and wailed. A big hulk of a man was vomiting; between vomiting, [he] was swearing in the most blood-curdling Yiddish against the boat, the food, the service, his fate, and the relatives who had taken it into their hands to bring him to America. We were all crammed in the passages, like Jonah in the whale. The engines were clattering, and the waves hammered against the boat. The more pious Jews put on their prayer shawls and prayed aloud morning and evening in congregation. Seldom had they prayed with such devotion, with so much sighing. Some of the younger people looked on with disdain. I discovered the usefulness of the beer-impregnated toasted bread: it was the only food my stomach would hold down. I sucked lemons for dessert.

As the boat came nearer the shores of America and the weather let up a little, the young people struck up acquaintances, gathered in groups and engaged in lively conversation. I sat at the periphery and soon I thought I was back in Russia or in the theatre at a performance of [Evgenii] Chirikov's *The Jews.*

"A Jewish worker is exploited doubly, first as a worker and then as a Jew. Even the peasant, the poorest of the poor, when he took justice in his hands, whom did he attack first? The landowner who exploited him? No, the Jew who was even worse off than himself."

To which came an immediate reply in terms equally familiar.

"Would it hurt less if a Jewish policeman instead of a Russian hit me on the head? Would I be better off if a Jewish capitalist robbed me instead of a Russian, American, or French[man]?"

And so on and on.

Then an older man broke in: "What about America? Can't you leave Russia for a while behind you?"

"Right!" shouted several people in a chorus.

Yes, what about America? How much did any of us know? I could not speak for the others, but I myself did not know very much. Having studied geography, I knew that New York was on the *Gudzonova Reka* [sic] (Hudson River). I knew about the Negroes from Harriet Beecher Stowe's *Uncle Tom's Cabin*. From [James] Fenimore Cooper's novels, I learned about the Indians. Cooper was very popular in Russia. It seemed that everybody who could read, read the *Leatherstocking Tales.*[1] And there was another American-English author very popular among Russian teenagers, Captain Mayne Reid.[2] Though born in England, Reid spent much time in the United States, fought in the American–Mexican War, and wrote widely of his American adventures. Here I may have even been in advance of many Americans. After my arrival in the United States, everyone I talked to knew of Cooper; but I hardly found anyone who had heard of or read Mayne Reid. Such differences in an author's popularity are not uncommon; Lord Byron and Edgar Allen Poe were held in greater esteem in Russia and France than in their own respective countries.

Back to my American education. An uncle of mine, who had been in the United States for three months and returned to Russia, tried to introduce me to American ways, customs, and language. In America, he said, the rule is "ladies first." A woman can make you marry her at the slightest pretext, so beware. When you address a man, you must say "mister, please." The American language has much in common with Yiddish. Yiddish *"lomp"* is American "lamp"; *"kum aher"* is "come here"; etc. Before you know it, you'll speak like a born American."

I forgot to mention that I also read a long essay on Washington and Lincoln (by Morgunov, I think) in which the author held Lincoln to be the greater man.

Of American art, I had practically no notion at all. Whistler was the only name I knew, but he was considered half, if not three-quarters, English. For the rest, I heard people say that America was a thoroughly materialistic country where art was not regarded too highly. I hoped they were wrong.

After eleven slow days of uneasy travel, we arrived at the New York harbor. We debarked at Ellis Island, "the isle of tears," and threw our baggage, bundles, bags, and boxes on the floor and prepared to wait. Before we were allowed to see our relatives, we had to go through a long interrogation and physical examination. It was a critical moment for everyone. There was an air of foreboding, apprehension, and hope. There were children whose fathers would hardly know them, and wives, sisters, and brothers in uneasy expectation. A considerable number would be refused admission.

To me America would be the beginning of a new life; to others, a final resting place; to all, a plunge into the unknown. This was the great divide in our lives; our lives split in two. We had all said farewell to our past with its many associations, customs, habits, to our ways of living and thinking, and to our friends and relatives (half our family stayed behind). Could we say hail to our present and future?

I was answering the examiner's questions mechanically. My mind was wandering. Memories came crowding into it, some pleasant, others horrid. Then, a blank wall: America, a vacuum which I could not yet fill with any definite imagery. Suddenly my name was called, and I was ushered into my brother's presence. We took the ferry and landed in Manhattan. The uncertainty of a month's pilgrimage was over. I looked up and down at the unusual environment. The skyscrapers, which later formed the subject of so many of my pictures, now looked forbidding, breathed a chilly indifference. But just as new sights were an object of curiosity to me, so apparently was I an object of curiosity to others, to judge from the way everybody stared at me. I was dressed in one of those embroidered Ukrainian shirts with a high collar (made familiar in this country by the Russian ballet), its tails hanging over the trousers and a cord with tassels tied around the waist. My brother looked at the people staring at me, then looked at me and said, "You'll need a new outfit."

My Americanization had begun.

PART TWO

1906-1920

Fig. 4 *Brooklyn Bridge,* lithograph, 1931.

AS A YOUNG MAN IN AMERICA

When Lozowick arrived in New York in 1906, he went to live with his brother in Newark, New Jersey. As a teenager, Lozowick attended the Barringer High School in Newark. He continued to draw, mainly for himself. His formal art training resumed when he enrolled in the antique figure class at the National Academy of Design in New York during the 1907–1908 academic year. He excelled in his studies, receiving the silver medal for this class. For whatever reason, Lozowick did not return to the academy until 1912, when he embarked on a three-year course of study. His teachers at that time included Leon Kroll, George Willoughby Maynard, Ivan Olinsky, and Douglas Volk. One of the events that remained prominent in Lozowick's mind was the Armory Show: "In 1913, in New York there was the international show of modern art, the first big show of modern art that fascinated me very much. I went there several times. I couldn't accept [it]; I didn't understand or whatever; but I was fascinated."[1]

As Lozowick approached the end of high school, he began to plan for his future. He decided that even an artist needed a good general education, so he applied to a number of universities and colleges. In his words,

> I got two favorable replies from two colleges, one at Wisconsin and the other at Ohio State. Ohio State appealed to me a little more. One of the reasons was that they said that "many of our students find employment, enough to support them while in

Fig. 5 *New York,* oil on canvas, ca. 1924–1926. Walker Art
Center, Minneapolis, gift of Hudson D. Walker, 1961.

college." So, I went to Ohio State, and it turned out to be true.
I did get enough employment. I got my meals at a fraternity. I
waited table.[2]

He recalled his college years with fondness. Arthur
Schlesinger, Sr., was his professor of American history. Lozowick became friendly with Schlesinger because his professor was interested in the political problems in Russia.[3]

> He invited me to his house. Especially in 1917, when the
> [Russian] revolution broke out, I was in college. He brought
> me in and invited a number of professors. Did I know anything
> about what was happening—the different parties, Bolsheviks,
> Mencheviks, socialists, revolutionaries? As it happened, I did.
> They were fascinated to no end to listen to what the clash
> was about.[4]

In his academic endeavors, Lozowick pursued a liberal
course of studies, completing a four-year program in three
years: "To me the studies were very easy. I wanted to do it in
less time but [the administration] wouldn't let me."[5] In 1918
he graduated Phi Beta Kappa.

In addition to his formal studies, Lozowick participated in
various collegiate activities and organizations:

> There was an intercollegiate Socialist Club of which I was a
> member. [There] was also the Cosmopolitan Club, [which in-
> cluded] members of various races. The policy [of the campus]
> was liberal. In fact, when I was in college, the first prime minis-
> ter of Israel, Ben Gurion, visited Ohio State University. We had
> a meeting with Gurion. He talked to us about his ideas. I was-
> n't a Zionist, but I was interested.[6]

Lozowick wrote his first manifesto on art, "Tentative Attitudes," while at Ohio State. It appeared in the student publication *The Sansculotte,* of which Lozowick was on the editorial board.[7] In this essay (see Appendix), Lozowick argued
that in the past art, which is based on emotions, assisted humanity in adjusting to the physical environment. In modern
times, however, the intellect as exemplified by the sciences
assists humanity in dealing with the world. Hence, he concluded that art is extraneous to contemporary life. Fundamental to Lozowick's reasoning was his presumption that to
be viable art must be relevant or express the relationship of
humanity to the social and physical environment. This view
remained constant in Lozowick's thinking throughout his life.

After graduation, he ". . . volunteered for the army—it
was right then when the war was on. I was in the army for
over a year"[8] (Figure 7). He was assigned to the medical section and was stationed in Charleston, South Carolina:

> When I got out of the army, I came back—I stayed around. I
> didn't have much to do. But I did get a little bonus from [New]
> Jersey—I think it was $700 or $800—and I got some money
> from the army. The army gave me a reduced rate of travel
> around the country. So that was my first trip across the country,
> practically the entire country. It took me some months. With
> the help of the army—whether [I received a free trip or a re-
> duced fare] I don't remember—but I do remember that they
> made it possible for me to make the trip in some way.[9]

Providing firsthand observation of the American terrain, this
trip was of immense importance in Lozowick's identification
with his new country and remained etched in his memory.
When later in his life interviewers queried him about the
sources of his work, he always credited this trip as essential in
introducing him to the technological character of America
during the early 1920s.

After his cross-country trip, Lozowick taught for some
months at the Educational Alliance Art School, an immigrant
settlement community on the Lower East Side.[10] While there
is no precise documentation of the dates of Lozowick's
classes, one of four outlines of lectures on the history of art
among Lozowick's papers is dated January 7, 1920.[11]

According to his own account, "By 1921, I decided to go
to Europe."[12] Actually, Lozowick appears to have left for Paris
in mid-1920. This is documented by the fact that his first article, on the subject of Russian Dadaist poets living in Paris,
appeared in the September–December 1920 issue of *Little Review,* initiating a relationship with this influential modernist
publication and affiliated gallery (by the same name) that
lasted until the late 1920s. Lozowick remained in Paris until
February or March 1922 when he moved to Berlin, where he
resided until the fall of 1923.

As background to the chapters that follow, it is important
to note that although the reasons prompting Americans to
travel abroad undoubtedly varied, one principal motivating
factor was a general feeling among American intellectuals'
that America's industrial and commercial environment was
inhospitable to creative activity. Harold E. Stearns best articulated this sentiment in his two popular books, *America and*

the Young Intellectual (1921) and *Civilization in the United States: An Inquiry by Thirty Americans* (1922). Lozowick recalls that Stearns' influential *Civilization in the United States* was "a wholesale arraignment of the futility and frustration that pervaded every phase of intellectual life in the U.S. and an expression of utter helplessness in the face of that situation."[13] In Stearn's opinion, intellectuals had only one recourse, to "get out" of America,[14] and he set an example by sailing for Europe as soon as he had submitted *Civilization* to the publisher.[15]

As Lozowick recounts in the following chapters, "Paris," "Berlin," and "Moscow," once abroad he was overwhelmed by the fascination that America held for European and Russian artists, writers, and intellectuals. His experience was shared by other American intellectuals living in foreign cities, such as Paris and Berlin. Edmund J. Wilson, Jr., comments on the ironic situation in which Americans found themselves:

> Young Americans going lately to Paris in the hope of drinking culture at its source have been startled to find young Frenchmen looking longingly toward America.
>
> In France they [Americans] discover the very things they have come abroad to get away from—machines, the advertisements, the elevators, and the jazz—have begun to fascinate the French at the expense of their own amenities. From the other side of the ocean the skyscrapers seem exotic, and movies look like the record of a rich and heroic world of new kinds of laughter and excitement.[16]

Stearns was one such American. Astonished by Europeans' infatuation with America that he found abroad, he wrote home: "As a spectacle, America is more poignant in Paris than in New York!"[17]

It is ironic that America's industrialized culture, from which young Americans fled, seemed to acquire a new luster from the distance of foreign cities. With Europeans expressing awe and envy at America's technological prowess, Americans living broad began to take pride in their homeland. Malcolm Cowley recalls that the chief benefit of his two years in Paris (1921–1923) was to free him from his feeling of inferiority, from "the prejudices of the lady whose French flour

Fig. 6 Lozowick as a young man, ca. 1915.

Fig. 7 Lozowick in army uniform, ca. 1919.

paste was so much better than the made-in-the U.S.A. product."[18] He came "to regard the dragon of American industry as a picturesque and even noble monster."[19]

This new pride in America resulted in a call for American artists and writers to reject foreign culture and to find their creative sources in native material. Matthew Josephson, an editor of the avant-garde monthly *Broom* put out by Americans living abroad,[20] observed that "the high speed and tension of American life may have been exported in quantity to

Europe, but we [Americans] are still the richest in materials. No city will quite equal what New York or Chicago or Tulsa have."[21] He urged Americans "to examine our home products sympathetically, to judge if they are not sprouting with an authentic beauty that justifies their outlandish departures from the past or from previous European traditions."[22] Noting that "the Old World is become [sic] fearfully americanized [sic],"[23] he cautioned that "it would be a strange surrender of our prerogative to imitate Europe, or Paris for that matter."[24] Surrounded by such widespread enthusiasm and pride in America's industrialized and mechanized culture, Lozowick adopted a comparable attitude, recalling that he turned to American subject matter in his work "perhaps in a spirit of nostalgia."

During this period of the early 1920s, Dada—an aesthetic of bizarre and iconoclastic art forms—was the dominant modernist style of poetry and painting in Paris and Berlin, as Lozowick relates in the next two chapters. America's fast-paced life, commercialism, and industrialism provided source material for much of Dadaists' syncopated, nonsensical poetry, as well as for the new machinist imagery that appeared in the works of artists such as Marcel Duchamp and Francis Picabia. As a consequence, Americans living abroad came to see the American culture they had fled in a new light. Harold A. Loeb, editor of *Broom* and a close friend of Lozowick, believed that Dadaists' iconoclastic and antiartistic use of American source material was essentially negative. He believed that for Americans to emulate Dada would result in the "immediate deterioration of the American product."[25]

In addition to Dadaists, Russian Constructivists also looked to America for inspiration but with a different purpose. America's industrial prowess provided both an example for postrevolutionary industry in Russia as well as new values for artistic creation, values of efficiency and utility that ultimately led to the Constructivists' desire to merge art with industry. Lozowick's account in Chapter 11 of his conversations with students at VKhUTEMAS, Higher State Art-Technical Workshops, and his observations of Vsevolod Meyerhold's biomechanical acting and mechanical stage sets all testify to

Russian Constructivists' fascination with the principles of order and reason that underlie industrialization. From correspondence between Lozowick and Loeb, it appears that Lozowick's trip lasted approximately six weeks during the summer of 1922.[26]

In response to the enthusiasm for the products and values of industrialization so highly accentuated by American engineering, Lozowick painted his first American cities—*Cleveland, Chicago, Pittsburgh, New York*—and made his initial drawings of machinist forms that he exhibited at the Gallerie Alfred Heller in Berlin in August 1923. According to his own account, his idea of the "Americanization" of art were formulated during his years abroad.

PART THREE

YEARS ABROAD
1920–1923

9

PARIS

When I was in heder one of the games the children used to play was inventing nonsense words and syllables and chanting them in rhythmic variation. The point was to see who could create longer and more complicated variations. Potentially the variations were endless. Here is an example:

Brendya brendya putya brissa

Bra brissa

Putya putya putya brissa

Bra brissa

putya putya putya bra

Brissas brissa brissa

putya bra

Brendya brissa

putya bra

Putya brendya brissa

Putya brissas putya bra

Bra

Brissa brissa

Bra

Brissa bra

Bra, etc.

Like Monsieur Jourdain, who did not know he was speaking prose,[1] we did not know we were composing poetry.

Years passed, many years passed. From the heder I went to a yeshiva, dropped my religious studies and took up my education in Russian, emigrated to America, studied art, went to college, was in the First World War (helping to make the world safe for democracy), and joined the post-war (lost) generation swarming by the thousands seeking culture in the capitals of Europe. Paris was my first stop. By this time, my childhood games—unconscious excursions into phonetic poetry—were completely forgotten. And suddenly they came back to me. All Europe seemed to be playing the same game.

The new poetry of which I speak was composed of vowels and consonants in combinations that looked like words but were unknown to any existing language. They were, in brief, visual and phonetic. Occasionally, punctuation marks, arithmetical signs, numbers, etc., were used. There was a proliferation of this poetry in the magazines of many countries (I almost said, in many languages)—Russia, France, Holland, Germany, Yugoslavia, and others. The following is a small sampling from a rich store.

First a poem published in a Paris magazine, *La vie des lettres et des arts* [The life of letters and arts] and written by a New Yorker.

PAROXYSMES

À Ezra Pound

..rrrR

— hs — hs — hS

!!! hooO

— hs — hs — hS

— rrroooR

! t — t vvvK

— — — — — o — O

!!! tsi — i — i — I

— *et sam* — *et sam* — *sam* — saM

?oha — Keink — — tsiH

! *rrroor* — O

— *atakak* — af — oh — tzziG

!!! tzziG

— tz — zi — iB
— rrakrrA
— rrA
— — — *rrak* — rA

? ar — as — tiM
! *akalas* — *ytar* — tarrR
— — — — O — z borrK
! zst — ak azaj — nihabast — O

— ozah — ah agnat — zinT
....
! zinT...........................
— *Ov* — *zrrro* ....R

— .... *rrr* ....O
!!! — sta — ta — aD
(Pierre Chapka-Bonnière
New York, 1920)[2]

The editor, Nicolas Beauduin, himself the inventor of poetry—"A trois plans"[3]—was evidently impressed by the
poem, for he wrote a three page "open letter" to the poet.[4]
He praised the poet's courage in carrying the art of poetry
beyond anything attempted heretofore:

> The new world, it goes without saying, cannot . . . be left
> behind Old Europe. . . .
> No half measures for you . . . you are the maximalists of
> poetry. You have not only rejected all intellectual methods, all
> logical constructions, all syntax, all esthetics—the WORD itself
> has been banished from your work.

According to M. Beauduin's assessment, this poetry is unbri-
dled individualism. Seeking to escape from the bonds of con-

vention, law, and faith, it works according to the laws of its own making, "to which it alone has the key." Phonetic, ideographic, it serves no social function. It is but an "exteriorization of lyrical emotion." It tries to register "the perturbations of the unconscious. . . . It challenges the very art of poetry." But precisely because of its radical departure from all known standards, it deserves the attention not only of the literary [world] but also of philosophers and aestheticians.

To pass now from Paris–New York to Berlin, Germany, and Rudolf Blümner, who writes about "absolute poetry."

"Absolute poetry" ("Die Absolute Dichtung," *Der Sturm,* July 1921), according to its elucidator Rudolf Blümner, is poetry to be heard rather than to be seen in print, for its value can be appreciated only when translated into the melody of the human voice *(hörbare Melodie)* in its infinite nuances, timbre, and sonorities, unaffected and unhindered by intellectual content *(Bedeutung).* Thus in the process of composing, the poet first becomes dimly aware of certain vocal resonances which later issue in the form of certain constructs of vowels and consonants. This poetry can, therefore, be fully apprehended only in the quality of these resonances *(. . . dass diese Dichtung . . . doch nur in ihrer Verklanglichung vollkommen aufgenommen werden kann).*[5] Another passage freely translated:

> Just as the painter utilizes creatively form–color according to his individual choice, that is, independently of intelligible meaning *(Bedeutung),* just as the composer arranges his tonalities with complete freedom, so do I combine vowels and consonants according to creative *(künstlerische)* laws.

Blümner ends his article on a note of warning to potential imitators who would find the task easy. Then follows the poem, ["Ango laïna"]: I quote the last section:

I éja
Alo
Mýu
Ssirio
Ssa

Schuá

Ará

Niija

Stuáz

Brorr

Schjatt

Ui ai laéla — oia ssisialu

To trésa trésa trésa mischnumi

Ia lon schtazúmato

Ango laína la

Lu liálo lu léiula

Lu léja léja lioleiolu

A túalo mýo

Mýo túalo

My ango ina

Ango gádse la

Schia séngu ina

Séngu ina la

My ángo séngu

Séngu ángola

Mengádze

Séngu

Ińa

Leiola

Kbaó

Sagór

Kadó[6]

■

From Berlin to Moscow.

The following is a phonetic poem by Aleksei Kruchenykh from his collection called *Piglets (Porosiata)*, dated 1913:

te ge ne

   ru ri

   le lu

       be

   tlk

   tlko

   kho mo lo

re k bukil

          krd krud

               nupr

               irkyu

               bi pu

Kruchenykh was the leader and theoretician of a large
group of writers, artists, and musicians—rebels very much
like their counterparts in Zurich, Paris, Berlin, or Rome.
They engaged in raucous brawls, relished public scandals,
were liberal in the use of profanity, and thundered imprecations against established mores and reputations. "A Slap in the
Face of Public Taste" [1912] is the title of one of their pamphlets. Kruchenykh also wrote prose and poetry in more or
less intelligible language, but his fame, such as it was—and
is—rests on his surrational or transrational poetry *(zaumnaia
poeziia)*. We have read the rationalization for the abstract phonetic poetry in previous pages. The following are a few random thoughts gleaned from his "Declaration of the Word as
Such":

> Thought and speech cannot catch up with the experience of
> inspiration; that is why the artist is free to express himself not
> only in the common (comprehensible) language but also in a
> personal (the creator is an individual) language that has no defi-
> nite meaning (not frozen), a transrational *(zaumnyi)*. The com-
> mon language is confining; free speech allows fuller expression.
> . . .
>
> Transrational language arouses and gives freedom to creative
> imagination without afflicting it by anything concrete. . . .
>
> Transrational creations can establish a universal poetic

language, born organically, not invented artificially like
Esperanto. . . .

One member of the Kruchenykh circle was the celebrated
artist Kazimir Malevich. Kruchenykh wrote an opera, *Victory
over the Sun* (performed in 1913 at the Luna Park in St. Petersburg) for which Malevich did the sets and the costumes,
[Mikhail] Matiushin wrote the music, and [Velimir] Khlebnikov (almost untranslatable but highly regarded by some
Russian critics) wrote a prologue.

In 1919, Malevich wrote a long essay entitled "Concerning Poetry" *(O poezii)*. It appeared in the official organ of the
Art Section of the Commissariat of Education. The poetry of
which Malevich speaks and that he extols looks in cold print
like the several samples we have seen previously. He assigns to
it, however, a rather unique function. For Malevich the true
poet is a magus, an orator, a servitor possessed by divine fire.
When such a poet creates his verse, he is performing a sacred
rite. In response to his inner tension, he invents his own language. The tremor of his emotion is transmitted to his entire
body, which, as it were, participates in "the liturgy" (Malevich's expression). [Malevich writes:]

> It is said that a thought once expressed becomes a lie ([Fe-
> dor] Tiutchev—L. L.) to which I would reply that while the
> use of words is inherent in the expression of thought, there is
> something more subtle, more fluid than thought . . . something
> you cannot express in words.
>
> This "something" every poet, artist, musician feels and seeks
> to express; but, when he undertakes to express it, this subtle
> fluid thing becomes perverted into Venus, Apollo, the Naiads,
> chrysanthemums, etc. Not a downy feather bed but a coarse
> heavy mattress with all its particularities.
>
> Reason and intellect destroy the spontaneous, uninhibited
> divine spark of the inner spirit. In the face of such a profound,
> soul-searching experience, mere craftsmanship, artistry, and
> beauty are only hindrances.
>
> The God or the Devil may speak through the poet.
>
> The highest spiritual evocation I consider speech without
> words, when delirious utterance escapes from the mouth,
> delirious beyond reason and intellect to fathom.

When the poetic flame ignites him, the poet stands up, raises his hands, bends his body, giving it the form which will present for the spectator a living, new, real church.

Oole Ele Lel Li One Kon See An

Onon Koree Ree Koasambee Moena Lezh

Sabno Oratr Tulozh Koaleebee Blestore

Teebo Orene Alazh

This is how the poet exhausted his high utterance; these words cannot be set in type and no one can imitate them.[7]

One could easily compile a large anthology of this phonetic poetry; for the moment, however, I shall cite no more.

After finishing the lengthy essay by Malevich, one feels a little cheated. To read a declamatory, sometimes purple, always solemn, essay which promises so much, and [to] find it end up in a meager quatrain is surely disappointing. There are reasons for this. The tone of the essay is like much else written by the modern artists, writers, and critics during the first years of the [Russian] Revolution. These artists, neglected, vilified, and ridiculed before the Revolution, suddenly found themselves invested with great power. The more established, conservative artists (with some exceptions) pursued a policy of watchful waiting, while the moderns—Malevich, [Wassily] Kandinsky, [Marc] Chagall, [El] Lissitzky, [Vladimir] Tatlin, and others—backed by the new state, undertook the reorganization of all art institutions, exhibitions, schools, academies, and museums. Hence, their pronouncements had a tendency to be couched in oracular, oratorical tones.

But there is another aspect quite startling and unusual in a professed revolutionary. The essay of Malevich harks back to the Bible, more specifically to the New Testament. What Malevich is advocating or, more correctly, preaching is glossolalia, the New Testament's "speaking with tongues": "And when Paul had laid his hands upon them, the Holy Ghost came on them, and they spake tongues and prophesied" [Acts 19:6]. Under the spell of deep religious fervor, ordinary speech failed them, and they resorted to a spontaneous outburst of unintelligible utterance. The New Testament does not condemn it. Some have the "gift of tongues"; others have the "gift of prophecy." Malevich and other moderns seemed to have had the gift of both.

In the essay Malevich refers to the Church, to liturgy, to the brotherhood of congenial spirits. Thus, when inspiration seizes the poet, [Malevich writes:]

> he will reach out to people and the people will reach out to him. He may thereby form a desert around himself. Those who are afraid of the desert will run. But he will reach out across the desert to the people and the people will respond. And if the people feel a kinship with him they will each greet him, each differently but all in unison.

With slight modification, this description might well apply to an early Christian community. The members of the community who "spake with tongues and prophesied" were, to use Spinoza's expression, "God-intoxicated," although to some of their brethren they appeared just intoxicated: "They are brimful of wine." This has a modern ring.

It is the Old Testament that cites an actual example of "other tongues." It is the famous writing on the wall of Belshazzar's palace: *Mene, mene, tekel, upharsin*. Although it was in a language unknown to any man, the prophet Daniel interpreted it (Daniel 5:25). There is no lack of modern Daniels.

Incidentally, one of the most tuneful songs of the WPA[8] era had a catchy, lilting refrain, which went:

Mene, mene, tekel, tekel, tekel

Mene, mene, tekel

Upharsin

Mene, mene, tekel, tekel, tekel

Mene, mene, tekel

Upharsin

It was a welcome change from the usual fare.

"Speaking with tongues" has continued well into our own day. Many saints of the church practiced it, and it was common among the Shakers and the Russian *Khlysty* (flagellants).[9] It had especially wide practice among the Mormons. Article 7 of Joseph Smith's "Articles of Faith" reads: "We believe in the gift of tongues, prophecy, revelations, visions, healings, interpretation of tongues," etc.

Feeling that I was in the line of an ancient and honorable tradition, I extracted from my childhood memory a number of "absolute poems," wrote them down, and introduced them with the following manifesto:

NÉANTISME

Lyrisme linéaire et syllabique

L'art moderne n'est pas supérieur à l'art ancien.

Ni certainement inférieur.

Il est autre—voilà tout.

Comme notre époque.

Il n'y a pas des progrès dans l'art (c'est

problématique s'il y'en a ailleurs).

Il n'y a qu'une progression.

L'art change.

Il ne s'améliore pas.

Par conséquent il n'y a pas de degrès de comparaison parmi les

oeuvres des différentes (ou d'une même) époques.

Un tableau, un poème, est une oeuvre d'art ou il n'est pas.

Alors pas de critérium?

C'est exact.

Il y en aura, peut-être, dans un avenir lointain, probablement le

jour, ou l'art sera mort. Pour le présent l'histoire de l'art et de

l'esthétique proclame bien haut (à ceux qui veulent l'entendre)

cette seule vérité incontestable: tout critérium est futile.

Que reste-t-il donc?

Le goût.

Le goût de la putain pour le roman boulevardier—

Le goût de Monsieur Bourget pour le roman psychologique—

Et ainsi de suite, sans fin.

Ils s'équivalent tous.

Chaque artiste (chaque individu) a le droit de

s'exprimer d'une façon aussi bien que d'une autre.

Le culte de l'incompétence donc?

Peut-être. Aucun mal à cela. Les esprits apparentés,

médiocres ou géniaux, sont réunis en communauté d'âmes

à l'exclusion de tout autre.

Le cercle des initiés peut renfermer dix personnes

(comme dix mille ou dix millions) c'est eux qui apprécient les

oeuvres de leur crû, et cela ne regarde qu'eux.

Pour l'artiste l'art est une crucifixion.

Une crucifixion de soi-même ou d'autrui.

Une crucifixion, mais aussi une rédemption.

L'art en soi est-il le sens de la vie?

Le contre-sens plutôt.

Le non-sens.

[NOTHINGNESS
Linear and syllabic lyricism

Modern art is not superior to ancient art.

Certainly not inferior.

It is other—that's all.

Like our times.

There is no progress in art (which is

problematic if some is made elsewhere).

There is only progression.

Art changes.

It does not improve.

Thus there are no degrees of comparison

among works of different (or the same) periods.

A painting, a poem, is a work of art or it is not.

So no criterion?

That's right.

There may be some, perhaps, in a distant future,

probably the day that art will be dead. For the present

the history of art and aesthetics proclaims very loudly (to those

willing to listen) this lone, unquestionable truth: any criterion is

futile.

What is left, then?

Taste.

The prostitute's taste for romance novels—

Monsieur Bourget's taste for psychological novels—

And so forth, without end.

They are all the same.

Each artist (each individual) is entitled to express himself one

way or another.

The cult of incompetence, then?

Maybe. There is no harm in that. The related spirits, mediocre

or genial, are gathered in a community of souls excluding all

others.

The circle of initiates may include ten persons (just as ten thou-

sands or ten millions) they are the ones who appreciate the

works produced in their midst, and that is nobody's else's

concern.

For the artist, art is a crucifixion.

A crucifixion of oneself or of others.

Crucifixion, but also redemption.

Does art in itself bring sense to life?

Counter-sense, rather.

Nonsense.]

I dispatched the poems and the manifesto to *La vie des lettres
et des arts* and waited, more with curiosity than bated breath.
A prompt reply came within the next few days requesting me
to meet with the editor. We met at his office and spent a few
pleasant hours talking about art, poetry, America, and France.
In view of the fact, he said, that poems of a similar nature had

already appeared in the magazine he would prefer to use the manifesto alone—for the time being—if I agreed. Which I did. As a gesture of fellowship, Monsieur Beauduin presented me with a volume of his poems (inscribed), *L'homme cosmogonique (poèmes synoptiques à trois plans)* [Cosmic man (synoptic poems on three levels)]). The next issue, which was February 1922, carried the manifesto.[10]

The manifesto did not set Paris on fire, but a few *habitués* of the [Café du] Dôme noticed the manifesto and spoke to me about it. One of them was the Russian poet Il'ia Zdanevich. He was one of the school founded in Russia by [Aleksei] Kruchenykh. The poetry of Zdanevich consisted of arbitrary word formations, sometimes a combination of syllables from different words, sometimes words deliberately misspelled, truncated, disguised, and often words completely unintelligible. He presented me with his book, *LidantIU fAram,* one of the oddest I have ever seen. For its exterior form alone, it deserves a place in some museum. In the frontispiece to the book, he gives his age as 1894–1973 (as of this moment, I do not know where he is or whether he is still alive).[11] There is also a guide to the orchestration of the book. Zdanevich regarded his work with the greatest seriousness. He maintained, against hostile criticism, that *LidantIU fAram* had a consistent line of development and that it was a labor of love as well as hard work. One may well believe it. Evidently the poet attached great importance to the graphic aspect of his poetry as well as to it phonetics (and content), for the typographic setting of the book is extraordinary. No two pages are typographically alike. Each page has several kinds of type— literally dozens. When all the available characters had been exhausted, Zdanevich made up his own from tail pieces, crowns, paragraph signs, leaf forms, etc. I am reproducing a double-page spread (pp. 52–53), which is indicative of the rest.

I heard Zdanevich recite his own work. It was a startling performance. He read, clicked his tongue, drawled, neighed, shouted, and ejected words that sounded familiar yet were strange; [he] gesticulated, almost danced, almost sang, and seemed to enjoy hugely the commotion, laughter, applause, and jeers of the audience. He could be serious, frivolous, and

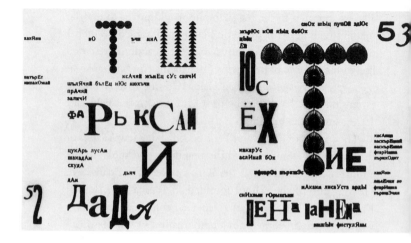

provocative. I saw a large poster on the streets of Paris announcing a lecture by "Ilyazd" (Il'ia Zdanevich) *"L'éloge de Il'ia Zdanievitch, nomme l'ange, sur lui-même"* (Eulogy of Il'ia Zdanevich, called angel, by himself). The poster then enumerated his attributes, to wit: *"crétin, lâche, traître, fripouille, assassin"* [cretin, coward, traitor, rogue, assassin], and more of the same—a true son of Dada.

Zdanevich introduced me to some literary circles. At one of them I met [Filippo] Marinetti, the machine-obsessed [Italian] Futurist who had decreed the death of Futurism years before but did not seem to be in a hurry to hasten that demise.[12] He invited me to a reading of his poetry. It took place in a back room of a Montparnasse café. Russians, Germans, Scandinavians, Frenchmen, Italians, and Americans formed a colorful audience. The room was thick with smoke, acrid with alcoholic vapors, and loud with the tongues of many nationalities. Everyone smoked, everyone drank, everyone talked. Silence was requested, and Marinetti rose to read. He recited with verve: Staccato words and phrases about speed, machines, and motors were thrown at the audience with a fine abandon. His hands and arms shot out and cut the air with the proverbial Latin impetuosity. Beads of sweat stood out on his forehead. He ended under a warm applause.

I saw him again after a short interval and came away with an inscribed copy of *Les mots en liberté futuriste* [Futurist words-in-freedom].[13] (I was accumulating quite a collection of inscribed books.)

Zdanevich was one of the many Russians I met in Paris. There was a large colony of them comprising all professions, all beliefs, and all social stations. They had their own clubs, charitable organizations, newspapers, magazines, restaurants, and book stores. Not a few were waiting confidently for the day ("soon, very soon") when internal counterrevolution or external intervention would restore them back to positions of power. Others tried to adjust to the realities of exile. And there were not a few who were willing to compromise with the Bolsheviks.

Occasionally, I used to sit at a table with a Russian who claimed to be nonpolitical. His chief interest was the cinema, for which he said he had written scenarios. His latest and best was—to take his word for it—truly epic in its sweep; it would just knock them for a loop in Hollywood. But wouldn't Hollywood trick the author out of his sensational plot? What did I think? Well, I thought it was a risk that might be worth taking. Yes, he would chance it. Would I be willing to translate a brief summary of his story? I would be, of course, properly compensated in due time. I would risk it, too, I said. And so I translated the story, which I remember quite clearly went as follows:

It is a tetralogy and begins in the year 1899 around Christmas when a young Polish couple, [who] is snowbound, is saved from being frozen to death by a young Ukrainian teacher, [by] the name of Mazurskii. As they all rest overnight in the hut of the forest warden, the young Polish woman, still a virgin, takes revenge on her impotent husband by giving herself to the Ukrainian teacher. "At the expiration of a period required by nature" (to quote the author), Stephanie Luboshchanskaia (for that is her name) gives birth to a child. It's a boy! Unable to bear his wife's infidelity, Pan Luboshchanskii commits suicide. He leaves his entire fortune to the newborn and also a letter to be handed him when he reaches the age of 18, in which the truth of his parenthood is told. Thus

Luboshchanskii hopes to induce the child to take revenge on his mother.

Tempus fugit. Comes the Russo–Japanese War (1904). Mazurskii, the Ukrainian, is sent to Manchuria. On the way, he meets Stephanie and her four-year-old son, but does not recognize them (the Hollywood touch). In Korea Mazurskii is taken prisoner by the Japanese. A Japanese married woman takes him as a lover but gets rid of him as soon as she finds herself pregnant. In the meantime, Mazurskii and two other prisoners get permission to go to America. Here he meets with much suffering and many adventures which end with his meeting and marrying a millionaire Indian squaw. The experiments of the Wright brothers stimulate Mazurskii and his friends to invent their own new type of airplane. Mazurskii and his friends together with Mazurskii's wife, the squaw millionaire, jointly take a trip to Europe on the newly invented airplane (1910). Before reaching Europe, a storm overtakes them. The plane goes out of control, is driven to Africa, where it crashes, killing everyone except Mazurskii.

Mazurskii is taken prisoner by a native Negro tribe. At once he is married to a Negress who, "at the expiration, etc.," gives birth to twins. Mazurskii is now an accepted member of the tribe and goes out hunting for elephants and crocodiles. The War of 1914 rolls around, soon involving Africa. Mazurskii is under Verdun (1915–1917). Then the Russian Revolution breaks out, and Mazurskii goes to Russia to join the Bolsheviks. He fights in the Russian–Polish War (1920) and, while there, orders the execution of a young Polish patriot, who is none other than Stephanie's son. Stephanie goes out of her mind.

The author then draws the international moral from the tetralogy, to wit: Thus, we have women of four races cohabiting with one man. The woman of the white race betrays her husband in order to have a child and thereby avenge the humiliation she had suffered at his hands. The woman of the yellow race wants to have a child by the white man in order to increase the population of her beloved fatherland and, thus, also to give joy to her husband who is away fighting a war. The woman of the red race marries the white man be-

cause she had won him in a lottery and had fought it out
with her white competitors in a duel. She made it a condition of her marriage that they were not to have children, as
she hated half-breeds. The woman of the black race rescued
the white man from the clutches of her fellow Africans who
were just about ready to make a meal of him. She wanted to
have lots of children, and she liked them light-skinned.

I translated the story and forwarded it to its proper destination. I did not think it would meet with a favorable reception. However, since then I have seen many Hollywood
smash hits that made me revise my original opinion. Some-
day it would not surprise me to be greeted from the screen by
the "millionaire squaw." Of course, her fingernails would be
manicured, and she would wear the finest silk underwear; and
as a climax, it would be discovered that somewhere in her
past there was an aristocratic white ancestry.

I came out of the army with a small bonus, which would not
have lasted very long in Paris. I also had a small monthly income through the help of a former fellow student [Louis
Rich] in college. Upon graduation, he found an editorial job
in the house organ of the Union of America Hebrew Congregations. He felt that a "cultural letter" from Europe dealing with artists, writers, actors, and architects would be of interest to the readers of the magazine *[Union Bulletin]*. I was
assigned to the job at $30 per article.[14]

My first victim was the sculptor [Léon] Indenbaum. Reproductions from his work had appeared in a magazine published on the [Ohio State University] campus. I was one of
several students working on the magazine, which was called
The Sansculotte. (Among its contributors were the architect
[N. J.] Donner; Jack Lewis; James Light (editor), who became
for a time one of the top theatrical directors in New York;
Kenneth Burke, the critic who was brilliant even then—he
wrote a fin-de-siècle sketch, "La Baudelarienne," in French,
which elicited high praise even from the French faculty of the
university; Louis Rich, who in his postgraduate days worked

on special assignments for the *New York Times;* and Boris Glossman, who developed into one of the best known American Jewish writers. We received illustrative material from George Bellows (who had studied at Ohio State University some years before) and John Sloan, among others. A brother of the Paris sculptor Indenbaum was a fellow student. He gave me his brother's address and a letter of introduction. Léon Indenbaum introduced me to many artists and helped me get acquainted with Paris. He gave me several reproductions from his works, which I forwarded with an article to the magazine in the mid-West [*Union Bulletin* was published in Cincinnati].

My next subject was the well-known poet and critic Iwan Goll. Despite his youth—he was then only about 30—he enjoyed a solid literary reputation both in France and in Germany. His contributions in prose and poetry appeared in such publications as *Die neue Rundschau* [The new review], *Die Aktion* [Action], *Das Kunstblatt* [The art sheet], *Le monde nouveau* [The new world], *L'Esprit nouveau* [The new spirit], and *La vie des lettres et des arts* [The life of letters and arts]. He was, thus, in his own modest way, working toward the rapprochement of the erstwhile enemies (somewhat like [Thomas Theodor] Heine before him). Such of his works as *Le coeur de l'ennemi* [The heart of the enemy], French translations of 14 German poets, and *Die drei guten Geister Frankreichs* [The three good minds of France], a critical study of [Denis] Diderot, [Stéphane] Mallarmé, [Paul] Cézanne, served to render the culture of each familiar to the other.

Iwan was one of the postwar poet–idealists, an internationalist, a humanist, and a firm believer in the ultimate regeneration of man. He had friends among writers and artists [throughout] Europe. He resented and subjected to sharp criticism everything that divided man from man and hampered his development. And he had a deep, abiding faith in the redeeming nobility of art.

One of Goll's poems is called "Der Panama Kanal." It is a hymn of praise to science, industry, and man's ingenuity that can transform a mosquito-infested, disease-ridden jungle into a place of health, comfort, and beauty. Oceans are united and men from all parts of the world come to trade goods, exchange opinions, and, hopefully, to shed prejudices. He admitted in later years that his vision was far too sanguine.

Another poem [by Goll] of a wide sweep is "Naomi." Although Goll was a pantheist and an universalist—in no sense a nationalist—"Naomi" pays tribute to the prophetic tradition in Judaism.

I spent many pleasant hours in the company of Iwan Goll and his charming wife, Claire, a fine poet in her own right. They were thoroughly steeped in the culture of Europe. Their circle of friends among artists and writers was enormous. The book *Le nouvel Orphée* [The new Orpheus], which Goll gave me, was illustrated by Georg Grosz, Robert Delaunay, and Fernand Léger.

(I met the Golls many years later when they were in the United States during the Second World War. Their faith was still broadly humanist, but considerably chastened; so many hopes shattered; so many friends turned into enemies.)

It was through Goll that I became acquainted with Ljubomir Micić, the founder of *Zenitisme* [Zenithism] and editor of *Zenit* (Zagreb-Belgrade [1921–1926]).[15] *Zenit* was an embattled Yugoslav magazine which championed avant-garde art in all its forms. One of its special features was to publish every author in his own language—French, German, Russian, and all the Balkan languages.

Personally, Micić was handsome, with his well-trimmed beard, and very agreeable company. His wife was a gracious hostess, and his house in the country, a delightful place to spend an afternoon or evening. An appetizing meal of French or Serb dishes, preceded and followed by just the right drink, disposed one to lively conversation and made clear what was meant by *"bon viveur."* We often met in the Café du Dôme, where he always brought his beautiful black dog. We would soon be joined by his friend Branco Polyansky. Polyansky explained how foolish and dangerous it was for young artists to show their work to Picasso in the hope of some favors. Instead, Picasso only appropriated their ideas and used them without acknowledgement in his own work. Polyansky was something of a lady-killer. He had no hesitation whatever [of] engaging in conversation women he had never met before. American women were his favorites.

We discussed everything. Micić hailed the escapades of Dada and was enthusiastic about the new Russian art and poetry. He had just published, in *Zenit,* Aleksandr Blok's poem, "The Scythians," in which the poet hurls a challenge to the Western world. We talked about the United States. They [Micić and Polyansky] were eager to learn from the "horse's mouth" all about modern America—[its] industries, architecture, and literature. I frankly admitted my limitations, but they were satisfied with whatever little I could offer. During one such leisurely conversation, the two Yugoslavs broached a scheme which they were sure would be highly profitable.

[Their scheme was based on the following:] Centuries ago, as is well-known, the Turks were in occupation of the territory now known as Yugoslavia. A certain rich and powerful Serb was forced to flee the country. Unable to take with him much of his money, jewelry, or other precious objects, and being, moreover, sure that the Turks would soon be expelled, he decided to bury his treasure. As a safety precaution, he drew a careful plan on parchment showing the exact location where the treasure was hidden. Unfortunately, events did not proceed as expected. The Turks overstayed their welcome. The merchant prince died. His family became impoverished. Ultimately, the Turks were driven out. The descendants of the rich merchant were still alive but no longer in possession of the property, but the parchment, having been handed down from generation to generation, was still in their hands. Micić and Polyansky knew that it was still available. All that was needed was sufficient capital to purchase the property. The compensation would be many times the investment.

They told the story in all seriousness. They felt that as an American it should not have been difficult for me to raise the necessary amount. It was a strange thing, an aberration, that to many Europeans, even intellectuals who might have known better, there was simply no such thing as an impecunious American.

Among the many Russians I used to meet at the different cafés, there was one who interested me for a special reason.

His name was Valentin Parnakh. He was of medium height, rather slight of stature, [with] a longish face, and a large head thrown back as if in an attitude of defiance. Picasso once made an excellent drawing of him, a fine character study. Parnakh wrote prose and poetry in Russian and French, did translations from and into each of these languages, but his main interest seems to have been the dance. He wrote, in fact, a book in French on the history of the dance,[16] and in his book, *Clambering Acrobat [Karabkaetsia akrobat],* an entire poem consists of diagrams indicating the movement of a certain dance.

I was privileged to see him dance once in private. It was a strange and absorbing performance. It did not resemble any dancing on the French, the Russian, or the American stage. He moved from floor to chair, from chair to table on which he executed a few pirouettes, and stretched his whole body upward as if trying to reach or lift the ceiling. It was more gesticulation and miming than what one would ordinarily call dancing. I was constantly reminded of his book of poems *The Clambering Acrobat.* There was no accompanying music, and yet it was a fascinating spectacle, more perhaps because of the dancer than the dance.

It was impossible to be bored in [the] Paris of the twenties!

I was not surprised at all to read several years later a surrealist tale by the eminent Russian poet Osip Mandel'shtam, "The Egyptian Stamp," in which Parnakh (under the name of Parnok) was one of the leading characters.

I never saw Parnakh after Paris, but his name intruded more than once on my attention. A few years after I read "The Egyptian Stamp," I came across a new book by Parnakh, which I acquired immediately. Written in Russian and published in the Soviet Union, it was called *Spanish and Portuguese Poets, Victims of the Inquisition.* The history and achievements of Spanish Jewry during the "golden age" have been well documented and described, and the work of the great poets and thinkers—Solomon Ibn Gabirol, Moses Ibn

Ezra, Judah Halevi—have been studied and commented on copiously. Parnakh's book deals with the little known post-exilic period and with poets who were thoroughly assimilated. They wrote in Spanish and Portuguese (unlike the poetics previously mentioned who wrote mostly in Hebrew). They were Marranos,[17] exiles, and refugees whom the long arm of the Inquisition tracked mercilessly wherever they were, from Holland to Brazil. Parnakh translated some of this poetry, related some of the biographies, and described the methods of torture (this had been done before). Although this was not the first work dealing with the subject, solid research has gone into assembling the pertinent facts. To me, the discovery that Parnakh was at home in the Spanish and Portuguese languages was a pleasant surprise and confirmed my regard for him. The last I heard of Parnakh was that he danced for some time at the Meyerhold Theatre.

■

Each café—the Dôme, the Coupole, the Sélect, the Rotonde—had its own loyal following. I wasn't faithful to any of them. I used to flit from one café to the other whenever and wherever I noticed someone or something of particular interest. One of the regular habitué's of the Café de la Rotonde was a man by the name Wolf who wrote under the Latin nom de plume "Lupus." He translated Yiddish literature, especially from Sholom Aleichem, into French. He stood out from the crowd by his shock of red hair. Always with him was his amie, a lively and voluble French woman. I always enjoyed sitting down at his table, particularly on the sidewalk, for an aperitif and conversation. Like his favorite author, Sholom Aleichem, Lupus liked to joke and tell or listen to anecdotes. His amie would ply me with questions about America.

"Is it true that in America when you get the call of nature there are no street *pissoirs* to relieve yourself?"

"Yes, it's true."

"Is it true that drug stores serve meals?"

"Yes, it's true."

"Is it true that society frowns on men openly having an amie?"

"Alas, it is true." (It was then—considerable progress has been made since.)

"What a barbarous country!" she would conclude.

Lupus also liked to inquire about America but in a more serious vein. One evening as I came to their table I had a story to tell. Earlier that day I had bought a paint set in a small polished box for outdoor sketching. While out, I stopped at the American Express for my mail. I stepped up to the window, put the box on the floor, and gave my name. It was no longer than a minute or two before I got through. I bent down to pick up the box. It was gone. I immediately reported it, but there was nothing the American Express could do except advise me to be more careful in the future. When I told the story to Lupus and his amie, he thought he could use it as an item for his *"chronique de la semaine"* [chronicle of the week]. He composed a brief note about an American artist recently arrived in Paris and anxious to create his first masterpiece on French soil but frustrated in this by certain practices common, alas, among some Parisians. Within a few days the magazine received a telephone call. If the artist would go to a certain café on Boulevard St. Michel, he could retrieve his box.

And so I got back my box. But why did the petty thief first steal the box, then return it? Lupus' amie, a born Parisienne, explained it this way. The thief made a mistake. He probably thought the box—small, pretty and nicely polished—contained silverware or perhaps even jewelry. When he discovered that it contained nothing more valuable than artist's supplies and when he read (or was told about) the notice, his native French gallantry got the better of him. I congratulated Lupus on his wide reading circle and treated everyone to an extra round of coffee.

Occasionally we would be joined by a character utterly atypical of the bohemian café crowd. He was Charles Rappoport, a prominent Communist writer, author of the definitive biography of Jean [Léon] Jaurès (assassinated on the eve of the First World War). In those days, Communists and non-

Communists met without fear of mutual contamination. Rappoport looked like Socrates in spectacles. Short, stockily built, with a pug nose, a dishevelled beard, and careless in appearance, he spoke in a cracked voice that carried across the street. Well versed in the social sciences and the literatures of Europe, he had a keen sense of satire. He was more than a match for Lupus in their friendly exchange of barbed thrusts. Once in a while, they would break into Yiddish, a language which both knew perfectly. This mixture of Yiddish and French gave an extra fillip to their conversation. Rappoport spoke excellent French, of course (and a number of other European languages as well), though with a thick Yiddish accent. I once asked him how many languages he spoke. "I speak six languages in Yiddish," he replied.

With an eye to posterity he devised his own epitaph: "No freedom without Socialism, no Socialism without freedom."

One day, a New York acquaintance said to me: "How would you like to splurge for a few days—eat in the best restaurants, ride around in taxis, all for free?"

"What's the catch?"

"No catch. A Japanese business man and his secretary are stopping over in Paris for a few days on their way to Berlin. You will act as their cicerone. Show them as much of Paris as time will permit."

The bargain was sealed, and I was introduced to the travelers. The businessman was an elderly gentleman, quiet-spoken and very polite. His secretary was a young girl, very small of stature and quite attractive in an oriental exotic way. They both spoke English well, though with an accent. I decided that our itinerary would be covered in taxis, stopping at points of special interest. First, I took them up to Sacre-Coeur and the Eiffel Tower for an overall view of Paris. During the few days our stops included the Opéra and the Arc de Triomphe, where we bowed to the eternal flame of the Unknown Soldier. I told them something about [François] Rude's statue *La Marseillaise*. We stopped at Notre Dame and the Sorbonne, where we took a walk on the university grounds, and I spoke about French college life. The man was silent most of the time, but she made up for the two. She kept on asking questions, to some of which I did not have any answers. We drove to Père Lachaise and the Murs de Fedérés.[18] I said a few words about the origin of the wall and the annual pilgrimage made to it. This was the only spot where the man evinced great interest and even showed some emotion. I took them to a cabaret on Montmartre and showed them three kinds of cafés—one on the Avenue de l'Opéra, another on Montparnasse—the Rotonde—and a third, a worker's café, in Belleville. And then it was time to part. They thanked me profusely—that is, she did, and he assented. My holiday was over.

About one year later, I met them again—in Moscow! She laughed out loud, and he smiled broadly. It turned out that the people I had in tow in Paris were not who I thought they were. She was his secretary—true enough—but he was not a business man. He was perhaps the most prominent revolutionary of Japan, Sen Katayama. She was Bertha Inomata and was on the way to Tokyo to join her husband, Professor Inomata of Waseda University.

Having hardly caught my breath from this surprise, a second and bigger surprise followed immediately. Bertha was not Japanese at all. She was a Russian Jewish girl. I couldn't believe it; she looked so Japanese. Whereupon she dispelled my doubt on the spot—she talked to me in Yiddish and Russian! This incident recalled to me the book by Dr. [Maurice] Fishberg, *The Jews* [: *A Study of Race and Environment*, 1911], in which the author refutes (or tries to) the notion that there is a pure racial "Jewish type." There are Jews, according to him, who look Mongol[ian], Italian, etc. Inomata would have made a perfect illustration for the book. In any case, Katayama–Inomata treated me to the best meal I had during that short stay in Moscow [summer 1922].

◼

As I sat at the Montparnasse cafés night after night, I witnessed the procession of celebrities (or future celebrities)—

Max Jacob, [Maurice] Vlaminck, [Chaim] Soutine, [Moise] Kisling, [Mikhail] Larionov, [Pablo] Picasso, [Eugène] Zak, [Isaac] Pailes, [Osip] Zadkine, [Albert] Gleizes, [Giorgio] de Chirico, [Adolph] Feder, [Marc] Chagall, Mané-Katz, [Tsuguharu] Fujita, [Serge] Charchoune, and many more. I was overwhelmed. Circulating among them was the popular model, black Aisha, sheathed in a turban or other picturesque headgear, talking and laughing and showing her glistening white teeth. Occasionally another model would make her appearance, Kiki, who was noted for her bawdy songs. From one of her songs, I recall this bit of gay information:

> . . . je suis m'en fou / . . .
>
> J'ai un grand trou . . .
>
> [. . . I am a madwoman/
>
> . . . I have a big hole . . .].

Many of the artists I met were to be in the Resistance during the Nazi invasion; many others perished in the concentration camps: Moise Kogan, Adolph Feder, Louis Marcoussis, Max Jacob, and many, many more.

The artists and writers one met at the cafés, because they came from so many different countries, presented a great diversity of character traits. Giorgio de Chirico, for example, seemed somber, spoke little but had a deliberate, logical consistency. (Sometime later I read his booklet on [Gustave] Courbet, which I thought very perceptive.)[19] The one-armed Blaise Cendrars, [in contrast], was highly vocal, ready to talk at the slightest opportunity, never short of a topic. He was probably the most traveled man there. He had visited every continent, including [North] America, and had worked at the most diverse trades. Unlike the other artists I met, he did not ask me about the United States; he told me. I got his book, *La fin du monde* [The end of the world], from Fernand Léger, who did the illustrations.[20]

Léger was one of my favorites, as a man and as an artist. Warm, friendly, he always made pleasant company. While there are paintings by [Georges] Braque and Picasso that are almost interchangeable, Léger is always distinctly himself, although undoubtedly a Cubist. I visited his studio. It looked like a workshop in good order: No fancy furniture, no drapes, some chairs, easels; several paintings lined up along the wall on which he worked simultaneously and methodically. And he was just as methodical in his choice of foods. We had dinner at one of the better restaurants in Paris. Léger knew exactly what wine or liqueur went with which course.

I was often surprised at the friendliness with which the artists and writers, with few exceptions, received a perfect stranger like me, of whose artistic *carte d'identité* they were totally ignorant. This helped make life in Paris extremely pleasant and stimulating. I attended various discussion groups, readings, and parties, often without an invitation.

One Saturday afternoon I went to an open house at Emma Goldman's. A well-known anarchist, she was deported from the United States to the Soviet Union together with her husband, Alexander Berkman. As might have been predicted, their views were too strongly in opposition to Soviet policy for them not to clash. They had to leave. (Another anarchist, Peter Kropotkin, returned to Soviet Russia voluntarily; and, though he did not actively cooperate with the Bolsheviks, he stayed on. Emma Goldman remained in Europe before settling permanently in Canada.)

When I arrived at Goldman's house, everybody was drinking hot wine. I had never drunk hot wine before, but I tasted it and rather liked it. I had known Emma Goldman by sight, having heard her speak in New York and having read her *Mother Earth*.[21] Most of the people present were strangers, but I spotted a Romanian with whom I used to exchange views occasionally at the cafés on Montparnasse. I sat down near him, and we sort of continued our café talk. Our conversation drifted to the international character of the artists' community in Paris. He mentioned his fellow Romanian, [Constantin] Brancusi, and my interest was aroused at once. I had heard a great deal and had seen some of his work, a few things in the original and more in reproduction. But sculpture, even more than painting, doesn't tell much in reproduction. I had never met Brancusi in person. Strange tales were told about him. He was spoken of as a Slavic peasant en-

dowed with occult powers, a kind of guru. His art was described in metaphysical and cosmic terms. I have always been
wary (I still am) of such labels, which explain little but mud-
dle a lot. More often than not, they are artificial creations.

(Once, on a visit to Japan, I was speaking to a museum director. I was seeking his advice on how best to get acquainted
with contemporary Japanese art. He was very generous and
helpful. Then he asked about American art. In the course of
our conversation, eager to show him how influential Japan is
in America, I told him how fashionable Zen Buddhism was
there, even among artists. Was Zen Buddhism also popular
among artists in Japan? I asked, expecting an affirmative reply.
He looked at me, smiled, and said: "American importation."

Importation—that is what many exotic labels are.)

In any case, I asked my Romanian friend whether he personally knew Brancusi.

"Indeed, I do."

"Would you introduce me to him?"

"I shall be glad to."

And so a meeting was arranged. In view of the tales I
mentioned earlier, I was somewhat apprehensive [about]
meeting Brancusi. As soon as I entered his studio, however,
my doubts were dissipated. He put me at ease immediately.
Plainly dressed, stocky, [with] strong sculptor's hands, a good
head of hair, and a full—though somewhat disheveled—
beard, he did look like a peasant, though, I thought, like a
peasant who was wise to the ways of the city slickers. There
was nothing odd or defiant in his appearance, yet he would
undoubtedly stand out in a Paris crowd—he looked so different from the overdressed, harassed urbanites.

Brancusi's studio, although full of things—stools and
pedestals—lacked the "artistic disorder" one associates with
an artist's workshop. The light was good, both for working
and for exhibiting the work done; it came from a skylight and
large window. I deliberately avoided discussion. To be sure, I
valued his judgment, but it was his work that interested me
more. I asked him to show me some of it, and he did as a
master showman. He exhibited his pieces from various angles
and in a light that would bring out the special surfaces of

metal, stone, and wood, their textures and configurations. I watched silently most of the time. Occasionally I would say something complimentary at which he seemed pleased.

I did put one question to him, the answer to which might have been obvious, but which I wanted to hear especially from him. The question was why he did so many versions of the same theme (or subject or conception) with but slight variation. His answer was that when a new version was created it did not mean that the old version was discarded; in the process of the search, each new embodiment of an idea became a new independent entity, sufficient unto itself, regardless of what came before or after.

We talked about life and art in Paris. I failed to discover the guru in him, but I found something more valuable, an unostentatious, friendly man who was not unaware of his own importance. Before I left I expressed my regret at lacking the means to purchase one of his works. I asked his permission to purchase from his photographer some pictures of his sculpture. Without saying anything, he took out a collection of photographs from which he let me choose several and firmly refused payment.

I speak a lot about the cafés, but, of course, I did not spend all my time there. During most of the day, I sketched, or wrote, or went to the museums. Whenever I visited the Luxembourg or the Louvre, I always took time out for a stroll in the street. In good weather the Luxembourg gardens were gay and colorful, a delightful spectacle—children everywhere chasing one another, floating boats on the lake, building castles; nurses and mothers hovering about them, gossiping cronies; young couples—mostly students—promenading along the alleys. After resting awhile and almost feeling at peace with the world, I would walk over to a nearby *confiserie* to have a cup of chocolate or tea and mouth-melting French pastry—delicious!

After the first few visits to the Louvre, I had my favorite rooms, to which I returned occasionally, as well as others, which I passed by or avoided. One section in the latter category was the Rubens Medici rooms. The tons of cascading, glowing, bulbous female flesh, masterly though it may have been rendered, was something I could take only a little at a time. Rembrandt, on the other hand—always one of my gods—I could contemplate again and again with deep spiritual satisfaction.

An aside. Shortly after the Second World War, I was in Amsterdam. Naturally, one of the first places to visit was the Rijksmuseum. I wandered from room to room in a kind of revery in the presence of the priceless treasures. Then I came upon a visiting group from Germany, young men and women perhaps between the ages of 18 and 20. They were guided by a man of middle age, evidently a professor of some school or college. There was a lively exchange of questions, answers, opinions, and speculations about the formal quality of the pictures, the social milieu in which they had been created, and the humanist message they embodied, etc. All this was conducted on a plane of gentility, urbanity, good humor, and friendliness. I looked at them and could not help thinking of the crematoria, of Dachau, of Babi Yar where my own two sisters were massacred. Could these well-mannered, well-dressed, well-behaved, fine-looking youngsters have goose-stepped to the strains of the Horst Wessel march, singing of their joy as they watched "Jewish blood spurting from the knife"? And the professor? Maybe they could or did.

But I immediately upbraided myself for having such thoughts. Didn't I always maintain that one could not condemn an entire nation for the crimes of an individual member? In fact, I was ready at that very moment to defend such a view—but the day was already spoiled for me.

Back to the Louvre. One of the rooms that was always delightful to visit was that of the small Dutch masters. Sometimes I walked from to room to room without any definite aim, like a flaneur on the boulevards. I would stop in front of a picture which, for one reason or another, attracted my attention and examine it without even knowing the artist's name. [After] I had stayed long enough in the museum to feel that sufficient unto the day was the good thereof, I would walk out and sit down on a bench in the Tuileries gardens to watch the passing scene, which in Paris is always full of interest.

I walked in the direction of Champs Élysées. There are perhaps too many statues in the Tuileries. However, they are not the eyesore that statues tend to be in so many other parks. Somehow they seem to belong. I came out on the historic Place de la Concorde, crossed it—not without a thought on its turbulent past—and continued through the park with its restaurants and showplaces. Sometimes the Guignol[22] was performing, and I would stop to watch the antics of Punch and Judy and listen to the commotion and the squeals and laughter of the children. Place d'Etoile was next and the streets radiating from it in all directions. A quick glance at the Arc de Triomphe and the *Marseillaise* by Rude, which reminded me of [Eugène] Delacroix's *Liberty Leading the People,* which again reminded me of Aleksandr Blok's "[The] Twelve," where Christ leads the red guards, and this in turn . . . but I am already across the Etoile and facing the wide prospect of Champs Élysées.

No place in Paris is more crowded, colorful, and alive with variegated throngs than the Champs Élysées on a bright summer afternoon: buses, carriages, bicycles, promenaders, shoppers, and flaneurs. The cafés are full to overflowing. It is the aperitif hour, the time to rest from the day's labors and to work up an appetite for dinner. Garçons bring out chairs and tables that are snapped up immediately. The only seats available are those inside; but, though I am exhausted, I will not settle for less than an outdoor seat. I wander from café to café until I finally spot a free seat at a table for two. I hasten to it. We go through the usual ritual. I bow.

"Permettez, Monsieur?"

"Faites, Monsieur, faites."

"Merci bien."

I take my seat and give my feet and my whole body a well-deserved rest. I order an aperitif; and, as I consume it, my entire being is suffused with a pleasant warmth and benevolence. I have a friendly chat with my neighbor about things of no consequence, and I watch and watch the passing pageant. Thoughts, ideas, and visions crowd upon one another with no logical sequence, flicker and disappear. A small, still voice upbraids me for spending "beyond my means." I waive it aside before my mood is spoiled.

"Take, therefore, no thought for the morrow: for the morrow shall take thought for the things by itself. . . ."

It has been a good day, a very good day.

■

Among the other museums which I enjoyed visiting were the Musée Guimet and Musée Cernuschi. They developed in me a taste for and love of Oriental art, which has persisted to this day. They prepared me for some of the inexhaustible and superlative artistic treasures of India and Japan when I visited those countries many years later. Subsequently, when I returned to the United States, I discovered what I had known only vaguely, how rich this country is in the art of the Orient.

■

Although I did not consider myself a tourist (I had a *carte d'identité* as a resident), I covered all the tourist's points of interest. One doesn't learn to love Paris all at once. The metro was not expensive, but I did most of my peregrinations and explorations on foot. I took in the theatres, the Folies Bergères, as well as the Opéra. And, of course, like everybody else, I went to Les Halles [the market], "the entrails of Paris." You get there in the wee hours of the morning, 4:00 or 5:00 (hardier souls come there even earlier, 2:00 or 3:00). Produce has been coming in all night long from everywhere and is now being distributed. You are assailed on all sides by noisy outbursts and harangues, for which the French are so well known, by pungent smells, by a bustle and scrimmage of porters, saleswomen, and truckmen. When action begins to slacken and the sun rises higher, the tourists—slummers— scatter to the several restaurants for the "specialty of the house," onion soup (you haven't tasted onion soup if you haven't had it at Les Halles). Then home to sleep.

I was beginning to feel half-Parisian when a friend who was about to leave for Berlin asked whether I would join him. I would and did.

On to Berlin!

10

BERLIN

Within my first few weeks, I criss-crossed Berlin in all directions to get the "lay of the land." Berlin was not Paris. There was no Île Sainte-Louis, no Sainte-Chapelle, no Montmartre, no Louvre, no Champs Élysées, etc.—the things that make Paris Paris. But there were approximations: the Tiergarten, Unter der Linden, Kaiser-Friedrich Museum, Museum für Volkerkunde. An approximation for the Rotonde was the Romanisches Café, an international gathering place for artists, writers, musicians, critics, hangers-on, and prostitutes (professional and amateur). Inside the Romanisches a cloud of smoke always hung over the din and the clatter of dishes, the clink of glasses and the animated dissonance of conversations. And conversation there always was—assertive, insistent, combative—in Russian, Hungarian, Polish, Yiddish, Swedish, and German too.

In the midst of the general hubbub I noticed a man with an enormously large head. Upon inquiry, I was told he was a great mathematician. Another odd-looking character was a dwarf by the name of Mendelssohn.[1] He was supposed to be related to the composer Felix Mendelssohn[-Bartholdy] and was himself a pianist and composer. Among the Russian artists, coming and going, were [Natan] Al'tman, [El] Lissitzky, [Isaak] Rabinovich (stage designer known especially for his sets to *Lysistrata),* [Isaachar Baer] Ryback, [Ivan] Puni (who later gallicized his name to [Jean] Pougny) and his wife [Kseniia] Boguslavskaia, Serge Charchoune ([he] began as a poet in Germany and ended up as a painter in France),

[Naum] Gabo, [David] Shterenberg, Mané-Katz, and [Hen-
ryk] Berlewi. Through Boguslavskaia I met briefly a young
Russian stage designer, [Pavel] Tchelitchew, who did colorful
sets for the Russian cabaret The Blue Bird *[Der Blaue Vogel]*.
He later settled in the United States, where he became famous
as a painter of strange and involved Surrealist compositions.

There was a wonderful group of Hungarians with whom
I became friendly: the critics [Ernst] Kállai and "Durus" [pen
name of Alfréd Kemény] and the artists [László] Péri and
[László] Moholy-Nagy. (Béla Uitz, another Hungarian artist,
was seldom seen in the cafés; he ultimately settled in the Soviet Union). They were all very articulate, and none more
than Moholy-Nagy. Ladislaus [László] Moholy-Nagy spoke
rather slowly, clearly, and with conviction. I thought his German superior in enunciation, clarity and sonority to [that of]
the native Germans. Perhaps as a foreigner myself I was not
competent to judge. It might have been a trace of the Hungarian accent which made his speech so melodious. I met the
group many times both in the cafés and elsewhere. I visited
Moholy-Nagy in Weimar and later at the Bauhaus in Dessau.
Together with the architect [Walter] Gropius, he edited a series of books on art, architecture, photography, film, and
crafts. He sent me the series when I returned to the United
States several years later. I reviewed some of the individual
volumes for the *Nation*.[2]

The work of Moholy-Nagy and Péri was nonobjective
(except for certain photomontages), related in its underlying
principles to the work of the Russian Constructivists. And
like those Russian artists, Moholy-Nagy attributed to his
work a social significance. The social meaning and function
of art was to Moholy-Nagy of prime importance. In this
connection I came across a minor but curious case of distortion applied to his thought. In his book, *Von Material zu Ar-
chitektur* [From material to architecture], a footnote reads as
follows:

> Die Taylorisierung, das System des laufenden Bandes u.a., sind
> Missverstandnisse so lange, als dabei den Mensch zur Maschine
> umgewandelt wird und seine mehrfache Leistung keinem an-
> dern als dem Unternehmer zugute kommt. (Vielleicht noch

dem Verbraucher, am allerwenigsten aber dem Arbeiter, dem wirklichen Erzeuger).

Here is the literal translation:

> The Taylor system, the conveyor belt, etc., are mistakes so long as they turn man into a machine and *his manifold contributions serve no one but the employer (perhaps the consumer also, but least of all the worker, the true producer)* (my italics).

And this is the way the translation appears in the English version:

> The "Taylor system," the conveyor belt, and the like are mistakes in so far as they turn man into a machine *without taking into account his biological basis"* (my italics).

I wonder whether Moholy-Nagy was aware of this "biology."

Almost every week, not to say every day, I met some member of the international avant-garde—sometimes in the Romanisches, sometimes at the Café des Westens, and also in private homes, as my circle of acquaintances grew. Theo van Doesburg, artist, architect, poet (under the name of [K. I.] Bonset), and theoretician of Neo-Plasticism [De Stijl],[3] was ready to explain his theories to anyone willing to listen, and I was willing. There was nothing of the bohemian about him. Well and neatly dressed, he looked more like a businessman than a rebel. He gave me several copies of *De Stijl,* the magazine which he edited and published.

A man more withdrawn and less conspicuous, but equally sure of his ideas, was Viking Eggeling, a painter better known for his abstract film. Like so many other creative persons, he was generous with his time, discussing freely his ideas without demanding to know my artistic genealogy. It was enough for him that I was a fellow artist (I began exhibiting in Berlin). Eggeling's abstract or "absolute" film, as demonstrated in his *Diagonal-symphonie* [Diagonal symphony], was to substitute for the single abstract a series of different abstracts arranged in dynamic sequence. From a large number of drawings more were eliminated than used. Eggeling's plans went further. He envisioned the creation of certain standard forms from which, as from blocks, one could build various structures, or, put differently, a series of notations from which a variety of compositions might be created. He also looked forward to the creation of abstract films in color. Unfortunately he died young, accomplishing only a small part of his pioneer efforts.

An artist of whom I saw a lot and with whom I became quite friendly was Lissitzky. Mild-mannered, soft-spoken, very gifted, yet modest, he was positive in his views, even though those views changed considerably over the years. The Revolution of 1905 brought to a head, out of the many accumulated grievances among the many minor nationalities, the demand for cultural autonomy, for the right to a national identity. Following, or alongside other nationalities, the Jews undertook a vast study of their national heritage. They organized groups for the gathering and recording of folk art in all its forms: legends, folk tales, songs, proverbs, superstitions, etc. They sent out expeditions of artists who traveled throughout the Pale of Settlement copying synagogue murals, illuminated marriage licenses *(ketubahs)* [contracts], folk drawings, paintings for the home and synagogue, embroidery, carving on holy arks, tombstones, etc.

Lissitzky was on one such expedition. He recounts the story and reproduces a number of copies he had made from the Mohilev synagogue in *Milgroim* (1923). Like Chagall, Al'tman, and Ryback, Lissitzky contributed his share to the creation of what the Jews like to think of as a national art *(Khad Gadya [One goat], Legend of Prague,* and others).[4] However, in his reminiscences of 1923, Lissitsky has a word of warning. These activities "according to the calendar are only a few years back but in life they happened epochs ago." To use the past as source for art or as proof that, like other nationalities, we [Jews] have a tradition, is anachronistic. "To us the living dog is dearer than the dead lion. We know that when the dog dies he becomes a lion."

A few years after the Revolution of 1917 Lissitzky made a complete break with the past. He joined the Suprematists and the Constructivists whose work he felt was more consistent with the needs and the ideals of the Revolution. His training as an architect and engineer had prepared him for his new tasks. With rule and compass he made his "objects" or *"Prouns" (Proekty uchrezhdeniia [ustanovleniia/utverzhdeniia] novogo,* projects for the institution [establishment/affirmation] of the new), "transfer stations between art and architecture." These nonobjective objects were designed with a skillful sense of spacial arrangement. Although they were purely artificial creations, they looked as though they might be drafts for some two or three dimensional constructions. In fact, they were done in correct perspective and foreshortening. They were not meant to appeal to the sense of beauty (though they did) but to the conception of order.[5]

Though Lissitzky believed in the usefulness of his various "objects," he constantly sought to create something more obviously utilitarian. He designed a room to house part of a Soviet exhibition in Berlin, a gallery in Hanover, and the Soviet section of the Press [Exhibition] in Cologne, etc.[6] He was coeditor of the Soviet magazine *[Izvestiia] ASNOVA* [News of ASNOVA][7] writing on architecture and city planning. In an issue in 1926 Lissitzky had an article on "Series of Skyscrapers for Moscow"—horizontal skyscrapers! In a very ingenious way, illustrated by maps, plans, and architectural renderings, Lissitzky attempts to prove how these "skyscrapers," carried on tall supports, would be preferable to the American type.[8] Alas, no one took him up on it, and it remained only an interesting project on paper, another and more complicated *Proun.*

Lissitzky [had] a restless and probing nature. Unlike Moholy-Nagy who, once he had discovered what he thought was the right thing, became a missionary for it, Lissitzky was forever finding, seeking, losing, and seeking once more. At one time, he even collaborated with Dada. The central contradiction in his career was that while he had a passion for the socially utilitarian, his gift lay in the realm of the imaginative (in a few instances he succeeded in combining the two). In the end, it was perhaps his achievement in the imaginative that was his contribution to the utilitarian.

Issachar Baer Ryback, who had accompanied Lissitzky on his expedition and who was now temporarily in Berlin, did not change his views on art with the coming of the Revolution. He greeted the Revolution, which, according to him, would now liberate the national energies and lead finally to the creation of a truly national art. Art, he insisted, must be rooted in national tradition, however poor it might be. He was eloquent in defending his views. [According to Ryback,] modern art has many elements in common with folk art, in anatomic distortion, disregard of perspective, nonrealistic color, etc. He illustrated those views in many of his pictures, particularly in his graphic drawing of the *shtetl* in its peaceful pursuits as well as its moments of terror. He even painted a Cubist picture, *L'Intran,* using Hebrew lettering instead of the French to prove that the national character of the artist will come to the surface even in an abstraction.[9] I am not so sure that the proof was very convincing.

I spent many evenings with [Ryback], his wife, and his friends—writers like [Ozer] Warshawski (the author of an interesting novel *The Smugglers;* he was massacred by the Nazis) and the artists, [Jankel] Adler, Mané-Katz, and others. Ryback loved to sing Jewish folk songs. Sometimes I would take my turn and sing Ukrainian songs.

Natan Al'tman, a gifted painter, graphic artist, and sculptor, would almost always be seen with some prominent Russian personality—[Il'ia] Ehrenburg, Aleksei Tolstoy, etc.

[Marc] Chagall was the star of the Russian constellation. Like the other Russian artists, he greeted the Revolution fervently ". . . in the bright glow of the Revolution we shall either perish or tread upon new paths. . . ." (Catalogue of Three Jewish Artists, [exhibition held] at the Jewish Cultural League, Moscow, 1922). In discussing Chagall's work, almost every writer sooner or later refers to its "Jewishness," which is natural in view of the numerous subjects that have come from his brush. As for most Jewish writers, they referred to him as *the* national Jewish artist. Chagall would agree but invariably ask, "Why only Jewish?" And he was right; for, beyond their Jewishness, his paintings and graphics have universal value. There is a painting by Chagall which seems to summarize the various elements in his art—Jewish, universal, whimsical, and nostalgic. It is a self-portrait showing the artist sitting in front of his own painting, *To Russia, Asses and Others,* placed on an easel. The face is treated cubistically; a seven-fingered hand holds the palette. To the [left] is the Eiffel Tower, to the [right] a view of Chagall's birthplace [Vitebsk]; the wall in the background carries an inscription in Hebrew, "Paris–Russia."[10]

■

When I left Paris for Berlin, I intended to stay in Berlin for only a few months, to give it "the once over" and return to Paris. But I became so much interested in what I saw, the people I met, and—not the least important—the lower cost of living (alas, at the expense of the local population, especially the lower income groups) that I decided to remain for a longer period. I began to paint in earnest. I had done some sketching in Paris, but in Berlin I began to work steadily and to exhibit. Within a short time, I had paintings at the Novembergruppe and the Juryfreie Kunstschau [Jury-free art show]. These were enormous exhibitions like the French salons or the American Independents [Salon of Independent Artists], including hundreds upon hundreds of paintings and sculptures. I also participated in the International Show at Düsseldorf in 1922, where heated debates were staged and manifestos issued.

My manner of working at that time was abstract and semi-abstract, though perhaps not as abstract as I thought. One day I took a painting to a frame shop to pick a suitable frame for a forthcoming exhibition. The picture was composed of some broken geometric figures in clear, bright colors. Instead of showing me samples of moldings for the frame, the shopkeeper kept looking intently at the painting. Finally, he turned to me and said, "Was soll das bedeuten?" (What might this mean?) I tried to explain to him that it had no literary meaning, that it was not meant to tell a story, that it was merely an effort to combine certain colors with certain forms in order to create a certain visual effect. He shook his head in disagreement. The explanation did not seem to satisfy him.

"The *Herr* does not think I understand or appreciate modern art, but I do. Artists come here for their frames, and I look at their pictures very carefully. Sometimes the artists even ask my advice. I know that the meaning of a picture is not always on the surface. Sometimes the artist speaks in symbols. And this is how I see your picture: To me it looks like a religious painting. Near the center I see the partial shape of a cross. That clearly refers to Christianity. Over to the right is an imperfect crescent—obviously Mohamedanism. And, down there, on the bottom, is an incomplete star of David—Judaism. You have here, *mein Herr,* a synthesis of the three great religions whose source is in the Old Testament and who each have their own prophet. Now that is a beautiful thought. Have I interpreted your conception right, *mein Herr?"*

It would have been the height of ingratitude not to agree with him. I complimented him on his discernment and, to myself, I thought that a wonderful art critic was lost to the world.

■

Now that I [had] decided to prolong my stay in Germany, one of the first things I proceeded to do was to learn more about Germany and the Germans. I registered at Friedrich Wilhelms Universität. I cultivated the acquaintance of some Germans. I began reading the newspapers and magazines, going to the theatres and cabarets, and familiarizing myself with current German literature.

Once I stepped into a bookstore and saw a row of paper-covered, inexpensive booklets, *Der Jüngste Tag* [Doomsday/day of judgment], among which were works by [Carl] Sternheim, Franz Jung, Walter Hasenclever, etc., all already somewhat familiar to me. Then I noticed the volume *Die Verwandlung* (The metamorphosis) by an author I hadn't heard of before, Franz Kafka. The title rang a bell but I did not quite know why. I opened the book and read the first paragraph: *"Als Gregor Samsa eines Morgens . . ."* (As Gregor Samsa awoke one morning after a night of restless dreams, he found himself in his bed transformed into a monstrous insect . . .). Now I knew. Of course, it reminded me of another "Metamorphosis," *The Golden Ass* by [Lucius] Apuleius. I bought the book. It was small, like a pamphlet, 75 pages long. When I returned to my room, I read it in one gulp, found it absorbing; and, thereafter, I read everything of Kafka's I came across.

I was intrigued by the two "Metamorphoses," the vast difference in time, in content, in style, and in the attitudes of the authors, and yet there was a certain parallelism between the two. Each author transforms his hero (if the term is appropriate here) into an animal—a revolting insect in one case, a frollicking donkey in the other—in order to expose the morals and manners in the author's own time and place—Rome of the second century, Germany of the twentieth. Each book is a satire, but what a world of difference between them. Apuleius' is comic satire—hilarious situations, lax sex morality, and adventurous mayhem; Kafka's is tragic satire—bitterness, meanness, alienation, and frustration. Unlike *Die Verwandlung, The Golden Ass* has a happy ending.

Reading the incredible tale by Kafka, I saw the very credible world of contemporary Germany. One might even go further and say (we all have the wisdom of hindsight) that a perceptive eye could have foreseen what an easy prey Germany could become to a doctrine like Nazism.

Browsing in one of the bookstores on Kurfürstendamm, I picked up three books that caught my attention: *Das Taschenbuch und Briefe an einen Freund* [The paperback and letters to a friend] by Otto Weininger; *Otto Weininger's Tod* [The death of Otto Weininger] by Hermann Swoboda; and *Otto Weininger* (biography) by Emil Lucka. I had read Weininger's main work (really the only one; the rest are just notes and letters), *Sex and Character [Geschlecht und charakter]* in Russian but knew next to nothing of his biography. The three booklets (purchased) supplied the information I lacked.

I now bought the book [*Geschlecht und Charakter (Sex and Character)*] in the original German and found both the book and the author amazing. In presenting and pursuing his argument, the author marshals proofs from anatomy, embryology, psychology, philosophy, literature, ethics, logic, and so forth, with copious references and quotations in half a dozen languages from Plato to Avenarius. This, in itself, is nothing extraordinary for any book in German that pretends to be scholarly. The amazing thing is that the author wrote it at the age of 23. Having written it, he seems to have concluded that his life's work was done in his vale of tears. He committed suicide.

Sex and Character is one of those books that creates a scandal for the moment and is then forgotten, except by some *Grübler* [brooder], who now and then digs it out from the dusty archives to bring it before the world for some special reason of his own. The first part of the book, the most easily comprehensible and logically consistent of the entire work, seeks to establish nothing less than the Law of Sexual Attraction in more precise, scientific terms than has been done hitherto. The thesis might be summarized as follows: Every human being is bisexual. Male and female in their adult lives, each retains in rudimentary form certain physical characteristics of the other. (In a Spanish museum, there is a portrait of a woman with a luxuriant beard of which any sea captain would be proud; and men have been known with fully developed breasts.) The proportions vary. We can express it arithmetically. Thus, in man it may be 9/10 M [male] plus 1/10 F [female] or again 3/4 M plus 1/4 F, etc., endlessly. The same, of course, is true in women with the proportions reversed. The Law of Sexual Attraction postulates the union of the separate fractions into one complete M and one complete F: thus, a man 9/10 M plus 1/10 F will find his complement in a woman 9/10 F plus 1/10 M, etc., ad infinitum.

This is stark realism compared with the mystic, fatal[istic], and irresistible "Elective Affinitives" in [Johann Wolfgang von] Goethe's novel *Wahlverwandtschaften [Elective Affinities]*. Weininger's thesis is not startlingly revolutionary. It sounds almost reasonable and even entertaining. It could provide interesting angles to the cartoonist and humorist. Having established his "law" with some objectivity, Weininger proceeds to "characterology," where prejudice takes over. The abstraction called "M" [male] embodies, according to Weininger, everything noble, heroic, creative, and good; "F" [female], on the other hand, [embodies] everything base, destructive, and evil. Supporting quotes and quotes [are given] in abundance. And now Weininger turns his attention to the Jews (Weininger was himself a Jew). What "F" is to "M," the Jews are to other nations. They are the most effeminate among nations. Like women, they are uncreative. They have never produced a single great man in art, literature, science, philosophy, or government (Jesus was the only exception, but he overcame his Judaism). The Jews cannot be truly religious nor can they be genuinely atheistic.

All this makes painful reading. Under the polished philosophical pilpul, one hears the rantings of a premature Nazi—a Jew converted to Protestantism. *Sex and Character* is really two books: one is the actual text; the other is an underlying, unexpressed, emotionally hidden undercurrent of some raging inner struggles. Weininger hated sex (or tried to convince himself that he did), and he hated the Jews but evidently could not overcome the obsession with either. The logical consequence: he rented a room in the house where Beethoven died and shot a bullet through his head.

Books were ridiculously cheap in terms of [the] dollar exchange. At about 50 cents a piece, I bought *Chinesische Landschaft Malerei* [Chinese landscape painting] by Otto Fischer and *Die Kunst der Japanischen Holzschnittmeister* [The art of the Japanese wood-engraving master] by Ludwig Bachhofer, two books that I can still look into with pleasure from time to time, even today. I became acquainted with the work of Eduard Fuchs, who wrote books of encyclopedic proportions. His best known work is perhaps *The History of the Erotic in Art* in three massive volumes.[11] The work contains hundreds upon hundreds of illustrations of the sex act in all its luscious variety. And this is what sold the book to foreigners, Americans and Swedes. And yet the text was probably more important to the author than the illustrations, though not too many people seemed to have read it. The book is a detailed Marxist interpretation of the social and individual attitude toward sex life from antiquity to the present. The long introduction explains the Marxist analysis of art. I once asked an American who bought the book whether he realized that he was bringing home a subversive work. He was puzzled at first; when I explained what I meant, he smiled and said that for the sake of art he was willing to overlook the author's scholarship.

Occasionally, as my means would allow, I went to the theatre to hear the reverberating echo of the thunder outside. German society was, to put it mildly, in a very unhealthy state. Inflation (it was a galloping inflation) was bringing ruin to families whose meager savings of many years were being wiped out in weeks or even days. Prostitution, beggary, drug addiction, and the blight of the *Schieber* [profiteer] were everywhere. (I was told of an American who bought a house in marks not in dollars. Several hundred dollars bought a house worth several thousand. The owner then moved to Paris where he lived on the income from the rent which was forwarded to him by one of the tenants. This blissful existence came to an end when the Nazis confiscated the house.)

Something of this turbulence reached the stage. Plays like [Ernst] Toller's *Masse-mensch* [Masses and man] and *Maschinenstürmer* [Machine-wreckers] and [Georg] Kaiser's *Gas*[12] made a brave attempt to interpret in theatrical terms the sickness of contemporary society, to cast some light on the darkness of postwar Germany, but the attempts were not wholly successful. One should give credit to the plays for being theatrical, i.e., full of action and movement. And they gave an opportunity to the Constructivist stage designers to go all out. But there scarcely was a living person on stage. They were "types," like the Woman, the Nameless One, the Engineer, the Billionaire, etc. One left the theatre disillusioned, apathetic, and hopeless.

A friend recommended that I go to see a new play which threw a challenge by the young to the old generation. I did. It was the *Vatermord* [Patricide] by Arnolt Bronnen, the story of a son's sexual hunger for his mother—with her encouragement—and the resultant hatred of his father. The most sensational scene is when the son murders his father (thankfully, behind the wings) and rushes out triumphantly on stage carrying his mother in his arms. Ultimately he casts his mother aside and struts out into the world to join the young against the old. I did not agree with my friend. I found the play crude and even revolting, containing nothing whatever "revolutionary." (I was not surprised to learn later that the "young," whose banner Bronnen carried, turned out to be [that of the] Nazis of whom he had become an ardent admirer.)

There is nothing in German literature and drama of the early twenties that approached the tragic power of [Otto] Dix's war pictures or the corrosive message of [George] Grosz's *Das Gesicht der herschenden Klasse* [The face of the ruling class].[13] Grosz was one of the great artists of the twentieth century. Much has been written about him, but there is still no adequate biography. Even his own writings do not reveal him fully. He was a man of violent extremes. I want to cite a little example of this. In a booklet on George Grosz by Willi Wolfradt *(Junge Kunst* [New art], 1921), a note written by the artist himself is appended under the title *"Statt einer Biographie"* (Instead of a biography). It is one vast, savage indictment of contemporary art and literature (as well as society), of speculation in art as a commodity, and of the artists and writers as willing, subservient tools of the ruling class:

> Your brushes, your pens which should be weapons are empty as straws. . . .
> Get out of your houses, however hard you may find it . . . try to understand the ideas of the working man, help him in the fight against the putrid society.

Grosz repeated this theme of "art as weapon" more than once elsewhere.

■

During the Second World War, Grosz was in the United States. I was a member of Artists for Victory. We organized exhibitions and made posters to solicit funds for the Red Cross, for Victory Bonds, etc. The Victory Workshop invited Grosz to submit a picture in support of the war effort. His reply, which we received on March 19, 1943 (and which I copied exactly as he wrote it), follows:

> In my opinion and experience in Art, I mean real ART [is] never a weapon.

If you mean propaganda, the popular illustration does much better propaganda and has much more to say for the masses and the average citizen than all the so-called finer artists together.

Very sincerely yours,
George Grosz

Perhaps the strangest thing in all this was that his new orientation did not lead to any remarkable development in his art. There may not be any direct casual connection; but, in any case, Grosz' best work is still in the past, which he now repudiated.

■

Of all the books I read at the time, none moved me as deeply as a collection of young (mostly) poetry edited by Kurt Pinthus under the title *Menschheits Dämmerung* [The dawn/twilight of mankind]. The author deliberately used the imprecise word *Dämmerung* [twilight/dawn] to indicate the modern poet's vacillation between the twilight and disaster of yesterday's nightfall and the dawn of a new and liberating daybreak. The poets Paul Zech, Georg Trakl, Franz Werfel, August Stramm, Georg Heym, Elsa Lasker-Schüler, Johannes Becher, Gottfried Benn, Iwan Goll, Jakob van Hoddis, and many others represented among them every style and every theme: the lyrical, the satirical, the comic, the tragic, the personal, and the social. In retrospect I find it hard to explain exactly why the appeal of the book was so powerful. Perhaps because it seemed at the time to put me in rapport with the intellectual climate of Germany in all its variety. Perhaps also because it was poetry that appealed not only to the eye or ear but to the mind as well.

Some years ago, I happened to have looked into the *Menschheits Dämmerung*. I was amazed at the vast changes of men and events in the course of the intervening years. Among the poets of the book, Van Hoddis had been dragged out of a mental institution by the Nazis and murdered; the gentle soul, Elsa Lasker-Schüler, died in Israel; Gottfried Benn, like the painter Emil Nolde, wooed the Nazis but was rudely jilted by them (after the war, they both regained their popularity); Johannes Becher became an active Communist; Alfred Wolfenstein and Walter Hasenclever committed suicide; Franz Werfel (a Jew) embraced Catholicism; Albert Ehrenstein died in exile in the United States; and Iwan Goll (and his wife Claire) were in the United States during the war where he edited the magazine *Hémisphères,*[14] in which he began to write in English.

■

I continued to paint and draw. In addition to participating in group shows, I had my first one-man show at the K. E. Twardy Book Shop on Potsdamer Strasse in late 1922.[15] I tried to develop something that I might call my own style. Physically far from America, I decided, perhaps in a spirit of nostalgia, that it would be an "American" style. This "style" expressed itself in the graphic utilization of what I conceived to be typical American industrial and mechanical subjects. True, such subjects were not exclusively American—certainly one found them in other countries, Germany for instance. But I thought that America was the greatest and most characteristic repository of such subjects. Thus, I made a series of ink drawings composed of parts of machines and structures joined in semiabstract designs. Then, I conceived of painting a series of American cities, each unique and yet characteristically American: New York for its skyscrapers [Figure 5], Pittsburgh for its steel mills, Minneapolis for its grain elevators, Oklahoma [City] for its oil wells, etc. The cities were to be recognizable yet not literal. Sketches of four cities, together with black and white designs and some imaginary stage sets, were included in my next exhibition in August–September 1923 at the Gallerie Alfred Heller on Kurfürstendamm in Berlin [Figure 8].[16]

To my great and pleasant surprise the critical reception was uniformly favorable. Dailies, like *B.Z. am Mittag,* and weeklies, like the *Berliner Illustrierte,* recommended the exhibition or gave illustrations. I also learned a useful lesson. One paper wanted to reproduce one of the pictures. An American

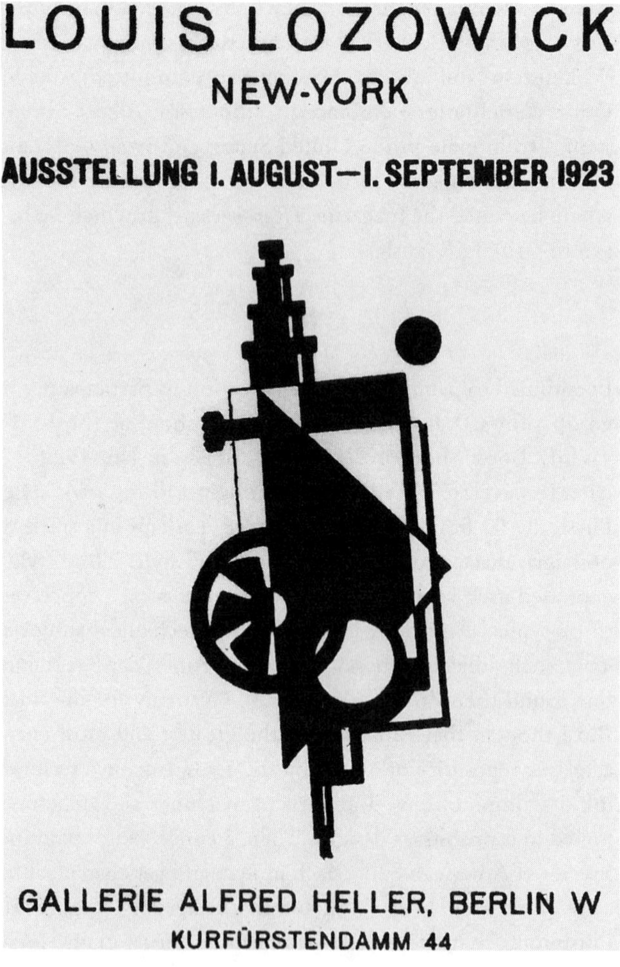

Fig. 8 Cover of exhibition pamphlet, Gallerie Alfred Heller, 1923, illustrating a "Machine Ornament."

friend advised me to ask for remuneration. Of course, I never heard from the paper again. The highly regarded magazine *Der Cicerone* printed an article on my work with four illustrations. The *Jahrbuch der jungen Kunst* [Yearbook of new art] for 1923, an annual for significant art in Germany and abroad, reprinted the article.[17] An Austrian magazine, *Das Zelt* [The tent], published an essay with four illustrations.[18] The French magazine *L'Esprit nouveau* [The new spirit], edited by [Amédée] Ozenfant and [Charles-Edouard] Jeanneret (Le Corbusier), used one of the city series to illustrate an article on *"Formation de l'optique moderne"* [Formation of the modern perspective] (no. 21).[19]

■

The "wave" even reached the United States. Shortly after my return in 1924, the *New York Times* Sunday magazine section had an article on the American cities with several illustrations. The interesting thing is that all of the references to my work stressed its Americanism. I myself jotted down several paragraphs on "The Americanization of Art," which ultimately saw the light in the catalogue of the "Machine-Age Show" held in 1927 in New York.[20] The *Little Review,* one of the sponsors of this show, reproduced some of my paintings in 1925.[21]

■

An echo of this flurry reached me in 1965 during the "Op [Art]" exhibition at the Museum of Modern Art in New York.[22] One of its participating artists, Henryk Berlewi, had been a boon companion in Berlin. We had many mutual friends; we went to cafés and exhibitions together, and together passed judgment on our betters. He was a gay blade, indefatigable in the pursuit of women. When I left Europe, I lost track of him. In 1963, I received a letter from him from Paris, announcing the organization of what he called *"Archives de l'art et de l'avant garde internationale. Directeur: Henryk Berlewi"* and requesting material for it. When he came to New York, he looked me up. One of the first things he said on meeting me was, *"Je suis toujours célibataire"* [I am still unmarried]. He brought his mother (she was not with him in Berlin), a spry 90-year-old lady, full of solicitude for her *chèr garçon.* We had a lively reunion—dinner, drinks, and reminiscences. He talked enthusiastically about the "heroic twenties" and said he was doing a book about the period. We exchanged pictures, and I gave him a number of rare documents on the "heroic twenties." In saying farewell he hinted delicately that I made a great mistake in changing my style of the twenties. I thanked him for the left-handed compliment. In 1967 I read a newspaper account of his death. I do not know whether he ever finished the book on the "heroic twenties."[23]

In the midst of painting and exhibiting, I had a lucky windfall. Harold Loeb of New York came to Europe in 1921 to launch "the best magazine in the English language." That was *Broom,* and its first editor was the "troubadour" Alfred Kreymborg.[24] Among the contributors were the writers James Stephens, Hart Crane, James Joyce, Gertrude Stein, Edna St. Vincent-Millay, Kay Boyle, and the artists Picasso, Brancusi, [Jacques] Lipchitz, [Francis] Picabia, [Marcel] Duchamps, Moholy-Nagy, Man Ray, and many more—certainly a most impressive roster. Having come across a few copies quite by accident, I noticed that the magazine had no Russian material. Yet, I felt that some of the Soviet art and literature being produced at the time in the general revolutionary ferment could make an important contribution to such a cosmopolitan publication. Accordingly, I wrote a brief article on Soviet art and sent it to Kreymborg.[25] A reply came almost immediately, friendly in tone and asking for more contributions. I was delighted, especially as a check was enclosed, which seemed to me quite generous. After Harold Loeb himself took over the editorship, I continued my contributions. I met Mr. Loeb in Italy, where he gave me a friendly reception. I wrote on Russian poetry, translated stories by [Vsevolod] Ivanov, [Il'ia] Ehrenburg, [Boris] Pil'niak, wrote notes on Russian writers, and even had one of my black and whites reproduced.[26] I became, thus, a kind of—I wouldn't say "ambassador"—but perhaps a minor "consul" to the court of *Broom*.

■

Having gone through an American university and art academy, having served in the American army, having studied
American history, art, and literature, and having voted in
American elections, I have always considered myself a full-
fledged—if only naturalized—American. At the same time, I
have retained a love of Russian culture and followed as much
as possible the development of its art and literature. It was,
therefore, natural that I should want to meet some of the
Russians that crowded Paris and Berlin when I came there.

Both Paris and Berlin had large Russian colonies with
their own publications, book shops, clubs, cabarets, and in-
terparty squabbles. Paris, however, seemed to be too much
self-centered, too much preoccupied with the fantastic dream
of a victorious return to Holy Russia. In Berlin this rosy
dream was more subdued. To be sure, there were Russians
who "knew" that, if not today, then surely tomorrow, will
come an invitation, as in the days of Riurik,[27] [to] "come
govern and rule over us." But their voices were lost in the active and turbulent life of the entire colony.

There was a greater literary activity [in Berlin] than in
Paris. Finer books and magazines were being published, and
Soviet publications were arriving in an unending stream.
Also, Soviet citizens, diplomats, writers, artists, and actors
were very much in evidence. There were also fairly large
groups of émigrés preaching reconciliation with the mother-
land on the basis of nonpolitical involvement. For example, I
read some pamphlets, like "Through Fire and Storm" and
"Our Own Face" by the social and literary critic Ivanov-
Razumnik [pseudonym for Razumnik Vasil'evich Ivanov],
defending this standpoint and attacking those who placed
party interest above the fatherland.

One of the most unique and short-lived Russian institutions in Berlin was the House of Art *(Dom iskusstva)*. The
House of Art was a cultural club in which the sole rule of
membership was "no politics." Actors, writers, artists, philosophers, and journalists met on Friday evenings in a German

café. "No politics" implied an unwritten truce under which the Left, the Right, and all gradations in between could be present, provided no political discussions took place. The meetings were devoted to debates, readings, analyses, and discussions. I attended readings of poetry of every style from the classical to Dada; I heard a lecture and demonstration (a most interesting one) on the use of the mask in classical, Oriental, and modern drama; I listened to discussions about children's theatre, modern art, philosophic terminology, and much, much more. I met (or at least saw) the writers Aleksei Tolstoy, Il'ia Ehrenburg, Andrei Belyi, Viktor Shklovskii, Marina Tsvetaeva, [Nikolai] Minskii, Ivanov, and the artists Ivan Puni, Al'tman, Gabo, Lissitzky, [Aleksandr] Archipenko, and the striking beauty, the illustrator Khentova, who was assiduously courted by several members of the group.

I was tremendously impressed by the concentration of talent and eagerly looked forward to every meeting. I heard someone say at one of the gatherings that Ehrenburg had just arrived with a wide selection of the latest Soviet publications. I approached him and asked whether I could read some of this material. "Yes," he replied, "but I cannot leave it out of my hands. If you wish to come to my apartment, I shall be glad to let you read anything you like." Of course I accepted the offer and went up to his room several times where I read some of the latest Russian poetry and the theatrical piece by [Vladimir] Mayakovsky, *Mystery-Bouffe*.[28]

It was one of the visitors from the Soviet Union who came close to wrecking the organization [House of Art]. The following is how I reported the event in *Broom*:

> German Berlin is astir.
> Isadora Duncan came from Russia flying in an aeroplane.
> But Russian Berlin is in even greater commotion.
> For Isadora Duncan did not come empty-handed; she
> brought some precious freight along, to wit:
> A poet,
> And a husband—
> All the same person, to be sure, the famous Russian Imaginist-peasant bard, Sergey Yessenin [Sergei Esenin].

Isadora Duncan and Sergey Yessenin will stay in Berlin for a time, take a flying trip to Paris and London, and in October depart for America where a well-known concert bureau has engaged them to tour the country. The bureau is reliable. Their success is assured.

To return to Berlin, however. The first thing for the couple to do was, naturally, to visit the Russian House of Art *(Dom iskusstva),* an institution where the great, near-great and would-be-great foregather without distinction of race, religion or previous condition of servitude, where talk and soda water flow in an unending stream; where theories and tobacco are consumed in alarming quantities (both meeting the same fate).

Everybody turned out for the festive occasion. The meeting was opened uncommonly early, to be precise: at half past ten P.M. which is not to say that Yessenin was there. He let the audience wait. The audience did. Long but not in vain. For as the midnight bell rang (he chose the psychological moment), Yessenin appeared arm in arm with Isadora Duncan. The windows shook. It was no tempest without; it was a thunderous applause within. Enthusiasm was boundless. No wonder some young chap forgot himself (which was not so bad), forgot the fact that the "House of Art" was non-political (which was far worse), and shouted: "Vive l'Internationale." (He meant the organization of course).

Isadora Duncan who did not know the rule of the House took up the cry:

"Chantez là." (She meant the song of course).

"Down with the Internationale!" broke in a white guard officer (he meant both, of course).

And then the fun began. The Whites (rather black) and the Reds (rather pink) were each determined to fight out the battle to the bitter end. It was the liveliest meeting in the history of this staid and lukewarm institution. Things went so far that Yessenin's fellow-Imaginist, the fine Circassian poet [Aleksandr] Kussikov [Kusikov], who had smelled powder in his Red Army days, wanted neither more nor less than to shoot the white [sic] guard officer, "like a puppy" as he eloquently put it.

Yessenin himself who had seen enough scandal in his Imaginist Club at Moscow to suffice a dozen other men a long lifetime, would not be discomfitted by a little incident like that. Anyhow, the Whites were completely routed and the Internationale rang out quite naturally, out of tune and with

overlapping stanzas, but none the less full-lunged and
enthusiastic.

Then Yessenin got on a chair and read.

Only Russians can read thus and only one of them,
Yessenin. Words that pounce on you, pummel you, lash you,
cut into your flesh, daze you.

It is the peasant revolution, million-voiced, that speaks
through the verse of Yessenin, the revolution with all its ex-
cesses and contradictions. A dualism can be traced through all
his work. The poet who at one moment declares himself so
harmless as not to touch a hare, is ready, at the next, to stick
somebody with a knife. The poet so humble as to tip his hat to
the cow on the sign of the city butcher shop, is sufficiently
daring to reform God himself. Tender and coarse almost in the
same breath:

> "Good night!"

> "Good night to you all!"

> "The scythe of evening rang out upon the glass of dusk.

> Somehow I feel like to-night.

> From my window to take a—on the moon."

> *(Confessions of a Scamp)*

The down-trodden are not sufficiently sophisticated, not
sufficiently schooled in the hypocrisies of civilization to mince
their words or check their instincts. They have an inestiguish-
able [sic] love of animal existence. That is why they are ready to
take bitter revenge for past wrongs, defend stubbornly present
privileges, and stake all for future freedoms.

Yessenin understands the downtrodden. If he is to be believed, only prostitutes and bandits can understand him. Calling
Nietzsche to witness, this might be a compliment to those who
appreciate the poetry of Yessenin, though they have not the
good luck to be prostitutes or bandits. Doubtless they possess
the requisite qualifications potentially, but they most have escaped their fate through mere accident (explanation of which
may be found in Freud—or in Marx). In this respect they are
not unlike Yessenin himself: "If I were not a poet, I would
surely be a crook and thief" *(In the Land of Rogues)*.

During the unprecedented upheaval in Russia, events have
been moving at a giddy speed. The poetry of Yessenin moves
synchronously with the speed of events. He piles novel image

upon image; he creates a new mythology; he invents new rhythms. The revolutionary trend will never quite be the same again. But it has already been arrested, rendered concrete and lasting in the poetry of Yessenin.[29]

■

Scandal followed Yessenin to the United States. A number of Jewish (Yiddish) writers arranged a reception and party for Yessenin. Some of the writers, being immigrants, knew Russian; others were sympathetic with the Soviet Union; still others went out of a sense of fellowship, and—to judge by what subsequently happened—there were a few deliberately bent on mischief.

The party went along swimmingly, and Yessenin, to no one's surprise, was getting drunk. At this stage, some unconscionable person or persons (I wasn't present at the party; I report what I read in the Yiddish press) began to feed Yessenin drinks of the most incompatible kind, with the result that he not only got more and more intoxicated, he became uncontrollable and had to be tied up. And there issued from his mouth a stream of abuse. One heard the dreaded (for Jews) word *zhid*. The next day Yessenin was unutterably miserable, contrite, and penitent. He pleaded innocence; he apologized. An uneasy peace was restored, but no magic could expunge the offending words. [The] wide American public was unaware (or dimly aware) of the scandal; it was confined to a tiny corner of New York, the Jewish East Side. And there it left a lasting mental scar.

■

Back to Berlin. The scandal in Berlin was patched up somehow; but after several months, the House [of Art] fell apart. The differences among its patrons were too sharp and getting sharper all the time. It reached a point when people of antagonistic political persuasions—people who had sat in the same room and had discussed jointly philosophical and cultural problems—refused to recognize each other when they met.

However there were still many exciting meetings held. One of them was a reading of poetry by Il'ia Zdanevich. It was perhaps less noisy than the one with Yessenin but more embarrassing.

Zdanevich was a Russian Dada poet living in Paris, where I had met him and heard him recite. There, he used to advertise himself as *"traître, crétin, assassin,"* among other compliments. An exciting time was, therefore, to be expected. And, indeed, he did not disappoint his public. He huffed and he puffed; he bellowed and he whispered; he leaped and he gesticulated. All this before an assemblage of scholars, poets, artists, and actors—a rarely distinguished [i.e., rarified] audience. Having heard his performance before, I was amused. I admired his guts and watched the reaction of the audience. Some looked puzzled; others were indignant. Faces expressed bewilderment, amusement, fascination, indifference, and resentment as they were assailed by a stream of unintelligible sounds in which one could occasionally catch a familiar syllable, half a word, and sometimes a phrase almost comprehensible, followed by a farrago of strange sounds. On the whole, the audience listened decorously. Zdanevich enjoyed himself immensely. There was a lively discussion after he had finished.

The aesthetic value of pure sound in various vowel and consonant combinations was discussed with great seriousness in several European countries, and not only among the Dadaists, as I had occasion to note earlier. I found a good deal of phonetic poetry in Germany: [Raoul] Hausmann, [Christian] Morgenstern, and others. But in the face of the German reality that stared insistently all around me, I lost interest. Unexpectedly, however, my interest revived, if only for a brief period. A book under the biblical title *Glossololiia* by Andrei Belyi appeared in 1922. Belyi was considered widely as one of the outstanding writers of the twentieth century. His *St. Petersburg* is esteemed a classic of modern Russian literature, and some of his other prose and poetic works are almost equally well known. Belyi was a mystic and a fervent disciple of Rudolf Steiner's anthroposophy. At the same time, he accepted Soviet power, for which he was roundly denounced. (He was not alone in such odd combinations of differing viewpoints. The poet [Aleksandr] Kusikov wrote a long poem *"Koevangelieran"* in which the New Testament and the Koran were called upon to support the Russian Revolution; and, of course, the famous poem by Blok, "The Twelve," has Christ leading the Red Guards.) In the preface to the book, Belyi says:

> *Glossololiia* is a poem about sound. Among the poems which I have written ("Christ is Risen," "The First Tryst") this is the most successful. I beg to receive it as such. To criticize it from the standpoint of science is utterly useless.
>
> *Glossololiia* is an improvisation on several sonic themes. As these themes arouse in me a fantasy of sonic imagery, I record them as they come.

Belyi develops a complicated and speculative system of translating sound, which he endows with color (quite unlike [Arthur] Rimbaud's), visual, and quantitative values. For example: *"We-ol,* a cloud; *na-weoln,* waves of the sea roll on; the sun shines, *sol-son!* And forthwith a golden stream splashes on the sand—*seln-seln!"* And a lot more of the same. Interspersed with poetry are studies of phonetics and excursions into history.

What attracted my most particular attention and touched a painful nerve of my memory was Belyi's startling analysis of the first word in Genesis, *"beréishis"* (in the beginning). It is the first word I learned in the heder under the vigorous accompaniment of ear-pulling and face-slapping by way of encouragement. This is certainly a novel and an unusual Biblical exegesis!

The last sentences in the book: "Long live the brotherhood of nations. The language of languages will destroy language. And that will be the Second Coming of the Word" (October 1917, Tsarskoe Selo; the book was published in Berlin in 1922).

Much of the spirit of the book is similar to that found in the article [by] Malevich on poetry [*O poezii,* see Chapter 9]: the same distrust of words in their surface, ordinary meaning; the same search for meaning behind and beyond the obvious; the same Biblical tone; and the same stress on brotherhood.

(Before and during the second World War the excursions into phonetic poetry and the esoteric hidden significance of sound were practially forgotten except as a curiosity.)

■

I met several Dadaists in Berlin who, among other things, also wrote visual poetry. But, perhaps through some shortcoming in my own makeup, I could not work up an enthusiasm for their noisy activity. Certainly they had a perfect right to have fun in their own odd ways, but I saw no great amusement or enlightenment in it. Their antibourgeois professions seemed to me dubious, if not spurious. They raised a terrible raucous and made terrifying faces, intending to frighten the bourgeois, who did not seem to be very much scared. To the refurbished old shibboleth, *épater le bourgeois* [to shock the bourgeois], the bourgeois exclaimed, *"Mais, c'est épatant"* [But, this is great].

■

In the sixties, I attended an exhibition of Dada and Surrealism at the Museum of Modern Art in New York.[30] On the sidewalk outside the Museum, a group of young men and women (and some not so young) paraded in protest against the "chi-chi" bourgeoisie inside who dared to appropriate the "antibourgeois" artists of another day. Alas, the young people in assorted hippy garb were wrong; the swanky crowd inside was right. Anti-art was now Art, and the terrible tigers of the twenties and thirties were now domesticated and purred like kittens.

■

Art, like politics, makes strange bedfellows. I could never understand how a man like Lissitzky, quiet, well-behaved, and straightforward, could belong to the group [Dadaists]. He was courteous, rather like a bourgeois himself (despite his genuine revolutionary faith). He was not flippant but rather serious about the views he held.

Another member of the group who did not seem the "type" was the painter, Arthur Segal, whom I had met at a number of exhibitions. After some experimenting, he developed a style of painting that was immediately recognizable as his. He divided his picture into two, four, or more planes, into which he put figures, or animals, or boats, etc. Everything (including the frame) was painted in prismatic colors.

Segal invited me to a party at his house. His wife seems to have had an independent income. In any case, there was good food, good drink, and good company. Among those present were [Raoul] Hausmann, [Richard] Huelsenbeck, and other well-known Dadaists, but I hardly recognized them—they were so normal. The conversation was lively and witty. There were one or two attempts at clowning; but, on the whole, the behavior was more proper than at many a party I attended in New York. I don't remember how it came about, but someone mentioned America, and somebody else suggested an idea (it may have been Hans Richter, though I am not sure) of how a lot of dollars could be made in America by the utilization of a special synthetic fiber (of which the speaker had personal knowledge, or maybe he was the inventor) in the making of automobile bodies. The speaker assured me that the fiber was strong, resilient, shock-resistant, long-lasting, and cheaper than steel and better. Was it meant to be taken seriously, or was it just another leg-pulling Dada spoof? I don't know, but I liked the people more than their public image.

■

Incidentally, I met one of the men present at that party many years later in New York. I was arranging a symposium on Dada and Surrealism for the American Artists' Congress to be held at the Museum of Modern Art, long before the exhibition in the sixties, when I discovered that one of the "top bananas" of Dadaism, Richard Huelsenbeck, was a resident of the United States. I made the discovery in a very Dadaesque manner. I got acquainted with an owner of a funeral parlor in Newark, New Jersey, by the name of Huelsenbeck. Was he, by any chance, related to the Dadaist of the same name? I asked. Yes he was. His relative was now living in the United States and was a practicing psychoanalyst. Thus, our symposium had one of the older Dadaists on the same platform with one of the youngest Surrealists, Salvador Dalí. It was an interesting symposium.[31]

■

While my fortune still lasted, I made several trips to a number of the larger German cities: Leipzig, Munich, Dresden, Heidelberg, Cologne, Nuremberg, and the neighboring charming medieval Rothenburg. I spent many hours in the galleries of Munich and Dresden. The latter, in particular, was a revelation to me. The *Sistine Madonna* by Raphael had a place of honor (it still does), separated from the public by a railing and a guard always in attendance. I preferred, however, such paintings as Titian's *Tribute Money* and [Jacob] More's *Portrait of a Man*. I was more affected by art at that time than I am now, and I was simply intoxicated before Correggio, Giorgione, and Rembrandt. A particular attraction, for reasons more historic than aesthetic, was the painting by [David] Vinckeboons, *Kermesa,* in which an artist is shown selling pictures amidst other merchants dealing in the greatest variety of goods. In my subsequent travels through the galleries of many countries, I always stopped to contemplate any picture that showed how artists of another day earned their livelihood, how and where they studied, what their relations were with their patrons, etc.

■

It is hardly possible to speak of Berlin in the twenties without touching on the prevailing sexual morality, at least as it looked to a tourist or a foreign visitor. There didn't seem to be any. The servant-maid who came to clean up the room, the woman to whom you gave your wash (and whose husband was at work), the kept-woman next door—all exhibited practically no power of resistance. One could perhaps explain it by the disillusionment with the war and the postwar situation, the failure of the revolution, the loss of the war, the constantly worsening economic conditions (the mark fell so rapidly, the meager savings of some families were wiped out overnight)—all combined to create this state of disarray.

Nationalist and antigovernment demonstrations were frequent, and sometimes bloody clashes occurred. I witnessed the severe beating of a man who refused to remove his hat while "Deutschland über Alles" [Germany over all else] was being played. He was stubborn and persistent. At first his hat was snapped off, and he put it on again. After he did it a second time, the mob descended on him and he went down. The strange thing to me was that despite his powerful physique he did not defend himself.

Almost every evening one could witness a repetition of the following scene. Two columns—one of men, the other of women—were walking slowly in opposite directions, like taking a leisurely evening stroll. Now and again a man would detach himself from his column and cross over to the column opposite to address a lady. If the answer was "no," he would venture for another try. If the answer was "yes," both would go off to a bar or a café, and a "friendship" pact was sealed for a day or a night, or whatever. A more formal way for these "chance friendships" [to occur] was to visit a café which had telephones on all tables. A man would call up a lady he fancied and invite her to his table; if she refused, there were others willing enough. Incidentally, there were not a few women who made the first advance. An American friend visited me in Berlin. When we sat down at our table (no telephones)—my friend received a "come-hither" look from an attractive woman at another table nearby. I did not see him till the next day.

There were *cabinets particuliers* [private rooms], so that it was not necessary to go home or to a hotel. The more expensive of these *cabinets* were well-appointed, separate rooms, to which attendants brought drinks or a meal, as requested by the clients. The cheaper bars offered little cubicles with curtains for an opening. The wine or *schnapps* was brought in to the patron, who attended to his business within hearing and almost within sight of the bar-flies. The women I am talking about were "honest" nonprofessionals. As for prostitutes of all ages, the place was crawling with them. It was easy to get trapped, pursuing what one thought was an amateur and being caught by a hardened pro.

Here an apology is certainly in order. Most of the citizens of Berlin did not fall into the category described above, but lived a quiet, inconspicuous life, worried over daily needs, working hard and earning little. Some of them surely began to look with favor on the wild ones beginning to appear in the streets, promising relief and projecting, in still faint outlines, the "thousand year Reich." But very few foreigners found their way into such families.

Homosexualism was openly preached and practiced. There were special cafés where the homosexuals [gathered]. They even published their own magazine. I think it was called *Freundschaft* [Friendship]. A friend and I ventured one evening into such a café on Nuremberg Strasse. It was a most bewildering experience. Many men were dressed as women, coy and giggling. They danced with men who were in their regular attire. There was kissing and hugging and whispers of endearments. It was a riot but we behaved as if everything was normal and nothing unusual was taking place, although some of the female disguises were so outrageously funny we could hardly keep a straight face.

Sex literature or plain pornography (it was sometimes difficult to tell one from the other) was widely sold. There were some truly scientific books like *Das Sexualleben unserer Zeit [in seinen bezeihungen zur modernen Kultur] (The Sexual Life of Our Time [in Relations to Modern Civilization])* by Dr. Iwan Bloch. One popular book by Dr. A[uguste] Forel was written in very simple language and was intended for the young, especially the newly married. Its instructions were so thorough; it even described a "do-it-yourself" method of making a *capote anglaise* [condom] from the entrails of a fish, how to wash it, dry it, and preserve it (cheaper than the commercial product, better and reusable). It was in one of those books (I forget which) that I found a somewhat cynical, though perhaps apt, definition of a kiss as "the ringing of a bell upstairs for permission to enter downstairs."[32]

The social atmosphere of Berlin was becoming stifling. Beggars, war cripples, *Shiebers,* and drug peddlers overshadowed even the frenzied race for physical gratification. (George Grosz was a perfect chronicler of the period.) I decided to leave, especially since the sources of my income were running dry. But first I wanted to go to Paris for a short stay, to say good-bye to a city I liked above all others in Europe.

11

| MOSCOW

A large and comprehensive exhibition of Russian contemporary art was held in Berlin in 1922 at the Van Diemen Gallery.[1]
Lissitzky did a fine cover for the catalogue and designed one
room especially for the exhibition. The exhibition received
wide publicity because, while there was a good deal of writing about and interest in Soviet art and while the work of
some individual artists had been shown in Berlin, this was the
first time that Soviet art could be seen comprehensively in its
variety. In addition to a number of Russian artists who had
been in Berlin before, there now came several more working in
various capacities with the exhibition. There was, thus, a large
contingent of Russian artists present: [Natan] Al'tman, [David]
Shterenberg (head of the Art Section in the Commissariat of
Education, immediately under [Anatolii] Lunacharskii),
[Ivan] Puni, [Naum] Gabo, [Marc] Chagall, and others.

I became acquainted with many of them. Once, in conversation over coffee and cake, some of them asked me
whether I would be interested in paying a short visit to the
Soviet Union. They would introduce me to more Russian art
and more Russian artists. They would show me the revolutionary changes that had been accomplished in the art institutions. I readily accepted the invitation, although a few of
the more conservative members of the House of Art urged
me to refuse. They warned me of dire consequences: my life
would not be safe; I would starve; I would be exposed to in-
fectious diseases, like typhus; I would not be allowed to leave

the country. But the temptation was too strong to resist. And so, in Oscar Wilde's words, "I overcame it by yielding to it."

One of the first artists my hosts took me to see was [Kazimir] Malevich. I had seen a number of his paintings and had read some of his writings (which seemed at that time even stranger than his paintings). Whatever one thought of his paintings or writings, he was undoubtedly an unusual man. But when I met him, I found nothing unusual in him. He was dressed simply in a gray suit, somewhat worn, and spoke in quiet tones. In the street I would have taken him for a minor clerk. A few young people who hovered around him seemed to hold him in great reverence. He obviously had some hidden charisma which took time to discover. We spoke briefly about art in Europe, in the Soviet Union, and in America. When I mentioned that I wanted to make a study of modern Russian art from before the Revolution to the present, he gave me a number of pamphlets, including his *From Cézanne to Suprematism*[2] and a rare copy of *Victory over the Sun,* a Futurist opera for which he did the sets.[3] The opera had been performed in 1913 in St. Petersburg under the accompaniment of catcalls and derision from the conservatives.

The career of Malevich as it passed through Impressionism, Cézanne, the Cubists, and the Futurists and culminated in *White on White* and Suprematism is generally well known.[4] There are, however, aspects of his career that are either little known or unknown at all, for example, his views on poetry. In a previous chapter [Chapter 9], I summarized his essay in defense of transrational *(zaumnaia)* poetry, the poetry of pure sound, vowel, and consonant combinations divested of all logical communicative content. This late echo of the Biblical "speaking with tongues" appeared in *Fine Art [Izobrazitel'noe iskusstvo],* a magazine published under the imprint of the Commissariat of Education, hardly the suitable platform. Even more unorthodox is an essay or manifesto which Malevich published in *Zhizn' iskusstva* (Life of art) on the occasion of the Exhibition of Petrograd Artists of All Trends, 1919–1923:[5]

THE SUPREMATIST MIRROR

The essence of nature is unchangeable in all its changing phenomena

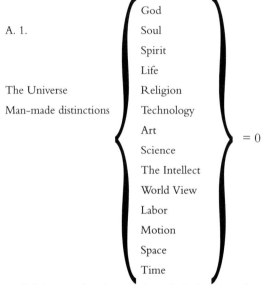

A. 1.

God
Soul
Spirit
Life

The Universe
Man-made distinctions

Religion
Technology
Art
Science
The Intellect
World View
Labor
Motion
Space
Time

= 0

1) Science and art have no boundaries because what is comprehended is innumerable, and infinity and innumerability are equal to nothing.

2) If the world's creations are God's paths and if "His ways are inscrutable," then both He and His path are equal to nothing.

3) If the world is the creation of science, knowledge and labor, and if their creation is infinite, then it is equal to nothing.

4) If religion has comprehended God, it has comprehende nothing.

5) If science has comprehended nature, it has comprehended nothing.

6) If art has comprehended harmony, rhythm, beauty, it has comprehended nothing.

7) If anyone has comprehended the absolute, he has comprehended nothing.

8) There is no existence either within or without me; nothing can change anything since nothing exists that could change
itself or be changed.

A. 2. The essence of distinctions

The world as nonobjectivity.

This is certainly metaphysics with a vengeance and contra-
dicts utterly the reigning Marxist philosophy of the Soviet
Union. Another unorthodox work by Malevich which relates
to this essay and the essay on poetry is "God Is Not Over-
thrown. Art, Factory, Church." Had Malevich read [Vladi-
mir] Lenin or [George] Berkeley?

I mentioned earlier [Chapter 9] that Malevich gave me an
out-of-print copy of *Victory over the Sun,* a Futurist opera for
which [Aleksei] Kruchenykh wrote the text, [Mikhail]
Matiushin composed the music, and Malevich designed the
costumes and scenery. The opera was performed in St. Petersburg in 1913. It began as a *succès de scandale* and ended as
a *succès d'estime*—at least in the opinion of some. Following is
a description of the performance by an eye witness (Benedikt
Livshits in *A One-and-a-Half-Eyed Marksman):*

The novelty and originality of Malevich consists primarily in
his utilization of light as a means of creating form, validating
the existence of objects in space.

Within the boundaries of the stage box, a pictorial stereom-
etry was born for the first time, a strict organization of volumes, reducing to a minimum the elements of chance thrust
upon it from without by the movement of human figures.
These figures were carved up by the blades of light. Hands,
feet, heads were disappearing by turns, because they were
merely geometric bodies for Malevich, subject not only to the
dissociation of the component parts, but also to their complete
dissolution in the pictorial space.

The only realities were the abstract forms which swallowed
whole the entire Luciferesque vanity of this world. Instead of
the square, instead of the circle to which Malevich already at
that time attempted to reduce his painting, he now found it
possible to operate with their three-dimensional correlates, the

cube and the sphere; and having discovered them, he proceeded
to demolish without pity everything that lay across the axis of
his choice.

Such are some of the less well known items in the career
of this strange man. I never met Malevich again, but I followed his activities, and I want to set down one more little
known but significant fact of his life. A few years before his
death, this artist whose Suprematism reduced art to its simplest, primordial elements—the zero point—painted a portrait of himself as a gentleman of the Renaissance! Dressed in
a characteristic costume of the period—cloak, vest, and hat—
his right hand is extended in an imperious gesture; his face
looks stern, as if addressing someone in a commanding tone.[6]
Why a gentleman of the Renaissance? Was it because of
his admiration for the period? Was it because he himself felt
that for his day he was as important as the Renaissance artist
was for his? Or was it just the satisfaction of a passing fancy?
Or something deliberately made for the critics to puzzle
over? I am not aware that anyone asked him.

My first impression of Moscow brought to mind Aleksandr
Blok's poem "The Sythians," the poem that offers the Western world the choice between a handshake and a clenched
fist. (I had recently read an analysis of the poem by an émigré
writer, Ivanov-Razumnik, who preached reconciliation with
Soviet Russia. According to him, the ideas in the poem could
be traced almost as far back as the "Lay of Igor's Raid" by
way of [Aleksandr] Pushkin, [Vladimir] Solov'ev, Andrei
Belyi, and others.)

I found Moscow an altogether unusual place, certainly little
like Paris or Berlin. The barbaric splendor of the Kremlin at
the center of the city, with its golden domes, its crenelated

walls and battlements; adjacent to it, the Cathedral of St. Basil, like no other cathedral in the world, with its garish red and green checkered towers and bulbous top—both the Kremlin and the cathedral set down on the vast Red Square. Many of the houses were small and pastel colored. (It was before the period of the "Stalinist Gothic.") The streets were alive with vari-colored crowds, endlessly moving with a pre-occupied restlessness. One could not help being infected by the general excitement. I met many people—writers, artists, and others. Almost everyone evinced immediate interest in America, not, however, in its art but in its machines. The two names heard most often in this connection were [Henry] Ford and [Thomas] Edison.

"Ah, America, wonderful machinery, wonderful factories, wonderful buildings; give us time—we'll have as much and more."

One lady put it even more emphatically: "We'll have it better" *(U nas luchshe budet)*.

In view of the critical condition in agriculture, industry, and housing, such a statement would seem wildly optimistic. But it was this wild optimism that brought the country out of its crisis.

One of the first artists I met was [Aleksandr] Rodchenko. He said: "You missed our important exhibition '5 x 5 = 25.' I'll give you a catalogue and take you to all the artists who had participated in it. This will give you an opportunity to get acquainted with some of the best work being done in the Soviet Union."[7]

The catalogue, which Rodchenko gave me, was itself a unique document of the period. It was handmade of bond paper—the kind used in the classroom—stitched together to make a little booklet. Each of the five artists was represented by five pictures; each had a section in the catalogue consisting of titles of pictures, a credo, and an original little picture made especially for the catalogue. It was, thus, really a collector's item. The five artists were Stepanova-Varst [Varvara Stepanova], known particularly for her sets for *The Death of Tarelkin;* [Liubov'] Popova, [known for her] sets for *Le cocu magnifique* [The magnanimous cuckold]; A[leksandr] Vesnin, a well-known stage designer and architect; [Aleksandra] Exter, a stage designer for the Tairov Theatre[8] [who] worked on the early experimental film *Aelita*[9] (I met her several years later in Paris and did an article on her puppets for the *Theatre Arts Magazine;*[10] and Rodchenko. I herewith translate Rodchenko's catalogue page:

16 Line, 1920
17 Graph, 1921
18 Pure Yellow Color, 1921
19 Pure Red Color
20 Pure Blue Color

1918

At the Moscow exhibition "Non-objective Art and Suprematism," I was the first to demonstrate Space Construction and to paint *Black on Black*.

1920

At the Nineteenth State Exhibition, I demonstrated for the first time Line as a factor in construction.

1921

The present exhibition demonstrates for the first time the three basic colors.

Rodchenko kept his promise and introduced me to the other participants in the exhibition. They were a dedicated group of Constructivists (with the exception perhaps of Exter), eager to expound their views. They believed that their work of the moment was experimental, a preliminary training, a transfer-station from contemplative art to industry, or life, or some wider realm where their talents and training would be utilized in a more practical and, at the same time, ideal, less self-indulgent manner.[11] I listened absorbed, although the arguments sounded vague and not very convincing. Some of the works seemed to me works of art in their own right, quite outside what might have been intended as their ultimate meaning or significance.

The most prominent member of the Constructivist fraternity was undoubtedly [Vladimir] Tatlin, and the work most discussed was his *[Project for a] Monument to the Third International*. I met him, and he was kind enough to give me two pamphlets, one describing in detail the *Monument* and the other devoted to him as an artist.

The *Monument to the Third International,* a synthesis of architecture, sculpture, painting, and engineering, was to be built as a structure 400 meters high, enclosed within a double spiral, leaning at an angle of 45 degrees, and supported by vertical steel columns. Enclosed within this structure were to be three stories, a cube (bottom), a pyramid [(middle)], and a cylinder [(top)] (echoes of Cézanne?), all revolving at the velocities of a year, a month, and a day, respectively. Of course, the building, being a near impossibility in engineering terms, remained in its planning stage, but it received a great deal of critical attention both in Russia and abroad.[12] Following is an excerpt from the pamphlet on Tatlin by the critic N[ikolai] Punin:

> The spiral expresses our spirit best, just as the equilibrium of
> the triangle expresses best the Renaissance. To realize this form
> means to create a dynamic principle with the same unsurpassed
> grandeur as the static principle was created by the pyramid . . .
> the spiral is the ideal expression of man's emancipation. Resting
> its heel on earth, the spiral flees from the earth, as it were, and
> becomes a symbol of renunciation, from all animal, mundane,
> and base interests. . . .[13]

One of the best stories by Il'ia Ehrenburg, "Vitrion" (illustrated by Lissitzky),[14] deals fictionally with Tatlin at work. And a laudatory article on Tatlin's *Monument* by the noted critic [Viktor] Shklovskii ends with the sentence: "The Monument is made of iron, steel and revolution."[15]

(Incidentally, not a few people made fun of [Tatlin's] revolving bodies in the *Monument*. Almost a half century later, Moscow built an enormously tall, thin television tower with a revolving restaurant at the top.)

Tatlin made other experimental inventions. He designed a glider, *Letatlin*[16] (a combination of the word for flying, *"letat',"* and the artist's name, "Tatlin"); and he designed work clothes. While many artists liked his work, engineers and scientists did not seem to be convinced. A story was told that he offered [to] some engineers to go to their factory to teach the workers the science of materials. In a spirit of reciprocity (and tongue in cheek), they offered him a course in mechanical drawing.

I met many more artists, writers, young art students, workers in the theatre, and others. I let it be known that I was [eager] to learn as much as possible about art and artists since 1917; and before long, I was flooded with books, pamphlets, announcements, posters, magazines, collections of poetry, prose, art criticism, and anthologies, printed mostly on bad newsprint. Many of those, though young, were already out of circulation and unobtainable. During those first years of the Revolution, the itch to appear in print was irresistible—pamphlets in every size, of every description, and on every conceivable subject. Here, for example, is one called *"Koryto umozakliuchenii"* [Trough of mental deductions]; here is a collection of poems by "Nichegoki" (from the word *"nichego,"* nothing). There had also been [a collection entitled] *"Vseki"* (from the word *"vse,"* everything). And here is something even more curious still: a tiny pamphlet in blue covers, [with] no name of [the] author, no place or date of publication, [entitled] "Lenin Versus Lenin."

Going through this material gave me a fuller view of the early period than any formal history could have done. [From one:]

> In the name of the great strides toward equality of everyone in the field of culture, let the free word of the creative personality be inscribed on the crossroads of walls, fences, roofs, [and] streets of our cities, villages, automobiles, carriages, trolleys, and on the clothes of every citizen. Let the pictures on the streets and squares, like iridescent rainbows, leap from house to house, to gladden and ennoble the beholder.

And again, from a Futurist manifesto:

> . . . artists and writers must take immediately pots of paints and, with the brushes of their mastery, cover the cheeks, foreheads, and breasts of the cities, railroad stations, and the perpetually racing herd of railway cars. Henceforth, let every citizen, as he walks along the streets, enjoy every instant the profound

thoughts of his great contemporaries, shine in the colorful brilliance of today's happiness, absorb the music, the melodies, the clamor, the blast of the splendid composers everywhere. Let the streets be holidays of art for all, so that everyone coming into the street, [will] feel exhilarated, [will] be inspired by the contemplation of beauty, instead of the present streets and their iron books (street signs) in which page after page carry messages of greed, cut-throat competition, self-seeking, mercenary rascality, venality, and base stupidity, which defile the soul and offend the eye. . . .

These extracts are samples of the somewhat overwrought, slightly wild outbursts with which the Futurists (an "umbrella" covering all modern trends)[17] greeted the Revolution of 1917. Near outcasts of yesterday, on the periphery of the established art world, they now felt that their day was at hand. The bolder spirits among them even went further; they discovered an affinity between themselves and the revolutionaries. Hadn't they been attacked by the prerevolutionary establishment, as the revolutionaries had been? Hadn't they created new art forms, as the revolutionaries had created new social institutions? There was even the matter of a semimystic prophecy. It was not taken seriously, but it certainly deserved some attention. The two most prominent Futurist poets had seen the Revolution coming and said so. In [Vladimir] Mayakovsky's poem "A Cloud in Trousers" occurs the following passage (1914):

I can see one, coming across the mountains

Whom no one yet sees

When the human eye stops unperceiving

The year '16 bursts forth

In a thorny crown of revolutions

Heading the hungry hordes

And I am its precursor among you

More striking still is the case of [Velimir] Khlebnikov. In an anthology called *A Slap in the Face of Public Taste,* published in

1912, a poem by Khlebnikov begins: "A glimpse of the year 1917." It then proceeds to enumerate by date the fall of many great empires of the past. The last line says cryptically: "Someone 1917." In his reminiscences of Mayakovsky,[18] the critic [Viktor] Shklovskii says:

> I met Khlebnikov in Petersburg (1913). I came over to him and said: "1917 is the fall of the Russian Empire?"
>
> "You are the first to have understood it," he said quietly . . . and added, "Can you lend me twenty kopecks?"

In any case, the modernists immediately offered their cooperation to the government and their readiness to serve in any capacity they might be found useful. The more conservative artists and art workers (there were exceptions in all camps) were hesitant and waited watchfully.

The young Soviet republic was in desperate straights, fighting desperately for its very existence on every front (one spoke frequently of "fronts" in those days)—military, economic, agricultural, diplomatic, and cultural—and certainly every [type of] help was welcome. Lunacharskii, head of the Commissariat of Education, met with a cool reception, sometimes a downright rebuff from the established artistic fraternity. In the leading art and literary magazine, *Apollon* [Apollo, in] late 1917, one could read, among other things, the following:

> After October 25th, there are no limits to our apprehension for the safety of Russian art and antiquities. Everything is possible in the land where the revolution is already stained with the worst crimes, where the dark masses commit not only the basest murders but also cultural suicide in which one feels a wild and malicious premeditation. The most precious national monuments, both religious and artistic, are subject to destruction and desecration.

And more of the same.

This was mere malicious gossip based more on hearsay than the truth. In fact, the young government, despite the invasion of foreign armies, raging civil war, starvation, and disease, found time and energy to pass decrees for the restoration of art and antiquities, including ancient churches and other monuments, decrees for the care of museums and other art institutions, and decrees against the export of valuable works of art. Lunacharskii placed in charge of its art section the modern artist David Shterenberg, who attracted artists of all shades to work with him on projects ranging from the reform of art education (the National Art Academies, rigidly conservative, were dissolved), to finding studios for artists, acquiring their work, opening art classes in factories, arranging traveling exhibitions, and engaging artists to decorate cities during revolutionary festivals (May 1, October 17, etc.).

It is a strange thing that art trends were born and died overnight and that painters, sculptors, and graphic artists turned out an unprecedented number of works. It is as if the artists were trying to compensate for the underconsumption of food by the overproduction of art. If art could have been used as food, Moscow would have had no need of rationing. There was a great variety of styles, almost always bolstered by a credo or manifesto. I shall not enumerate them, mainly because—making due allowances for national differences—analogous work could be seen in Western Europe. I would like, however, to say a few words about an art to which I found no parallel elsewhere, not because of its outstanding qualities but because of some interesting extraneous factors. The school coined a name for itself, *"Zorved"* (a cross between vision and knowledge or insight).[19] I shall let one of its members, [Mikhail] Matiushin, speak for it:

> *Zorved* signifies a physiological change of former methods of observation and involves an entirely new way of reflecting the visual. . . .
>
> New data have established how space, color, and form affect the brain center by way of the occiput. A series of tests conducted by members of *Zorved* have clearly demonstrated the sensitivity of the visual centers found in the back of the head. . . .

In other words, the artists of *Zorved* faced the object, if I may say so, with the back of their head. The results were not spectacularly different from works by artists who faced their objects *en face* or others who discarded objects (as subject) altogether.

In addition to exhibitions by individuals or groups, there were also non-jury shows on a larger scale, regional or all-Soviet. The *Art of the Commune [Iskusstvo kommuny]* (of which I was given a full set—an indispensable source of information on the period) tells of a meeting where such an exhibition was being planned. The artist [Natan] Al'tman had just asked for a resolution to invite all art societies to participate and to make the exhibition a big public event, thus bringing art closer to the people. Thereupon a member of the World of Art *[Mir iskusstva]* got up angrily and delivered himself of the following:

> Al'tman's idea that art is accessible to everyone is not to our taste. We are for the few. Art cannot be spread about to all and sundry. It is divine, majestic. Any attempt on this sanctuary will have to be answered before God. The theses of the speaker sound like a joke to us. It presents a challenge. Art is indeed something bourgeois. Politicians at the present cannot abide the bourgeois. But the bourgeoisie has its place in art, because for art the "riff-raff" still exists. Al'tman's theses are unacceptable to us. . . .

[With that, the speaker] stalked out of the room.

This and similar kinds of behavior tended to strengthen the anti-intellectualism among certain revolutionaries who could not forget the vacillations, ambivalence, and self-delusions of many prerevolutionary writers, critics, and philosophers. Paris, Berlin, New York, and Prague kept their memories alive [Aleksandr Blok], in his epic poem of the Revolution, "The Twelve," gives this unflattering picture of the "internal émigré":

And who is that? Long hair

And whispering under his breath

"Traitors"

"Russia is ruined"

Must be a writer

Magniloquent

Vasilii Kamenskii, as befits a Futurist, is more brusque and also more vituperative. I saw an announcement of a lecture he had delivered: Title: "The Story of a Son of a Bitch"; subtitle: "The History of the Russian Intelligentsia."

I should perhaps add a few words about another oppositional element that made the early years of the young republic hectic and turbulent. I mean the Anarchists. The Anarchists had representative groups in a number of large cities of the Soviet Union. One of their number, Makhno, led his own army in Ukraine, alternately collaborating and fighting against the Red Army. The Moscow contingent was vocal, active, and conspicuous. It had its own headquarters and its own paper, *Anarchy [Anarkhiia]*. *Anarchy* showered high praise on modernists like [Aleksandr] Rodchenko, [Nadezhda] Udal'tsova, [Aleksandr] Drevin, and others. But, as an antiauthoritarian organization, the Anarchists were opposed to the many artists organized under government patronage, and they were not shy in stating their position. "Bolsheviks of Futurism," says an issue of *Anarchy* (1918):

> State Futurists issue a decree, order the shooting of the innovators, [who are] more extreme than you, the anarcho-rebels. The new Commissariat of Art wants to organize creativeness along the lines of a political party. Creativeness requires no official sanction of a ruling party . . . we put ever new fetters on ourselves and chain ourselves to the walls. Here is a professional union, and we are at its feet, at the feet of the *chinovniks* [bureaucrats] elected by ourselves . . . throw [off] the trumpery of every force! Arise!

So far as is known, the appeal met with no response. Incidentally, Malevich contributed several items to *Anarchy*.

The eminent critic Viktor Shklovskii, a friend and supporter of the Futurists (he considered himself one of them) and certainly a supporter of Soviet power, wrote a criticism, in one respect similar to that of the Anarchists, and he received a response, a sharp one, from no less a man than

[Leon] Trotsky. In an article in *Zhizn' iskusstva* (Life of art), Shklovskii said inter alia the following: "The most serious mistake made by contemporary writers on art I consider [to be] their effort to equate the social revolution and the formal revolution in art." And further: "Art has always been free from everyday life *(byt),* and its color has never been reflected in the color of the flag above the ramparts of the city."

Then Shklovskii makes five points to prove his position. In his *Literature and Revolution,* Leon Trotsky refuted (or tried to) each of the five points in turn, then gave Shklovskii a lecture on sociology and a dressing down for good measure.

■

One evening a friend suggested that we visit some schools and get acquainted with the younger generation of students. I immediately agreed. The first place we came to was a middle-sized room, rather dimly lighted and full of young people noisy with talk and laughter. Most of them seemed to be engaged in what appeared to be physical exercises of all kinds—swinging over bars, leaping over obstacles, doing acrobatic stunts on a ladder, making somersaults, and suddenly exploding with laughter when something did not seem to go right. Was this a gymnasium? I asked. No, it was a class for young actors in biomechanics, the discipline favored or invented by [Vsevolod] Meyerhold and very popular among the young. Briefly, biomechanics required of the actor that he be complete master of his "biologic machine" in all its faculties and functions. The actor should have such perfect control of his body that he could pass instantly from motion to repose, from fencing to the dance, from gesture to pantomime, and from walking to acrobatics.[20]

"Very few of them," said my companion, "will ever reach the stage. But, in the meantime, they are enjoying their physical exercises and the companionship."

When they learned that there was an American in their midst, they surrounded me and showered me with questions.

"What kind of training do the actors get in America? How do they make their living? Do they know about biomechanics?" Etc.

I had to confess that my knowledge of the American theatre was limited to a number of plays I had seen and read and a few actors I had known.

"Do you think we'll ever be able to visit America?"

"I sincerely hope so."

When I left, they all sang out a collective farewell.

Next we went to VKhUTEMAS, the Higher State Art-Technical Workshops.[21] The attendance was much smaller, less exuberant, though not less enthusiastic. There were many kinds of odd-looking objects scattered around the room, some in wood, others in metal, attached to stands or by themselves, and some sketches that looked like mechanical drawings. They looked half-familiar, and I dropped a remark to the effect that the Weimar Bauhaus was engaged in somewhat similar projects and experiments. My casual remark drew a sudden, loud, and collective protest.

"No, no, no, what we are doing is something utterly different. In the West, they are seeking new forms, trying to justify them on esthetics grounds. They are still trying to create art. We have not been infected by esthetics contagion *(zaraza);* we are against art. We are students of Constructivism; we study the space relations between objects, the character and properties of many materials, always with a view to their ultimate utilization."

Their talk was very interesting, though not too convincing; but I did not press the point.

"See our instructor, Comrade Rodchenko."

Then came the inevitable interrogation about America. Was I ever in Detroit, and did I go through the Ford factory? Yes, I was, and I did. Did I ever visit the steel mills of Pittsburgh? I did. I am afraid that my description of what I saw lent itself more to the painting of pictures than to the creation of Constructivist objects. The talk continued on other aspects of America—the cities, the villages, the way of life, and the theatre. They were eager for knowledge about other lands as well; and when the interview was over, they gave me the same warm and noisy farewell as I had received at the other studio.

The next time I saw Rodchenko he took me to meet the famous *ménage à trois.* We found all of its members at home:

Osip Brik, the critic, his wife Lily, and the poet [Vladimir] Mayakovsky. I was agitated and looked around the room with eager curiosity: first, of course, Mayakovsky whose poetry I had admired for its original versification, its unconventional imagery, its striking phrase structure and word coinage, and—yes—its narrative power;[22] next Lily, Mayakovsky's inamorata, to whom in the course of many years he dedicated so many of his poems. She was attractive, though far from the raving beauty one heard about. I must have been under the influence of the gossip that circulated about her, because as I looked at her walking about the room, swaying a little, then gliding into her chair, she gave me the impression of being spoiled, affected, and snobbish. Her sister was, at the time I am speaking of, abroad in Berlin I think, where she met and married [Louis] Aragon and later became known in French literary circles as Elsa Triolet.

Mayakovsky was exactly as I imagined him to be: tall—when he stood up he towered above everybody in the room—his features clear-cut and well articulated. His voice was a baritone-basso; he spoke in clipped sentences; and as he spoke, he chopped the air with his hands. I thought he would make an excellent subject for some sculptor, but none of the sculptures I was to see in subsequent years did him justice. Although I came chiefly to speak to Brik, it was Mayakovsky who interested me more. But I was plainly over-awed. The only thing I could bring myself to say was, "Do you believe in the Constructivist theories?"

"Of course. 'Give us a new art / one / that would pull the republic out of the mud,'" he quoted from his own poetry ("Order No. 2 to the Army of Art").

"And, what do you think?"

I told him what I thought. I don't think he was impressed.

Then Brik took over. Occasionally Rodchenko put in a word. You could feel that Brik was repeating what he had said before, probably more than once, and what he would say again, more than once. In fact, in one of the pamphlets I took with me from the Soviet Union, I found an article under his name which repeated what he said to me almost verbatim:

The trouble with you—and we have some citizens of the Soviet Union talking the same way—is that you forget the Revolution of 1917. The October Revolution was a social upheaval of unprecedented scope. It shook society to its very foundations and transformed all institutions, root and branch. Wouldn't you expect such a transformation to affect art? Unfortunately many workers in the arts do not realize that; they continue to act as if nothing happened. Take one phase of it, by way of example, so called pure and applied art. Pure art was the repository of the highest creative values—paintings, sculpture, and churches; applied art, the embellishment of objects of use—furniture, textile, cigarette cases—was mere workmanship. We look upon it differently. To us, sculpture is the same kind of labor as cabinet-making, and painting is as much a craft as weaving. We work toward a state where the worker and the artist meet on the same ground in the industrial process, where the worker will approach his labor creatively and the artist will apply his talents to the effective functioning of production. This is Constructivism.

And much more to the same effect. He even said as a kind of afterthought: "It takes as much talent, as much creative ability to design chintz as to paint a landscape, and the chintz might be more important to us at the present state of the republic."[23]

I had not come to argue but to learn, and so I thanked Brik for his time and went out to learn more.

Incidentally, I must pay tribute to one artist who did more perhaps than anyone else to help me meet artists, writers, and theatrical people and to supply me with much printed material on the subjects that interested me. He was David Shterenberg, the head of the Art Section under the Commissariat of Education. He gave me, among other things, the first and only issue of *Fine Art (Izobrazitel'noe iskusstvo)* with articles by [Wassily] Kandinsky (stage design), Malevich (poetry), Shterenberg (art front), and others, richly illustrated. I still have a photograph of myself and Shterenberg taken in Moscow [Figure 9].

Osip Brik was one of a brigade of critic-ideologues who preached the doctrine of Constructivism. That doctrine im-

Fig. 9 Lozowick and David Shterenberg, Moscow, 1922.

plied, among other things, that art must be eliminated but that the artist should be retained as a factor in the productive life of the country. How this was to be accomplished was explained by the critics at great length in an involved rhetoric, which was sometimes difficult to follow. They were much more lucid and definite in their negative attacks on art itself.

The artists themselves, the adherents of Constructivism, who greeted the Revolution so enthusiastically, were anxious to do something more practical than the mere creation of paintings and sculptures. They continued to turn out "counter-reliefs," *"Prouns,"* "space constructions," "colored planes and volumes," etc.;[24] but somehow they came to believe that these creations were already beyond art though not yet integrated into the productive process; they were "transfer stations" between one and the other. The artists adjusted to their usual practice, believing at the same time that they were transcending it. But the dilemma remained. There was no such dilemma for the critics.

I spoke briefly of Brik's views. I shall speak even more briefly, just barely mention, a few others. [Boris] Arvatov's special abomination was the easel picture and sculpture. [According to Arvatov,] the easel picture did not spring full-blown from the head of Zeus. It assumed its present form gradually, parallel with and a result of the step-by-step development of capitalism and the accumulation of private fortunes. Whether as vehicle, object of exchange, commodity, or as expression of individual ideology, it is flesh of the flesh—bone of the bone—of the capitalist system, the system of commodity, production, and exchange. The easel picture or sculpture decorates the house of the bourgeois; it expresses his egotistic philosophy; it is the favorite child of private enterprise. To try to saddle the working class and the revolution with it is to commit a crime against both.

The writer, [Boris] Kushner, is even more direct:

> Art is as dangerous as religion. If religion is opium for the people, then art is carbon monoxide. Religion held the masses in darkness, in slavish submission. Now art makes an assault on the emancipated masses; it tries to lure them into the palaces of the beautiful. Art is thoroughly permeated with the most reactionary idealism; it cannot be materialistic. . . .[25]

Finally, a climax of sorts is reached in the book *Constructivism* by [Aleksei] Gan in which the very first line states unequivocally: "We declare irreconcilable war on art."[26] After this punch line, what follows is anticlimactic:

> Art is indissolubly connected with ideology, metaphysics, [and] mysticism.
> It originated in the epoch of prehistoric culture when technique consisted in rudimentary tools.
> It passed through the handicraft kitchen of the Middle Ages.
> It was deliberately warmed over by the hypocrisy of bourgeois culture and has finally bumped into the mechanical world of our century.
> Death to art.
> It had a natural origin.

It had a natural development.

It has naturally come to its demise . . .

Our annals begin with October 25th, 1917 . . .

The social-political order determined by the new economic substructure causes the creation of new forms and means of expression.

The emerging culture of labor and intellect will be expressed by intellectual-material construction.

The first slogan of the Constructivists is: Down with speculative activity in artistic labor.

We declare . . . irreconcilable war on art.

Paraphrasing Gan's positive approach to Constructivism:

As the stout child of the Revolution, Constructivism operates under the discipline of *tektonika* [tectonics] (the binding force between ideology and form), *faktura* (property of materials), *konstruktsiia* (convergence of all factors in the purposive process of construction).[27]

It was not recorded how many projects were successfully carried out under this triple discipline.

[The year] 1922 was a critical period for the Constructivists and other modernists. They were fighting a rear-guard battle against the encroachments of a constantly growing opposition. A number of prominent moderns—Chagall, Kandinsky, Gabo, [Antoine] Pevsner, and [David] Burliuk—left the country permanently and settled in Europe or America. In a few years, the Constructivist group was beginning to fall apart. Some, carrying their ideas to their logical conclusions, actually went into industry. Others, like Tatlin and Al'tman, turned to the theatre. Lissitzky did his last *Proun* in 1924 and thereafter was active in making posters, designing books, and doing architectural planning.

[The year] 1922 [also] marked the organization of AKhRR, Association of Artists of Revolutionary Russia. Its declaration of principles speaks for itself:

Our civic duty before mankind is to record in monumentally artistic forms the greatest moment in history in its revolutionary upsurge.

> We shall represent our day: the life of the red army, the life
> of workers, the peasantry, the participants in the Revolution,
> [and] the heroes of labor.
>   We shall render the true picture of events, not the abstract
> gimmicks which discredit our Revolution before the interna-
> tional proletariat. . . .[28]

AKhRR called this "heroic realism." In vain did the critic
[Nikolai] Chuzhak dub it "heroic servilism"; in vain did others accuse the AKhRR artists of being hypocrites, time-
servers who fawned on the powers that be. The organization
grew by leaps and bounds. It had some powerful backing.
The theoretician [Nikolai] Bukharin, who was something of
an artist himself, sponsored it. And if the Futurists and Constructivists could boast of their own poet, Mayakovsky,
AKhRR, too, had its poet, the popular Dem'ian Bednyi.

And while the Constructivist group was falling apart, it
left a most powerful legacy in the theatre. How this came
about makes an interesting story. In 1921, Meyerhold visited
the exhibition "5 x 5 = 25," which I described earlier. He
was obviously interested because he came again. He talked
with the artists several times, discussed their ideas, and finally
asked whether they would be interested in working with him
and experimenting with some of their ideas in the theatre.
The result was that two members of "5 x 5," [Liubov'] Popova
and [Varvara] Stepanova, in collaboration with Meyerhold,
did the sets for *The [Magnanimous] Cuckold* (Popova) and *The
Death of Tarelkin* (Stepanova). (Another member, Exter,
worked similarly with the Kamernyi Theatre.)

The idea fell on fertile soil, and many theatres adopted the
technique, often with variations of their own. (I myself got
into the act. In 1926, a few years after my return from Europe, a former pupil of Meyerhold, Marion Gering, who had
seen reproductions from my paintings in the *Little Review,* invited me to do Constructivist stage sets for *Gas* by Georg
Kaiser [Figure 16]. The play was produced at the [Kenneth
Sawyer] Goodman [Memorial] Theatre in Chicago.[29] It received some favorable reviews. My sketch for the sets was reproduced in a book on theatrical decoration by Sheldon

Cheney.)[30] One of the best of those theatres was GOSET,[31] the State Jewish Theatre, which was sometimes jokingly referred to as the Meyerhold branch on Malaia Bronnaia Street. That was an exaggeration—GOSET was among the most original theatres in Moscow.

The existence of the [State] Jewish Theatre was made possible by the Soviet policy regarding its many nationalities. In essence, this policy guaranteed each nationality its cultural autonomy. For the Jews, who had no territory of their own, this was of special importance. The Revolution abolished the many restrictive and repressive anti-Jewish laws of the Tsarist regime, and the result was almost immediate. In an amazingly short few years, there was an unprecedented outburst of cultural activity; one might almost say a renaissance. Collections of poetry, short stories, novels, and critical studies of high merit appeared in regular succession. There were magazines, newspapers, and schools in the Yiddish language to meet the demand of the swelling Jewish population in the large cities. (In the first turbulent years of the Revolution and Civil War, it was far from safe for the Jews to remain in the villages and small towns; and so, there was an exodus from them and an influx into the big urban centers.) Moscow, like other large centers, had its Jewish Cultural League where meetings, discussions, poetry readings, and exhibitions were held at all times. I found, for example, a catalogue of a recent exhibition by the artists Al'tman, Shterenberg, and Chagall with a flamingly revolutionary credo by Chagall.

■

I spent a pleasant time with a number of Jewish writers who presented me with some books and a magazine called *Shtrom* [Current] that had a most interesting cover by Chagall. Here, too, I came across some work by Lissitzky in what might be called his middle period. As I stated in my Berlin letter [Chapter 10], his interest before the Revolution was in the Jewish past. After the Revolution, he turned to themes and styles of a more universal significance. From 1917 to about 1920, he moved between one and the other. Perhaps his most ambitious and interesting work done during this period is [his illustrative work for] *The Legend of Prague* by M[oshe] Broderson.[32] This *Legend* was designed in a nationalistic style, even with religious overtones. The lettering was designed by a Torah scribe (Torah is the Pentateuch inscribed by hand on a parchment scroll and recited in the Synagogue). The *Legend* was printed in 110 copies, 20 of which were colored by hand, decorated in the manner of an illuminated manuscript; [it was] rolled like a Torah scroll, and, again, like a Torah, placed in a beautiful case.

■

Back to the [State] Jewish Theatre [GOSET]. I had the good fortune to attend two of its most successful productions, *The Sorceress* "according to [Abraham] Goldfaden," and *At Night in the Old Market Place* "according to [Isaac] Peretz." [Aleksei] Granovskii, the director of GOSET ([later known] as [Solomon Mikhailovich] Mikhoels [Vovsi]), altered sometimes drastically the plays he produced according to the needs of the actors but mainly for ideologic reasons.

The Sorceress, a tearful melodrama about an orphan and her tribulations at the hands of an evil stepmother, was turned into a spectacle of which Goldfaden had never dreamed. Granovskii was drawn to Goldfaden's melodrama by its folk character. Under the dross of lachrymose sentimentality, there was the gold of folk humor, folk speech, and folk tradition. Granovskii retained the fast-moving plot of *The Sorceress* and turned the melodrama into a riotous comedy, a comedy that laughs at its own plot even while it uses it—a carnival in the spirit of a Jewish *Commedia dell'Arte.* (For the Jews did have their own *Commedia* in the Purim players. These wandering, primitive amateurs, recruited mostly from the local population, performed on the most secular of the Jewish holidays, Purim. The plot, revolving around the Biblical story of Esther, was freely improvised in song, dance, and recitation, and in ample allusions and sharp barbs aimed at the local "big shots," a practice not ordinarily permitted.) Granovskii deliberately utilized to the fullest the abandon and spontaneity of the Purim plays, as well as their use of stock types and broad, primitive humor. Thus, *The Sorceress* passes, in rollicking review, the ever-present personages of the small town: the sorceress *(makhshefa)*, the orphan *(yesoma)*, the minstrel *(badkhan)*, the marriage-broker *(shadkhan)*, and others. It should be emphasized, naturally, that tradition was transformed here by a highly sophisticated sensibility. This was especially notable in the music by [Iosif] Akhron, the stylization of the acting, and the conventionalization of the sets by [Isaak] Rabinovich.

The sets were Constructivist, consisting of platforms at various levels, ladders, and steps designed in such a way as to allow the actors to move up, down, over, and under in all directions. Indeed, the actors never seemed to stop moving, climbing, and swinging. The spectacle was a complex processional which sought to exhibit through song, dance, and gesture the exuberance, the love of life of *amkho* (the plain [common] people), and to expose and to ridicule the old order in its cruelty, hypocrisy, exploitation, and obscurantism. The exaggerated makeup, the near-frenzied movement, the acrobatics, the grotesquerie, and the background music held one spellbound and well-nigh obliterated whatever message the play meant to convey.

The next play I attended was *At Night in the Old Market Place* "according to Peretz." How liberally "according to" was interpreted may be seen in the case of *At Night,* in which a poem of about 1,000 words was converted into a full mystery play. *At Night in the Old Market Place* is a tragedy; but like *The Sorceress*, which is a comedy, it embodied a castigating indictment of the old Jewish world. A mystery play with scarcely any plot, it revealed a poignant picture of a decrepit world, which was accentuated to the pitch of the macabre by the fine music of [Grigorii] Krein, the excellent scenery by [Robert] Fal'k, and the thoroughly controlled bodily movements and gestures of the actors. Fal'k created an abstracted version of the old market place, framed by the symbols of church and synagogue in a hieratic rigidity on opposite sides of the stage, and heightened the funeral atmosphere of the play by ghastly masks and costumes. This was the dying world of priests and rabbis, traders and prostitutes, writhing in its last agonies and clinging desperately to its old superstitions. The dead regulate the customs of the living, and the living are putrid with the germs of decay. The last judgment is upon them; and when the dead rise, the difference between the dead and the living disappears.

The effect of the two plays on me was profound. Although I saw subsequently both in the Soviet Union and in Western Europe, practically the entire repertory of the Jewish State (sometimes also called the Academic) Theatre [GOSET], no other plays affected me as powerfully. In the fifties, when the theatre was no longer in existence, I passed along Malaia Bronnaia where the theatre used to be. The street was quiet. Now and again someone hurried by, casting a curious glance at me—a stranger staring at a building across the street, a building no different from any [other] building on the block. I stood reminiscing for a while, then shook my shoulders and was on my way. *Sic transit. . . .*

One evening I went to see *The [Magnanimous] Cuckold* at the Meyerhold Theatre, the most controversial in Moscow. One could hardly recognize it as the play by [Fernand] Crommelynk performed at the Théâtre del Oeuvre in Paris. The stage was bare—no curtain, no proscenium arch, wings, backdrop, or flood lights. On the background of the bare wall of the building with its open brickwork, one saw a simple, skeleton-like construction, a scaffolding designed by Popova consisting of one large black wheel and two small ones, red and white, platforms at various levels, revolving doors, stairs, ladders, chutes, and square, triangular, and rectangular shapes. The wheels moved fast or slow according to the intensity of the action in the play [Figure 10]. The costumes of the actors were all alike, made of blue denim, like workers' clothes. The actors wore no makeup. Speech, however, was not the speech of ordinary conversation, but a kind of standardized, syncopated recitation. The movement of the actors was acrobatic—up the ladders, down the chutes, through the doors, and around the constructions with leaps, somersaults, and dance and march steps, with zest, rapidity, and vitality that kept the

Fig. 10 Liubov' Popova, set for *The Magnanimous Cuckold,* 1922.

audience in constant tension. I admired the mastery of the production. I admired his [Meyerhold's] daring in the use of such unorthodox methods, but I was also puzzled by some of them. It was only years later, when I saw more of his productions, particularly the superb *Inspector General,* that I came to admire and appreciate him as one of the truly great men of the theatre.[33]

Whatever reservations I may have had about the staging, I had none at all about the acting, for the actors were magnificent. I asked Meyerhold's permission to be present at a rehearsal, which he readily granted. The actors, as they went through their paces, kept constantly deferring to Vsevolod Emil´evich [Meyerhold], and it was amazing to watch how expertly Meyerhold demonstrated every role, including those of the women. When I mentioned, in the course of conversation, that I was to be in Paris shortly, he asked me to convey his warmest greetings to "the great French master," Picasso. I promised to do so.

I took leave of my hosts and thanked them for the many kindnesses they had shown me. They all wished me well and exclaimed in unison: "Come again. Come again."

I returned to Berlin where I had to answer a million questions about the Soviet Union: the theatre, art, conditions of living, etc. Then I went to Paris, eager to deliver the message from Meyerhold to Picasso.

"Ah," exclaimed Picasso, *"Moscou, Moscou,* wonderful city. Quite often we listen to the bells of the Kremlin playing the 'International.'" Picasso was flattered to receive the greetings from Meyerhold. We spoke about the theatre and the arts in Moscow. I asked him whether he knew that there was an extensive literature about him and his work in Russia, that while some regarded it very highly, others considered it the work of the devil incarnate. He said he had heard something about it but really knew very little. Then I added, "In view of such diversity of views about your work, can you point to anyone whose opinions coincide with yours, who most truly understands you?"

"Qui sait?" he replied, "perhaps this one," and he showed me a book about him [written] in Japanese.

■

To look ahead some years. In 1926, I did an article on Chagall's circus series for the *Theatre Arts Magazine.*[34] I sent the article to Chagall and received a very friendly letter in return and an invitation to visit him in Paris, if I ever came there. In 1927, I was in Paris and accordingly paid him a visit. He was most friendly and, in appreciation, presented me with an etching of his, a self-portrait with a *dédicace.* We talked of many things, one of them being the kind of reception his work might get in America. In the course of our further conversation, I asked him the same question I had asked Picasso five years previously.

"Who do you think writes most truly about your work?"

Without hesitation he replied, "You, you truly understand what I am trying to say."

That was the last time I ever asked that question of anyone.

◼

I returned to Germany where I remained until it became quite trying to stay there much longer. I decided to spend a few weeks in my favorite city, Paris. Paris was beautiful. I felt that it put on its finest raiment just for me. I was less than eager to go back [to America] and face the uncertain (to put it mildly) prospect of earning a livelihood. And I kept postponing the date of my departure. My French friends could not understand my hesitation. They would have been happy to exchange *la ville luminère* for the "land of opportunity," where they were sure fortune awaited anyone of capability. I did not argue for or against. I just quoted the immortal expression of Marcel Duchamp: "Sélavy." And who could gainsay *that*?

PART FOUR

1924–1945

BACK IN AMERICA

As Lozowick relates in Chapters 10 and 11, he returned to
Berlin after his trip to Moscow. In a letter dated September
12, 1922, Lozowick wrote, "I am just back from Russia,"[1]
placing his return to Berlin in mid-September. He remained
in Berlin until the fall of 1923, when he returned to Paris for
a brief visit before sailing for New York.[2]

Soon after his arrival in New York, Lozowick became acquainted with Katherine S. Dreier, initiating a long personal
and professional relationship with Dreier and the Société
Anonyme. On February 2, Dreier invited Lozowick to submit two works to the Société Anonyme's forthcoming exhibition of Russian Suprematism and Constructivism and to
give a talk in conjunction with the show.[3] Lozowick had the
distinction of being the only American artist included in this
important early exhibition in America of Russian avant-garde
art. His lecture entitled "The Suprematists of Russia" of February 19, 1924 (see Figure 11) became the basis of *Modern
Russian Art,* which the Société Anonyme published in 1925.[4]
This was the first book on the subject of Russian Suprematist
and Constructivist art published in the United States. The
text was an expansion of Lozowick's essay, "A Note in Modern Russian Art," which had appeared in the February 1923
issue of *Broom*. Appropriately, the cover of *Modern Russian Art*
(Figure 14) is based on Lissitzky's cover of the *Broom* issue
(Figure 15) in which Lozowick's original essay on the subject
had appeared.

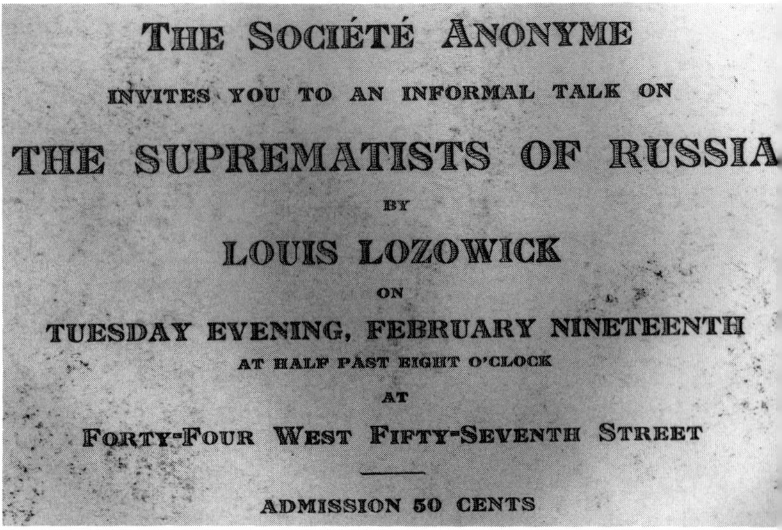

THE SOCIÉTÉ ANONYME

INVITES YOU TO AN INFORMAL TALK ON

THE SUPREMATISTS OF RUSSIA

BY

LOUIS LOZOWICK

ON

TUESDAY EVENING, FEBRUARY NINETEENTH

AT HALF PAST EIGHT O'CLOCK

AT

FORTY-FOUR WEST FIFTY-SEVENTH STREET

———

ADMISSION 50 CENTS

Fig. 11 Announcement of lecture for Société Anonyme, February 19, 1924.

In 1926 Dreier included two of Lozowick's paintings in the International Exhibition of Modern Art mounted by the Société Anonyme and held at the Brooklyn Museum.[5] It is significant that Lozowick wrote Dreier requesting that his paintings not be placed in the Russian section, stating that "for reasons of education, outlook, etc., I prefer to be included in the American section,"[6] a statement that indicates Lozowick's strong identification as an American. Again, Dreier invited Lozowick to give a lecture in conjunction with the exhibition (Figure 12) and to review the exhibition for *Nation*.[7]

In addition to lectures and articles commissioned by Dreier, Lozowick lectured and wrote many articles on modern art. Soon after his return to New York, he resumed his association with the Educational Alliance Art School, giving two lectures on modern art in early 1924 (Figure 13). He also wrote articles on Natan Al'tman, Marc Chagall, Fernand Léger, El Lissitzky, and others, which appeared in Jewish and avant-garde publications (see the Selected Bibliography).

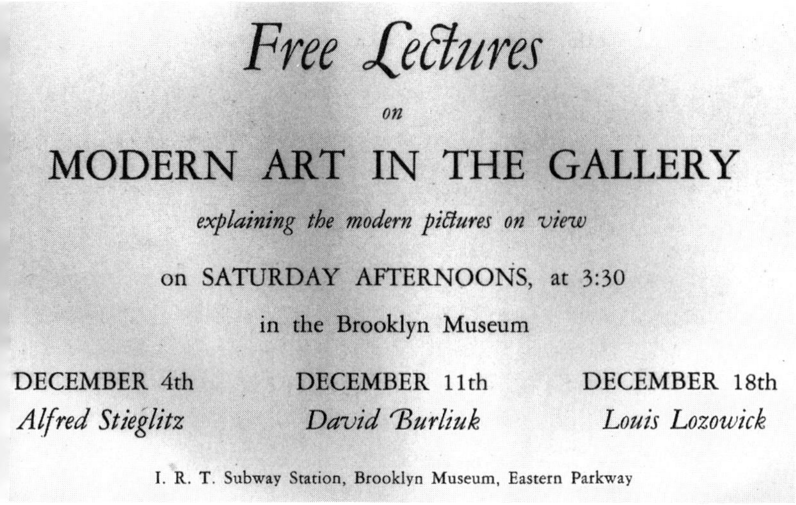

Free Lectures

on

MODERN ART IN THE GALLERY

explaining the modern pictures on view

on SATURDAY AFTERNOONS, at 3:30

in the Brooklyn Museum

DECEMBER 4th	DECEMBER 11th	DECEMBER 18th
Alfred Stieglitz	*David Burliuk*	*Louis Lozowick*

I. R. T. Subway Station, Brooklyn Museum, Eastern Parkway

Fig. 12 Announcement of lectures in connection with International Exhibition of Modern Art, Brooklyn Museum, 1926.

The years 1926 and 1927 were extremely productive for Lozowick. It was during this period that his ideas about America's industrialization culminated in a body of work of the same theme. Expanding the urban and industrial themes of his "City" paintings and ink drawings done in Berlin, he painted a new series of ten "American Cities" and drew more "Machine Ornaments." Selected works were exhibited at the Society of Independent Artists' annual exhibitions and were reproduced in *Nation* and *New Masses*. The first major exhibition of Lozowick's City paintings and Machine Ornament drawings was held at J. B. Neumann's New Art Circle in January–February 1926. It was prophetic that in the room adjoining exhibition of Lozowick's work Neumann mounted an exhibition of the work of Charles Sheeler; together, Lozowick and Sheeler today are considered to be seminal figures of American Precisionism—work of the 1920s and 1930s that depicted the American industrial landscape in an ordered and laconic style of precise execution that in its imagery and principles reflected the machine age in America.[8] Although shar-

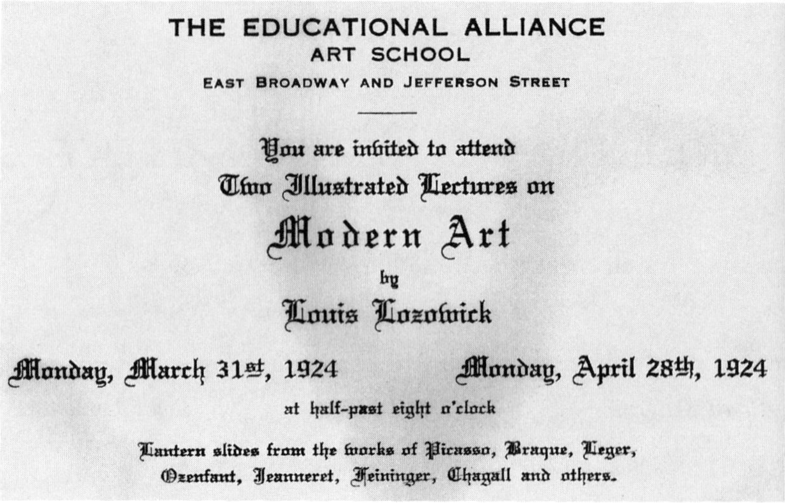

THE EDUCATIONAL ALLIANCE
ART SCHOOL
EAST BROADWAY AND JEFFERSON STREET

———

𝔜𝔬𝔲 𝔞𝔯𝔢 𝔦𝔫𝔳𝔦𝔱𝔢𝔡 𝔱𝔬 𝔞𝔱𝔱𝔢𝔫𝔡
𝔗𝔴𝔬 𝔍𝔩𝔩𝔲𝔰𝔱𝔯𝔞𝔱𝔢𝔡 𝔏𝔢𝔠𝔱𝔲𝔯𝔢𝔰 𝔬𝔫
𝔐𝔬𝔡𝔢𝔯𝔫 𝔄𝔯𝔱
𝔟𝔶
𝔏𝔬𝔲𝔦𝔰 𝔏𝔬𝔷𝔬𝔴𝔦𝔠𝔨

𝔐𝔬𝔫𝔡𝔞𝔶, 𝔐𝔞𝔯𝔠𝔥 31𝔰𝔱, 1924   𝔐𝔬𝔫𝔡𝔞𝔶, 𝔄𝔭𝔯𝔦𝔩 28𝔱𝔥, 1924
at half-past eight o'clock

𝔏𝔞𝔫𝔱𝔢𝔯𝔫 𝔰𝔩𝔦𝔡𝔢𝔰 𝔣𝔯𝔬𝔪 𝔱𝔥𝔢 𝔴𝔬𝔯𝔨𝔰 𝔬𝔣 𝔓𝔦𝔠𝔞𝔰𝔰𝔬, 𝔅𝔯𝔞𝔮𝔲𝔢, 𝔏𝔢𝔤𝔢𝔯,
𝔒𝔷𝔢𝔫𝔣𝔞𝔫𝔱, 𝔍𝔢𝔞𝔫𝔫𝔢𝔯𝔢𝔱, 𝔉𝔢𝔦𝔫𝔦𝔫𝔤𝔢𝔯, 𝔆𝔥𝔞𝔤𝔞𝔩𝔩 𝔞𝔫𝔡 𝔬𝔱𝔥𝔢𝔯𝔰.

Fig. 13 Announcement of lectures at Educational Alliance Art School, 1924.

ing many formal and thematic qualities, it is important to note that Sheeler and Lozowick developed their formal and thematic focus independent of each other. Lozowick has stressed his independence from Sheeler and emphasized his debt to European and Russian avant-garde art, especially Russian Constructivism, which shared the precise technique, geometrically ordered compositions, and industrial themes that are associated with Precisionism:

> It was like Huxley and Darwin both discovering the struggle for existence independently, where there is a certain air, a certain atmosphere. I wasn't, nor have I ever been, influenced by Sheeler in any way. My forms were arrived at independently of his. If there was any influence, it was from the Europeans, the Constructivists.[9]

One of Lozowick's most important projects during 1926 was his set for Marion Gering's production of Georg Kaiser's *Gas,* which was performed at the Kenneth Sawyer Goodman Memorial Theatre of the Art Institute of Chicago in January–February 1926. According to Lozowick, Gering, a former pupil of Meyerhold, "had seen some of my mechanical drawings, and he asked me if I would be interested in doing a set for *Gas.* I said I was very interested as I had seen the Berlin production of the play and I liked it."[10] For this project, Lozowick translated several of his Machine Ornaments into wooden structures built of wood, metal, and wire, added a motor-driven wheel, and projected images of an airplane and a steamboat (Figure 16).[11] The inspiration for these sets clearly was Popova's set for Meyerhold's production of *The Magnanimous Cuckold* (Figure 10), which, according to Lozowick's account, had both surprised and excited him when he saw it in Moscow in the summer of 1922. As the first Constructivist-inspired stage set mounted in America, Lozowick's set for *Gas* is a landmark. In an explanatory article, "'Gas': A Theatrical Experiment," which appeared in conjunction with his set designs in the International Theatre Exposition of February 27 to March 15, Lozowick asserted that the machine imagery of his set represented "the crystallization of a vision fashioned by the rigid geometric pattern of the American city: the verticals of its smoke stacks, the parallels of its car tracks, the squares of its streets, the cubes of its factories, the arcs of its bridges, the cylinders of its gas tanks."[12] This statement is significant because it indicates that by 1926 Lozowick equated the industrial materials and machinist imagery of Popova's set with America's urban and industrial landscape.

Other projects reflecting Lozowick's assimilation of the ideas of Russian avant-garde artists whom he had met in Berlin and Moscow was the commission for a window display and a backdrop for a fashion show for the department store Lord & Taylor's centennial celebration, which was held in March 1926. As with his recently completed set for *Gas,* Lozowick was inspired by the theme of the American industrial and urban landscape. For the window display, Lozowick placed a mannikin wearing a fabric of abstracted machine-like forms before a backdrop that featured his nocturnal version of *New York* (Figure 17). For the accompanying fashion show, Lozowick reworked selected Machine Ornaments into large free-standing structures placed at the ends of the plat-

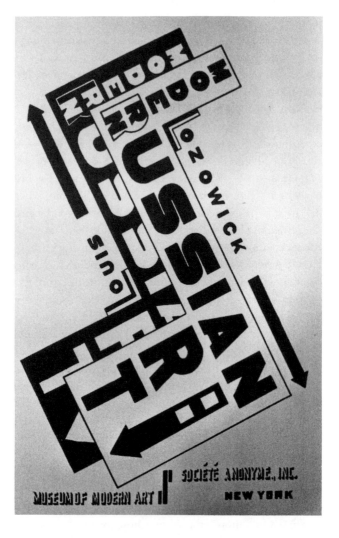

Fig. 14 Cover of *Modern Russian Art,* 1925. Photograph courtesy of the editor.

Fig. 15 El Lissitzky, cover of *Broom,* February 1923. General Research Division, The New York Public Library, Astor, Lenox, and Tilden Foundations.

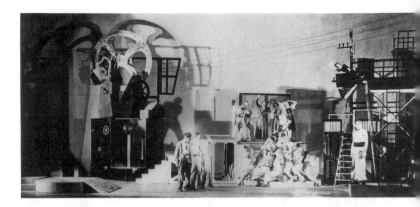

Fig. 16 Set for *Gas,* 1926.

form and displayed other Machine Ornaments on a large
backdrop. The backdrop and the skyscraper-like end structures were connected by geometric shapes that decorated the
platform itself (Figure 18). A garment designed by Lozowick
featuring machinist imagery reminiscent of Léger was worn
by one of the models. Like the set for *Gas,* Lozowick's commission for Lord & Taylor was related to the utilitarian direction espoused by the VKhUTEMAS students he had met in
Moscow. Like so much of the Constructivists' work—especially the *Prouns* of his close friend Lissitzky—the projects for
Lord & Taylor represent an intermediate stage between fine
art and utilitarian application.

The international Machine-Age Exposition of May 1927
highlighted the dominance of the machine as the source material for imagery and aesthetic criteria. Lozowick recalled
that he met Jane Heap who "asked me to help organize the
Machine-Age Show. She was really the head."[13] He was a
member of the Artists Committee, which included such important artists as Charles Sheeler, Charles Demuth, and Man
Ray, all of whom used machinist imagery in their work. This
was the second occasion that Lozowick was associated with
other American Precisionists (the first being the Neumann
exhibitions of Lozowick's and Sheeler's work). For this significant exposition, Lozowick designed a poster (Figure 19); and

Fig. 17 Window display for Lord & Taylor, March 1926. *Little Review* (Chicago, Ill.). Records, 1914–1964. UWM Manuscript Collection 1. University Manuscript Collection, Golda Meir Library, University of Wisconsin-Milwaukee.

a full range of his work—"American Cities," a group of Machine Ornaments, his set for *Gas,* and his Lord & Taylor window display and fashion show—were exhibited. In addition, four Machine Ornaments were illustrated in the catalogue along with Lozowick's essay, "The Americanization of Art." In this important manifesto, Lozowick articulated ideas that had occupied him since he was in Berlin and resolved the conflict that he had expressed in "Tentative Attitudes" (see Appendix for both essays). Whereas in 1917 he could see no

Fig. 18 Backdrop and platform of fashion show for Lord & Taylor, March 1926. *Little Review* (Chicago, Ill.) Records, 1914–1964. UWM Manuscript Collection 1. University Manuscript Collection, Golda Meir Library, University of Wisconsin-Milwaukee.

accommodation for art, which he defined as founded on emotions, in the contemporary era in which the intellect, as exemplified by the sciences, was the dominant means by which humanity could understand the environment, now he proposed that works of art could in fact assist humanity in relating to the modern machine age by adopting the principles underlying technology and engineering—rational order, functionalism, and precision—as the basis of art. The intellect (not emotions) became the common ground whereby the modern age could be assimilated by the artist for meaningful and socially relevant works of art.

At the same time that Lozowick was expanding his Cities, making more Machine Ornaments, and exploring applied art—all of which were rooted in his contact with European and Russian avant-garde art—he joined the staff of the *New*

Fig. 19 Poster of Machine-Age Exposition, May 1927.
Photograph courtesy of the editor.

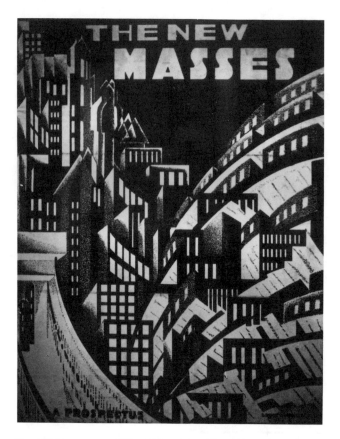

Fig. 20 Prospectus of *New Masses*, December 1925: cover (above) with illustration of *New York* by Lozowick and cartoon (opposite) by William Gropper (Lozowick is shown seated in right background with a "Machine Ornament" drawing). Photograph courtesy of the editor.

Masses, a monthly publication that was initiated during 1925 by writers and artists who had worked on two earlier leftist publications, *The Masses* (1911–1917) and the *Liberator* (1918–1924).[14] Lozowick recalled

> I was one of the founders of the *New Masses*. I was at the very first meeting. . . . The program was published in a four-page leaflet. It was a prospectus of what the *New Masses* was

going to be and what it was intending to do. And what it was intending to do, in brief, was to follow the old *Masses* and to have a variety of points of view, all liberal but a great variety. In fact, it said "nonparty but liberal." It was not going to be a magazine of any party. I did the front page and [William] Gropper did the back page, which was a caricature of the people who were present.[15]

The prospectus of the new publication, which appeared in December 1925, featured Lozowick's drawing of New York at night on the cover and included a caricature by Gropper of the organizers, with Lozowick shown with one of his Machine Ornaments (Figure 20). The two objectives of the new publication—the revival of American art based on contemporary life and the association with working men and women—were fully compatible with Lozowick's work and sympathies at the time. During 1925 and 1926 he was formulating his idea of the "Americanization" of art, a direction that he believed would revitalize American art. Not only did Lozowick serve on the editorial board of the *New Masses* during the late 1920s, but his Cities and Machine Ornaments appeared frequently in the *New Masses* as evidence of a vital new direction for American art that reflected the urban and industrial landscape. It is noteworthy that in joining the staff of the *New Masses* in 1925, Lozowick initiated nearly two decades of association with activist organizations, affiliations that were a logical expression of his outrage at social inequity and cruelty that he had witnessed as a child in Ukraine and that he observed in America during the 1930s.

During 1927 and 1928 Lozowick made a second trip abroad. It was occasioned by two one-person exhibitions of his work: one at the Museum of Western Art in Moscow, which was held in January 1928, the other at the Galerie Zak in Paris, which was held July 11–25, 1928. Both exhibitions included drawings and lithographs, the latter Lozowick's preferred medium during the late 1920s and thereafter. During this trip, Lozowick not only saw former friends and acquaintances in Paris, Berlin, and Moscow but met Sergei Eisenstein, Aleksandra Exter, and Aleksandr Tairov. On his return to New York in the summer of 1928,[16] he again wrote articles on the art, theatre, and cinema that he had seen in Russia, this time commenting on the demise of Constructivism and the rise of a new realism.

He also resumed his involvement with the *New Masses,* which was becoming increasingly dominated by political radicals under Michael Gold who became editor-in-chief in June 1928. Gold focused the publication more narrowly on the plight of workers and encouraged "workers art," by which he meant work that either was produced by workers or that reflected the viewpoint of workers.[17] In response to the drive for a realistic and socially oriented art, Lozowick developed a formal synthesis of representational exactitude modified by geometric elements that recalled his earlier semi-

Fig. 21 *Birth of a Skyscraper,* lithograph, 1930.

abstract compositions; his subject matter also altered slightly, now showing workers engaged in urban construction and in factories (Figure 21). Of his move toward greater realism, Lozowick recalled

> I changed to a more realistic [style]. I do not think it was due to a feeling of guilt but it was due to a feeling that this was a little bit more adequate to the times. But I still retained the formal qualities that were found in my earlier work. . . . My work was

industrial, factories and so on. I always believed, then and now, that this does not necessarily represent capitalism; it represents something that will ultimately be the property of the worker.[18]

Opposing those who urged that art be used as a propaganda tool, Lozowick consistently and forcefully asserted that art was separate from politics. On one occasion in 1929 he chastised a reader for confusing art with politics, stating that "art has its own specific problems of importance to the artist and to the worker. People who make flying excursions into sociology and esthetics would do well to remember this."[19] The following year he wrote "Lithography: Abstraction and Realism," in which he enumerated some of the lithographic techniques that could be used to vary texture and lighting effects (see Appendix). A prominent spokesperson for leftist artists, Lozowick's essay "Art in the Service of the Proletariat" (see Appendix) was published in *Literature of the World Revolution,* the organ of the Soviet Union of Revolutionary Writers, in 1931. In this essay, Lozowick outlined "a variety of revolutionary stages" and stated that revolutionary artists seek "a synthetic style" using "the highest technical quality" to "help the effective delivery" of their social content. Defending his own industrial subject matter as relevant to workers, he asserted that the themes of the city and construction represent one direction of revolutionary art, because "the American worker inevitably lives and works with cities and machines."

Recognizing Lozowick's prominence as artist and spokesperson of the American Left, the Moscow-based International Union of Revolutionary Writers (IURW) invited Lozowick to join an international group of writers to tour Soviet Central Asia in 1931. This, Lozowick's third return to his native country, occurred from late spring to early fall. He was joined by Joshua Kunitz, his good friend and a fellow member of the John Reed Club. On route to Russia, Lozowick met Adele Turner, whom he married later in the year (Figure 27).

In addition to his involvement with the *New Masses,* Lozowick participated in various organizations founded by *New Masses* staff members. These included the short-lived left-

JOHN REED CLUB
63,W.15

Lectures on Literature and Art
Sunday Afternoons - 2:30 p. m.

Sunday, June 5th: **Louis Lozowick** on *The Marxian Approach to Art*

Sunday, June 12th: *Symposium* on **Literature and Art of the World Revolution**

These are the next two numbers in the series of sixteen JRC lectures and symposiums, designed to set forth the proletarian theory of art, literature and criticism with special reference to the present situation in America.

AT THE CLUBROOMS   ADMISSION 25c.   BRING YOUR FRIENDS

Fig. 22 Announcement of Lozowick lecture on "The Marxian Approach to Art" at John Reed Club, 1932.

wing theatre groups, the Workers' Drama League (1925–1927) and the New Playwrights Theatre (1927–1929)[20] and, most important, the John Reed Club (1929–1934).[21] Lozowick was an organizer and charter member of the John Reed Club and served as its executive secretary in 1931 and its international secretary in 1932. In addition, he taught lithography and lectured at the John Reed Club Art School and exhibited in the Club's exhibitions (Figures 22 and 23). He was a speaker at the Club's symposium on the topic "Should Art Be National?"—a controversial subject that set John Reed Club artists, who advocated a Marxist-Leninist revolutionary art committed to enhancing workers' class consciousness and illuminating problems in the context of the international struggle of workers, against the chauvinist subjects of the "American School" promoted by Thomas Hart Benton and Thomas Craven, which left-wing artists considered reactionary. Lozowick alluded to these opposing camps in "Towards a Revolutionary Art," which appeared in 1936 (see Appendix).

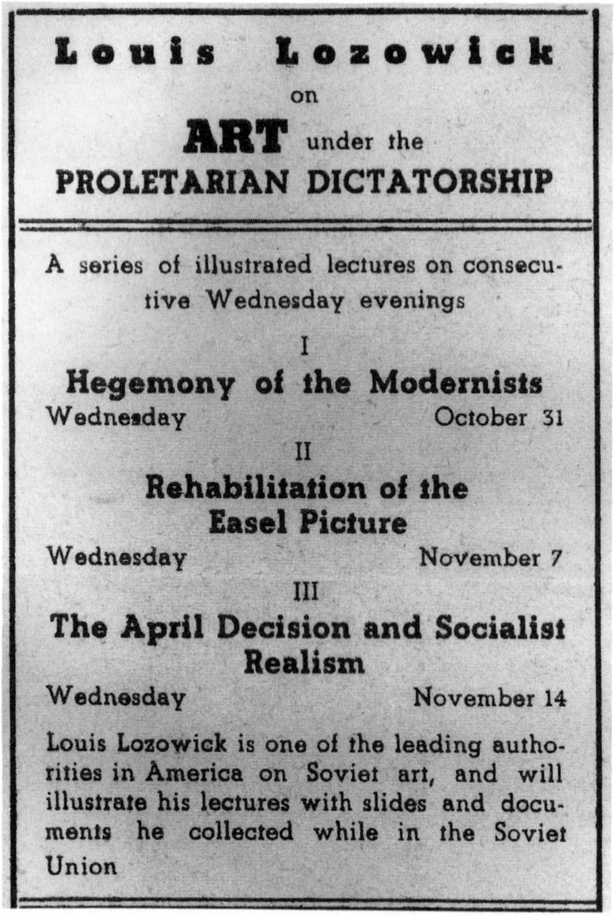

Louis   Lozowick

on

ART under the
PROLETARIAN DICTATORSHIP

A series of illustrated lectures on consecu-
tive Wednesday evenings

I

Hegemony of the Modernists
Wednesday   October 31

II

Rehabilitation of the
Easel Picture
Wednesday   November 7

III

The April Decision and Socialist
Realism
Wednesday   November 14

Louis Lozowick is one of the leading authorities in America on Soviet art, and will
illustrate his lectures with slides and documents he collected while in the Soviet
Union

Fig. 23 Announcement of Lozowick lectures on "Art under
the Proletarian Dictatorship" at the John Reed Club School of
Art, 1934.

In a letter of 1933, he states that "earning any kind of a
livelihood is at present for me a full-time and blood sweating
job."[22] His lithographs of Hoovervilles, demonstrations,
strikes, and lynchings reflected his increased political activism
during these years (Figure 24). On occasion he depicted himself in the role of protester or victim, as in *Tear Gas,* a litho-

Fig. 24 Demonstration of John Reed Club and Artists' Union: Lozowick is in the middle, between the two banners on the left, 1934. Louis Lozowick Papers, Archives of American Art, Smithsonian Institution.

graph of 1934, in which Lozowick himself is the demonstrator (Figure 25).

With the disbanding of the John Reed Club in 1934, Lozowick, like other left-wing artists, continued his activities on behalf of artists through the Artists' Union,[23] whose purpose was to lobby for government support for artists, and, more importantly, in the American Artists' Congress, a broadly based Popular Front organization that was dedicated to combating war and fascism. He served as the Congress' international secretary, chaired its cultural committee, and participated in its exhibitions, most noteworthy the "America Today" graphic exhibition of 1936. He also taught at the American Artists School,[24] which succeeded the John Reed Club School of Art. In "Towards a Revolutionary Art" of 1936, which appeared only months after the first American Artists' Congress, Lozowick discussed revolutionary art based

Fig. 25 *Tear Gas* (self-portrait), lithograph, 1934.

on Marxist principles in the context of the history of social art of the nineteenth century and encouraged artists of all political persuasions in their efforts to relate their work to contemporary social conditions.

During the late 1930s, he continued to produce lithographs and was intermittently employed by federally funded art programs, most notably by the Graphic Division of the Works Progress Administration (WPA). He painted two

Fig. 26 *Red Tea Pot,* lithograph, September 1973 (signed for the artist after his death by his widow, Adele Lozowick).

WPA murals—one depicting the building of the Triborough Bridge, the other the skyline of New York—for the New York Post Office at 33rd Street. As WPA projects provided economic relief, lessening the hardship that had contributed to the politicalization of artists during the early 1930s, Lozowick returned to the formal concerns and subjects of his earlier work. Recalling his early City compositions and subjects of construction sites and factories of the 1920s, he reintroduced formal elements of lines and geometric shapes in his depictions of factory and construction sites and city street scenes, achieving a new synthesis of abstraction and realism.

In 1945, the Lozowicks moved to South Orange, New Jersey, where Lozowick lived and worked until his death in 1973. While much of his life in South Orange centered around his son Lee, who was born in 1943, Lozowick nevertheless remained active in numerous artistic organizations and traveled worldwide. He continued to work in lithography, and his work after 1945 demonstrates a synthesis of richly textured surfaces, innovative designs, and realist imagery,

Fig. 27 Louis and Adele Lozowick, ca. 1933.

drawing on many of the elements of his earlier work (Figure 26). In recognition of his superior achievement in the medium of lithography, the National Academy of Design elected Lozowick to the rank of National Academician in the Graphic Arts Section in 1972.

In "Credo," which appeared in 1947, Lozowick made his last formal statement on the nature and purpose of art (see Appendix). Reiterating ideas that appear in all his artistic statements since 1927, he asserted his long-held belief that industrialization characterizes modern times and, hence, should be reflected in the imagery and in the character of art. Further, he maintained that although art is reflective of life, it nevertheless is separate from it. It is noteworthy that although earlier manifestos had appeared in publications ranging from the avant-garde to left-wing, this last published manifesto ap-

Fig. 28 Lozowick with son Lee, 1946.

peared in a Yiddish American publication on Jewish American artists. Although best known as a Precisionist whose art reflects the rationalism and imagery of industrialization, Lozowick's ethnic identity, rooted in Ludvinovka, Guermanovka, and Vasil'kov, is a continuing context for his art, as it was for his life.

APPENDIX

Statements on Art

Tentative Attitudes (1917)
Auditur Est Altera Pars

Strange to say, there still are men who take art seriously—what a pity! An infinity of problems require solutions, numberless movements demand participation; and yet hosts of men, some of them very able, devote their time to art—a phenomenon that has outlived its usefulness and is going fast to extinction. What a waste of energy!

Every phenomenon has its root in necessity; the law of cause and effect is as applicable to art as to everything else. Now art is a product subjectively of the emotional life and objectively of environmental influences. In the progress of mankind the emotions are of the highest importance. They served in the early stages as excellent means for meeting the exigencies of daily existence; they were defensive and preservative attitudes aiding man to cope with environment. Through fear primitive man avoided danger; through love sought society. To function more efficiently the emotions needed exercise, and art appeared on the stage. Primitive art is grossly materialistic and practical. It treats of the primitive man's immediate and essential interests—nutrition and reproduction, chiefly satisfaction of his stomach and propagation of his kind, and is, so to speak, an appeal through example. It raises the primitive man's emotional state to the necessary pitch and trains it for proper orientation in any given circumstances. Thus the savage is able to fortify his capacities for defense on one hand and to strengthen his social ties on the other.

With greater progress, the social instincts become more and more deeply rooted in human consciousness. Intellect, through the instrumentality of various inventions, wards off external attack more effectively, controls powers of nature more efficaciously. In consequence emotion as a guide is superseded by intellect. Life becomes gradually organized on the basis of reason instead of blind instinct.

In ancient and Medieval ages art was still vitally connected with life, although not in the same degree as among the savages. Today art has become a privilege of the few, the luxury very significantly tucked away in museums, and—still more significantly, perhaps—an object of apologetic critics. It has, however, no longer any important function to perform. One factory is a greater force in the establishment of *social harmony* than all the novels and dramas *(pieces-a-these* not excluded) ever written. Any science, astronomy, biology, etc., gives more scope to the *imagination* than all the epics and lyrics in existence. One ordinary love affair gives a deeper *emotional experience* than all the romances combined.

Having no important function to perform, art lives by mere power of inertia, while its momentum acquired through the ages is growing weaker. It will doubtless crop out in the future as an atovistic [sic] survival—a sort of spiritual vermiform appendix—but whatever value it possesses will be taken on one hand by science and the other by life itself. Art as a distinct social institution, since it has no root in necessity—is doomed to inevitable extinction.

From *The Sansculotte* 1, No. 1 (January 1911): 14.

The Americanization
of Art (1927)

If one were to grant the allegation that America possesses a meager cultural heritage and lacks the weight of established tradition, it would by no means follow that material for creative activity is wanting. The intriguing novelty, the crude virility, the stupendous magnitude of the new American environment furnishes such material in extravagant abundance. To the truly creative artist the fallow rawness of the field should prove only an additional incentive to its intensive cultivation. The artist's task is to sift and sort material at hand, mold it to his purpose by separating the plastically essential from the adventitious and, in this manner, enrich the existing culture and help to establish a new tradition.

The history of America is a history of stubborn and ceaseless effort to harness the forces of nature—a constant perfecting of the tools and processes which make the mastery of these forces possible. The history of America is a history of gigantic engineering feats and colossal mechanical constructions.

The skyscrapers of New York, the grain elevators of Minneapolis, the steel mills of Pittsburgh, the oil wells of Oklahoma, the copper mines of Butte, the lumber yards of Seattle give the American industrial epic its diapason.

Environment, however, is not in itself art but only raw material which becomes art when reconstructed by the artist according to the requirement of aesthetic form. The artist cannot and should not, therefore, attempt a literal soulless transcription of the American scene but rather give a penetrating creative interpretation of it, which, while including everything relevant to the subject depicted, would exclude everything irrelevant to the plastic possibilities of that subject.

Every epoch conditions the artist's attitude and manner of his expression very subtly and in devious ways. He observes and absorbs environmental facts, social currents, philosophic speculation and then chooses the elements for his work in such fashion and focuses attention on such aspects of the environment as will reveal his own esthetics vision as the essential character of the environment which conditioned it.

The dominant trend in America today is towards an industrialization and standardization which require precise adjustment of structure to function which dictate an economic utilization of processes and materials and thereby foster in man a spirit of objectivity excluding all emotional aberration and accustom his vision to shapes and colors not paralleled in nature.

The dominant trend in America today, beneath all the apparent chaos and confusion is towards order and organization which find their outward sign and symbol in the rigid geometry of the American city: in the verticals of its smokestacks, in the parallels of its car tracks, the squares of its streets, the cubes of its factories, the arc of its bridges, the cylinders of its gas tanks.

Upon this underlying mathematical pattern as scaffolding may be built a solid plastic structure of great intricacy and subtlety. The artist who confronts his task with original vision and accomplished craftsmanship will note with exactitude the articulation, solidity and weight of advancing and receding masses, will define with precision the space around objects and between them; he will organize line, plane and volume into a well knit design, arrange color and light into a pattern of contrast and harmony and weave organically into every composition an all prevading [sic] rhythm and equilibrium. The true artist will in sum objectify the dominant experience of our epoch in plastic terms that possess value for more than this epoch alone.

A composition is most effective when its elements are used in a double function: associative, establishing contact with concrete objects of the real world and aesthetic, serving to create plastic values. The intrinsic importance of the contemporary theme may thus be immensely enhanced by the formal significance of the treatment. In this manner, the flowing rhythm of modern America may be gripped and stayed and its synthesis eloquently rendered in the native idiom.

The whole of mankind is vitally affected by industrial development and if the artist can make his work clear in its intention, convincing in its reality, inevitable in its logic, his potential audience will be practically universal.

And this is perhaps as high a goal as any artist might hope to attain.

From *The Machine-Age Exposition* (New York: Little Review, 1927), 18–19.

Machine Ornament (1929)

While it may sound almost hackneyed and provincial to speak now of the interrelation between art and industry, the fact is that, contrary to prevalent opinion, the exact nature of this interrelationship has never yet been the subject of a competent or thorough investigation. Moreover, the extent of the effect exerted by industry on art has been somewhat exaggerated. Considerable in architecture, less so in painting, still less in music and literature, it is practically negligible in applied arts.

A close study of existing ornament in wallpaper, textile, masonry, iron work, furniture, embroidery, etc., would give little or no clue to the fact that we are living in an industrial world; existing ornament forms a repository of every motif known to history: primitive man's birds, snake, fish; Egyptian lotus and scarab; Greek acanthus and honeysuckle; Indian crocodile; Medieval gargoyle, etc.—all mixed with indiscriminate tolerance. The stock or traditional motifs has been drained to turn the modern interior into a cluttered shop of unhygienic curios and the exterior into a conglomeration of decorative inanities. An aesthetician with a penchant for sociologic speculation would not be wrong perhaps to detect in this phenomenon a parallel to the economic Law of Conspicuous Waste.

This condition is one of the many things that point to an obvious and recognized disparity between life and art. Egyptian and Greek ornament reveal unmistakably their source in contemporary life. The development of ornamental animal motifs among hunting tribes and plant motifs among agricultural tribes are clear proofs that the primitives drew on those environmental factors upon which their existence depended.

In its constant evolution, however, and the growing complexity, life left behind it the point at which art had once touched it. A con-

flict developed between old expression seeking to perpetuate itself
and new circumstances tending to destroy it. During this process,
ornament has become so repetitious, overloaded and trite as to constitute a serious problem to everyone interested in applied art.
Whether one recognizes the social implications of art or believes in
the complete autonomy of aesthetic expression, the need for some
sounder based and more substantially planned applied art will be
generally admitted.

I shall here try to outline tentatively, though by no means hastily,
what seems to me possible procedure towards the solution of the
problem. A cursory glance at the frieze of a building, the carving of
furniture, the design of wallpaper, the embroidery of a dress and a
thousand other objects where ornament is used will show at once
that familiar and historic ornament is *organic,* that is, based on the
conventionalization of plant, animal or human form. The machine
and its products open an inexhaustible source of new *machine* ornament based on the conventionalization of inorganic, mechanical,
geometric form. And just as older organic ornament—concentric,
asymmetric, repetitive—used animals and plants in whole or in part
(wings, scales, leaves, figures), so can the new machine ornament use
machinery and its parts (cams, wheels, shafts, cogs, screws) in a co-
ordination of imitated, borrowed and suggested shapes to achieve results similar in scope and application.

Unpublished manuscript, Louis Lozowick Papers, Archives of
American Art, Roll 1336: 2316–2317.

Lithography: Abstraction and Realism (1930)

Lithography, like wood-engraving and etching, is so often used for illustrative, literary purposes that representation has come to be considered its characteristic trait. As a matter of fact, lithography not only lends itself to abstraction, but close analysis will show that even in the work of the most conservative artists conventions are employed which are basically abstract. When the graphic artist draws the outline of a tree or a house or a human face, and fills parts of this outline with black or gray to represent shadow, leaving other parts white to represent light, he is having recourse to a convention that has no counterpart in actuality. The graphic artist converts a three-dimensional multicolored world of light and darks. And it is the manner in which this conversion is accomplished by the effective distribution and arrangement of black, gray, and white areas, lines and spots that distinguishes the good lithograph from the bad.

This essential trait in graphic art makes it easily comprehensible why it is so generally practised among the moderns. The modern artist asserts something like the following: a house is constructed to answer a definite function which is, according to Corbusier, that of a machine for living in; when transferred by the artist to canvas or paper this house at once acquires a new function, that of a machine for eliciting aesthetic emotion ([Amédée] Ozenfant). Certain parts of this house, however necessary in practical application, may prove to be entirely superfluous as compositional units in a picture. It is the duty of the artist then to change in shape and appearance, to remove the roof or windows, etc., until it conforms to his compositional scheme. This explains in part the widespread use of distortion and deformation among the moderns of all schools.

Lithography in common with painting has employed symmetric, asymmetric, circular, diagonal, etc., compositional patterns, but there are certain technical procedures which are peculiar to itself. Lithography is a more flexible medium than etching or wood-engraving. By the use of pen and lithographic ink one can make a linear drawing as fine as a dry point; by varying the width of the stroke or by scratching, a wood cut effect can be easily obtained; a skilled use of brush and lithographic ink in different degrees of concentration and dilution will produce the effect of a "wash." Naturally, the best results for every art are achieved within its own proper field, and that for lithography is tone in infinite gradation from the most subdued, softest silvery grays to the blackest velvety blacks. The grainy surface of the stone lends the tone a special, a specific textural quality.

The flexibility of the lithographic medium creates endless possibilities for experiment. Contemporary American lithography is rich in examples: the fine pencil strokes and textures in [Yasuo] Kuniyoshi, the combination of wash, brush, and crayon in [Ernest] Fiene and [Adolphe] Dehn, the wavy line and dots in Wanda Gag that lend a romantic shimmer to the most commonplace scene, the scratched white lines on a black background in [George] Biddle, the lines and dots and crosshatch in Stuart Davis and [Jan] Matulka, etc. Here are a few more tricks of the trade. If you use fine or coarse spatter, then apply pen or brush to it, or scratch parts of it; if you flood the stone with black, then scratch out parts of it with a fine or dull needle, or rub sandpaper on it, or run a "jumper"[1] over it; if you place thin paper over lace or metal or wood, rub a lithographic block over it and then transfer that to stone. In all these cases you get a corresponding variety of effects. Though this may sound like a series of laboratory exercises to an outsider, it forms the daily routine of a practitioner.

The great danger of extreme preoccupation with formalism is that it is likely to degenerate into decoration and ornamentation; it has indeed done so in many cases, though more in painting than in graphic art (and more in Europe than in America). Born of a healthy contemporary impulse formalism gradually drifted away from close contact with life into experiment for the sake of experiment and even distortion for the sake of distortion. However, the last several years have witnessed a reaction against extreme abstraction. German expressionists, Italian futurists, French cubists have turned from dissection of natural objects to the creation of perfectly comprehensible still lifes, portraits, and genre pictures. A theoretic justification was at once found, of course. Abstraction has always been only a means. There is no theoretic reason why the technical gains of abstraction cannot be used in the representation of an actual scene. The fact that a drawing resembles in certain respects a concrete object does not necessarily mean that it cannot at the same time be also a fine work of art.

Furthermore, many of these artists lay stress not on reality as such but on contemporary reality. Michelangelo, Rembrandt, Goya, Watteau, Chardin, Daumier show differences as much in subject matter as in technique. Great changes in the history of art have been thematic as well as stylistic. With the new tendency (which is common to graphic no less than to other arts) there is again the danger of being so absorbed in representation as to fall into photographic actualism. Against this, however, the experience of a quarter of a century stands guard.

A parallel tendency toward moderation is also evident in America. The transition is perhaps easier here because American artists never went to the extremes practised in Europe, certainly not the graphic artists. Given the fluidity of contemporary American life, the riches and variety of its contemporary themes is [sic] inexhaustible. The passing scene is excellently suited to the graphic artist in general, and to the lithographer, because of the technical elasticity and resourcefulness of his medium, in particular. If the graphic artist can avoid the danger of ornamental abstraction on the one hand and photographic actualism on the other, if he can apply the force of the new technical equipment to the wealth of new themes, no prospect for what he might accomplish would be too hopeful.

From *Space* 1, No. 2 (March 1930): 31–33.

Art in the Service of the Proletariat (1931)

On numerous occasions whenever American artists are called upon to express their views on their work or in art in general they invariably adopt an attitude of aggressive individualism. They declare that art is autonomous and that the artist is independent from masses and classes. This proves—if proof is necessary—how effective the ideology of the ruling class dominates the average artist. A moment's thought should expose the hollowness of such claims. Economically the artist is, of course, dependent for his livelihood on dealers, galleries, patrons. Besides, all of his methods, themes, etc., are historically conditioned. The fact, however, is that the very vehicle the painter uses—easel painting—the themes he selects—portrait, landscape, still-life—the individualistic philosophy he professes, all are a result of post-Renaissance capitalist development.

The battles that artists have fought have been battles of a purely formal nature. The academy whose practice is a mixture of Classicism, Romanticism, and Impressionism, is a powerful widely ramified organization with branches in all large and many small cities, with connections in government circles and a sure control of the art market. The modernists have been fighting this intrenched [sic] institution for twenty-five years and are now coming very close to victory. The downhill movement of post-war imperialism and the resultant general disillusion has turned the attention of art patrons away from disagreeable reality into the realm of formal and abstract experimentation. One collector after another has joined the camp of the modernists. Special museums have been opened for their works. [Roger Ward] Babson, the great financial authority on stocks and bonds and the money market, has found it necessary to send out a special weekly letter (a Babson Chart) recommending modern art as a good investment. Modern art has arrived. Needless to say the modernists have no contact whatever with the working class. They are satisfied to produce for few patrons than the proverbial Four Hundred.

It is in such an unfavorable atmosphere that the few American revolutionary artists have to carry on their work. These artists are grouped mainly around the John Reed Club and the New Masses. Their activity flows along several lines. They organize meetings and discussions to expose the class character of bourgeois art, to fight the influence of that art on the masses, and to agitate for the consolidation of proletarian forces. They offer their services to the working class in his [sic] political and economic battles by preparing posters for demonstrations, staging pageants, decorating workers plays, illustrating shop papers, and so on.

Within the field of art proper, the work of the revolutionary artist, while always maintaining a working-class orientation, shows certain varieties of method and theme. In the revolutionary political cartoon the artist's task is to make an annihilating attack on the capitalist regime in all its aspects, to show how inimical its existence is to the emancipation of the working class.

Here a variety of revolutionary stages must be noted. The American worker inevitably lives and works with cities and machines. But instead of portraying the apocalyptic city of the German Expressionists or the man and inhuman city of the Italian Futurists, the American revolutionary artist pictures it more as a prognostication than a fact. He departs from realistic appearance and paints the city as a product of that rationalization and economy which must prove allies of the working class in the building of socialism. The revolutionary artists are gradually working towards the acquisition of a synthetic style. They insist on the highest technical quality, not however at the expense of the message but only as something that can best help the effective delivery of that message. They have profited by the experiments in the art of the last twenty-five years. Thus they utilize the clear-cut laconic precision of certain younger artists; they take liberties with natural appearance whenever their theme requires it. They strive towards a style which must develop and mature as the revolutionary movement grows.

Daumier, one of the great forerunners of revolutionary art said, *Je suis de mon temps.* The American revolutionary artist would revise this to read: *Je suis de ma classe,* and make it clear beyond a doubt that *la classe ouvrière* is meant. For the American revolutionary artist is

above all the representative of the class of proletarians in their struggle for the overthrows [sic] of the capitalist system and for a new socialist society.

From *Literature of the World Revolution* (Moscow), No. 4 (1931):
126–127.

Towards a Revolutionary Art (1936)

When a new art current emerges, persisting over a long period of time, comprising a large number of adherents, exhibiting continuity of development, embodying a solid system of principles, we are justified in assuming that a fundamental change in society has taken place. In a broad generalization: Italian art of the fourteenth century, Dutch art of the seventeenth century, French art of the nineteenth century—each compared with the century preceding it might be taken as characteristic illustrations. Similarly—perhaps in even broader generalization—the emergence of a revolutionary art in the Soviet Union as in Japan, in Mexico as in Hungary, in Holland as in the United States, points to the presence of a revolutionary world situation, is in fact both a symbol and a product of that situation.

The capitalist press in a moment of unconscious clairvoyance has referred to the revolutionary artist as "class-struggle" artists. Excellent appelation [sic], for it identifies the revolutionary artist unmistakably. Like the artist of every age worth considering, the revolutionary artist proceeds from direct experience of immediate reality, knowing, however, that experience and reality have no meaning except in concrete connotation. The revolutionary artist proceeds from the patent factor that the class antagonisms, always present in capitalist society, have reached the acute stage of open class war. When capitalism "plans" industry by curtailing production, "solves" starvation by destroying food, and degrades the human personality, science and art to cash payments (to limit ourselves to a few short items), the conclusion is inescapable that the basic assumptions underlying capitalist society have lost their validity; that it has reached a stage of insoluble internal contradictions which only a shift of power can resolve.

In all parts of the world there are signs of incipient and open revolt against the system. The organized working class, joined by
growing numbers of intellectuals, farmers and other elements, and
guided by the philosophy of Karl Marx, is the only force that can
abolish it. Artists, like others, whether they want it or not, whether
they know it or not cannot remain outside of the situation described. We notice, in fact, everywhere the parallel process of fas-
cization and radicalization of art as representative of the two forces
in conflict. (The meaning of the so-called American school is trans-
parent. On one hand it attempts to corner the art market against
foreign competition; on the other hand it is the first step in the direction of a more aggressive chauvinism, a home style. Whether it
will also take the last step will depend entirely on how far reaction
travels in the United States.)

When the revolutionary artist expresses in his work the dissatis-
faction with, the revolt against, the criticism of the existing state of
affairs, when he seeks to awaken in his audience a desire to participate in the fight, he is, therefore, drawing on direct observation of
the world about him as well as on his most intimate, immediate,
blistering, blood-sweating experience, in the art gallery, in the bread
line, in the relief office. But as already indicated experience to him
is not a chance agglomeration of impressions but is related to long
training, to habits formed, to views assimilated and entertained at a
definite place and time; to him experience acquires significant
meaning by virtue of a revolutionary orientation. In sum, revolutionary art implies open-eyed observation, intense participation and
an ordered view of life. And by the same token revolutionary art
further implies that its provenance is not due to an arbitrary order
from any person or group but is decreed by history, is a consequence
of particular historic events.

Although the revolutionary artist will admit partisanship he will
most emphatically deny that it need affect unfavorably his work.
Obviously, if disinterestedness were in itself a guarantee of high
achievement all the tenth-rate Picassos would be geniuses; if social
partisanship resulted necessarily in inferior art Goya and Daumier
would have to be erased from the pages of art history. Nor does partisanship narrow the horizon of revolutionary art. Quite the contrary, the challenge of a new cause leads to the discovery of a new
storehouse of experience and the exploration of a new world of actuality. Even a tentative summary will show the vast possibilities,
ideologic and plastic; relations between the classes; relations within
each class; a clear characterization in historic perspective of the cap-

italist as employer, as philanthropist, as statesman, as art patron; the worker as victim, as striker, as hero, as comrade, as fighter for a better world; the unattached liberal, the unctuous priest, the labor racketeer; all the ills capitalist flesh is heir to—persons and events treated not as chance snapshot episodes but correlated among themselves shown in their dramatic antagonisms, made convincing by the living language of fact and made meaningful from the standpoint of a world philosophy. The very newness of the theme will forbid a conformity in technique.

Strictly speaking, contemporary revolutionary art is not altogether new. It already has an impressive history and many precursors of great talent. Almost as soon as industrial workers organized as a class in the early part of the nineteenth century, pictures began to appear which showed labor in its social position and historic role. [Philip] Tassaert, [Philippe] Jeanron, [Jankel] Adler, [Eugène] Laermans, [Gustave] Courbet, [Honoré] Daumier and many others pictured the working class in its daily occupations as well as on barricades and in strikes.

If contemporary revolutionary art stems in a continuous line from the artists enumerated, it descends in a collateral line from many more, throughout the ages. For the overwhelming mass of art across all history—Egyptian, Byzantine, Renaissance, Dutch, French, etc., has been art derived from social experience and directed to social ends, an art frankly partisan for one or another historic class.

Thus, the revolutionary artist has a rich cultural heritage to draw upon, absorb and utilize in his efforts toward the formation of a style appropriate to his needs. But just as no style can be created out of a vacuum, so no style can be carried over from one period to another without change. Certain elements in the cultural heritage such as the religious genre and pure abstraction are not usable at all. Other elements may have to be radically modified. The problem of how to utilize the cultural heritage will be best solved in practice—revolutionary art being still in process of formation. As an extreme instance one may take the revolutionary artist who has recourse to the method of surrealism. Like the surrealist he records within the same frame a series of events, distributed over several points of space and time (the surrealists are the latest but by no means the only ones to use this device which is, in fact, quite ancient), but unlike the surrealist he gives the events logical unity and ideological meaning; like the surrealist he uses a meticulous technique but unlike him he rejects its mystical application. Where the surrealist postulates irrationalism and automatism, the revolutionary artist must substitute reason, volition, clarity. The message will fail of its object unless it is clear and forceful; the meaning will not carry conviction unless it is effective. And this, by the way, is only another aspect of the form–content relation. It is therefore a perversion of the truth to accuse the revolutionary artist—as is done so often—of disregarding the problem of form. Beginning with Marx and Engels (who presumably knew their own minds) the importance of formal excellence in art has been stressed by every Marxist who has written on the subject. The Marxists maintain, however, that while all artistic creation implies formal organization, it cannot be reduced to it, much less exhausted by it. Content and form are mutually interpenetrating; both derive from social practice, are outgrowths of social exigencies.

To illustrate by example (one among many) from the history of Christian art: Early Christianity was a movement of the enslaved, the impoverished and oppressed; their art of the Catacombs (second and third centuries) followed the style and imagery of Roman fresco painting and incorporated in their work the humble subject-matter from their own life and beliefs; stone masons, agricultural works, the figure of Christ (Orpheus) as the Good Shepherd, all done in subdued colors and treated with a directness and simplicity which invite intimacy between image and audience. With the spread of Christianity among larger masses, with the rise of a priesthood and the growing entrenchment of the church as part of the state apparatus, new elements came into Christian art (fifth and sixth century): the formal dignity of the Byzantine, elaborateness and solemnity. Art emerged from the underground catacombs to make its abode in caste-ridden houses of worship. The image of Christ as the Good Shepherd gave way to the concept of Christ as Lord, as powerful ruler with all the attributes of regal authority, throne, scepter, splendid raiment, an increasing army of royal attendants (pictorial elements these, inseparably both content and form). The resplendent colors, the precious stones, the rigid formal dignity served as a wall to keep the congregation at a reverent distance. Christianity had become the state religion, admirably responsive to the needs of the ruling autocracy.

In this example which could be profitably analyzed in greater detail, we see with striking clarity how old forms are grafted on new contents, how new forms evolve to meet new social situations, how reciprocally related are all the elements involved and how contingent on the underlying class structure. If historic precedent is any indication the revolutionary artist may look confidently to the develop-

ment of a style appropriate to his aims. For the present, revolutionary art is still a direction but a direction well defined as to its source
and its goal.

A revolutionary orientation must ultimately affect even the treatment of old genres such as still life and landscape. Which brings up
the question of whether the revolutionary artist should at all deal
with them. The formation of a revolutionary art is not the task to be
achieved by one world or even by one artist. It is the labor of a movement; whether one painter or another occasionally paints a still life or
a landscape is, viewed in large perspective, of little consequence.

A more serious question is: can the artist who has been trained
in the dispassionate contemplative tradition change into a participant
and revolutionary? Unquestionably yes—with reservations—even as
the conditions under which he lives and to which he must adjust
himself, change. In proportion as his ideology forms and matures
and becomes part of his mental make-up his art will seek to express
his feelings and thoughts. But the process is not mechanical; it depends on the mobility of character in the individual artist, on how
set he is in his ways; it may be very painless with certain artists, very
slow with others and all but impossible with some. The process
should be in every way encouraged—it cannot be forced. But again,
in a movement of such major proportions the behavior of a few single artists is inconsequential.

We are in the midst of a vast, decisive transformation, economic,
social, cultural by which no one is unaffected. Where among contemporary art currents can we look to the expression of this
momentous event? In the moribund symbolism of the doddering
academy? In the "hypnagogic" trances of the surrealists? In the
tabloid thrills of the American school? Whatever else might be said
about revolutionary art, it does not play sycophant to "disinterested"
collectors, nor cater to the speculative needs of the dealers. It grows
out of profound conviction of the artist and the living issues of society. Fortified by a revolutionary tradition (present—if neglected—in
American art as in the art of other countries) the revolutionary artist
stands before an ideal and a task to which all artists not directly interested in the maintenance of the *status quo* can rally. To make art
auxiliary to the building [of] a new society is not to degrade but to
elevate it. An art to be valuable must be historically on time. Revolutionary art makes sure to be in the vanguard rather than in the
rearguard of history.

From *Art Front* 2 (July–August 1936): 12–14.

Credo (1947)

From the innumerable choices which our complex and tradition-laden civilization presents to the artist, I have chosen one which seems to suit my training and temperament. I might characterize it thus: Industry Harnessed by Man for the Benefit of Mankind.

Obviously this is not in itself art but the raw material in the sense that religious fervor was raw material for the Medieval artists, or mundane satisfaction for the Renaissance artists, or the inexhaustible variety of the visual world for the nineteenth-century artist—raw material that must be hammered and shaped into art.

When Giotto painted St. Francis, faith and conviction came first; problems of form and color followed. We could do no more with a contemporary theme; and we should attempt no less.

I have chosen an idea which seems to offer rich rewards to the creative artist if he communicates it to the spectator in the precise pictorial language appropriate to it. I cannot say in what measure I have succeeded, but it has been great fun trying.

From *100 Contemporary American Jewish Painters and Sculptors* (New York: YKUF [Yiddisher kultur farband] Art Section, 1947), 126.

MAJOR EXHIBITIONS
(One-person and group)

"Louis Lozowick—New York: Ausstellung," K. E. Twardy Book Shop, Berlin, June 1922.

"Louis Lozowick, New York," Gallerie Alfred Heller, Berlin, August 1–September 1, 1923.

"Paintings and Drawings by Louis Lozowick," J. B. Neumann's New Art Circle, New York, January 18–February 4, 1926.

"Lithographs by Louis Lozowick," Advertising Club, New York, February 1926.

"International Theatre Exposition," Steinway Hall, New York, February–March, 1926.

"International Exhibition of Modern Art Assembled by Société Anonyme," The Brooklyn Museum, New York, November 19, 1926–January 1, 1927.

"The Machine-Age Exposition," Steinway Hall, New York, May 6–26, 1927.

"Drawings and Prints by Louis Lozowick," Museum of Western Art, Moscow, U.S.S.R., January 1928.

"Exposition de dessins et gravures de Louis Lozowick," Galerie Zak, Paris, July 11–25, 1928.

"Lithographs by Louis Lozowick," Weyhe Gallery, New York, October 28–November 9, 1929.

"Paintings, Drawings, and Lithographs by Louis Lozowick," Weyhe Gallery, New York City, March 23–April 4, 1931.

Fig. 29 *What Never Happened,* ink and pencil, 1970.

"Oil Paintings, Water Colors, and Original Lithographs by Louis Lozowick," Courvoisier Galleries, San Francisco, March 7–19, 1932.

"Projects for Murals by Hugo Gellert, Louis Lozowick, Wm. Gropper, and A. Refregier," Decora Gallery, New York City, March 10–31, 1932.

"Prints, Drawings, Paintings by Louis Lozowick," Stendahl Gallery, Los Angeles, April 1932.

"Paintings and Lithographs by Louis Lozowick," Weyhe Gallery, New York, April 6–18, 1936.

"American Realists and Magic Realists," The Museum of Modern Art, New York, February 10–March 1943.

"Prints by Louis Lozowick," Smithsonian Institution, Washington, D.C., March 27–April 23, 1950.

"Louis Lozowick: A Retrospective Show," YM-YWHA, Newark, New Jersey, May 1–15, 1960.

"The Precisionist View in American Art," The Walker Art Center, Minneapolis, Minnesota, November 13–December 25, 1960. The exhibition was also shown at the Whitney Museum of American Art, New York, Detroit Institute of Arts, Los Angeles County Museum, and San Francisco Museum of Art.

"Louis Lozowick: Paintings and Drawings, 1923–29," Zabriskie Gallery, New York, January 3–21, 1961.

"Louis Lozowick," Argus Gallery, Madison, New Jersey, Fall 1965.

"Louis Lozowick," Bloomfield College Art Gallery, Bloomfield, New Jersey, January 8–26, 1968.

"Louis Lozowick: Graphic Retrospective," Newark Public Library, Newark, New Jersey, February 28–March 28, 1969.

"Three Contemporary Artists: Drawings 1920–1970" (Louis Lozowick, Katherine Schmidt, and Morris Kantor), Zabriskie Gallery, New York City, January 23–March 6, 1971. Shown concurrently: "Louis Lozowick: Works of the Last Decade," January 23–February 1971.

"Abstraction and Realism: 1923–1943 Paintings, Drawings, and Lithographs by Louis Lozowick," Robert Hull Fleming Museum, The University of Vermont, Burlington, March 14–April 18, 1971.

"Louis Lozowick: Lithographs," Whitney Museum of American Art, New York, November 21, 1972–January 1, 1973.

"Louis Lozowick: Drawings," Zabriskie Gallery, New York, November 25–December 23, 1972.

"Louis Lozowick: Lithographs and Drawings," Newark Public Library, New Jersey, December 20, 1972–January 31, 1973.

"Precisionist Louis Lozowick: Paintings and Lithographs," Dain Gallery, New York, January 2–31, 1973.

"Louis Lozowick 1892–1973," Department of Art and Music, Seton Hall University, South Orange, New Jersey, October 14–November 11, 1973.

"Louis Lozowick 1892–1973: Retrospective," Hunterdon Art Center, Clinton, New Jersey, June 16–July 14, 1974.

"Louis Lozowick: Lithographs and Drawings," The Art Corner, Millburn, New Jersey, October 6–26, 1974.

"Louis Lozowick: Drawings and Lithographs," National Collection of Fine Arts, Smithsonian Institution, Washington, D.C., September 12–November 23, 1975.

"Louis Lozowick: Paintings, Drawings, Prints," Lunn Gallery/ Graphics International Ltd., Washington, D.C., October 4–November 5, 1975.

"Louis Lozowick's New York," Associated American Artists, New York, January 5–31, 1976.

"America as Art," National Collection of Fine Arts, Smithsonian Institution, Washington, D.C., April 30–November 7, 1976.

"The Golden Door: Artist-Immigrants of America, 1876–1976," Hirshhorn Museum and Sculpture Garden, Smithsonian Institution, Washington, D.C., May 20–October 20, 1976.

"Urban Focus: Industrial Drawings by Louis Lozowick; Photographs by Berenice Abbott, Ralph Steiner, and Ralston Crawford," Zabriskie Gallery, New York, September 28–October 23, 1976.

"Lozowick: The Full Range of His Prints," June 1 Gallery, Bethlehem, Connecticut, September 17–October 9, 1977.

"Louis Lozowick, American Precisionist, Retrospective," Long Beach Museum of Art, California, February 26–May 7, 1978.

"Lithographs and Drawings by Louis Lozowick," Summit Gallery, Ltd., New York, March 27–April 20, 1979.

"Louis Lozowick (1892–1973): Works in the Precisionist Manner," Hirschl and Adler Galleries, Inc., New York, February 16–March 15, 1980.

"Louis Lozowick's Lithographs," Hom Gallery, Washington, D.C.,

December 5, 1980–January 10, 1981.

"America: Dream and Depression 1920/40," Akademie der Kunst, West Berlin, Germany, November 9–December 28, 1980, and Kunstverein, Hamburg, West Germany, January 11–February 15, 1981.

"Louis Lozowick (1892–1973): Bridges," Zabriskie Gallery, New York, October 18–November 8, 1981.

"Louis Lozowick: American Precisionist," Kornbluth Gallery, Fairlawn, New Jersey, October 18–November 8, 1981.

"The Prints of Louis Lozowick," Associated American Artists, New York, November 1–November 24, 1982.

"The Prints of Louis Lozowick," National Museum of American Art, Smithsonian Institution, Washington, D.C., November 5, 1982–April 10, 1983.

"Louis Lozowick Lithographs," Brunner Gallery and Museum, Iowa State Center, Ames, Iowa, December 1–January 13, 1985.

"Louis Lozowick: Urban Images," Vanderwaude/Ananlaum Gallery, New York, February 20–March 30, 1985.

"Louis Lozowick: Images of New York," Sylvan Cole Gallery, New York, October 12–October 31, 1985.

"Lithographs of Louis Lozowick," Hirschl J. Adler Galleries, Inc., New York, September 25–October 25, 1986.

"The Machine Age in America, 1918–1941," The Brooklyn Museum, New York, October 17, 1986–February 16, 1987; Museum of Art, Carnegie Institute, Pittsburgh, April 4–June 28, 1987; Los Angeles County Museum of Art, August 16–October 18, 1987; The High Museum of Art, Atlanta, December 1, 1987–February 14, 1988.

"Louis Lozowick, Oils and Drawings," Sid Deutch Gallery, New York, October 6–October 31, 1990.

"Painting A Place in America: Jewish Artists in New York 1900–1945," The Jewish Museum, New York, May 16–September 29, 1991.

"Louis Lozowick Centennial Exhibition," Associated American Artist Gallery, New York City, December 2–December 31, 1992.

Group Exhibitions

Lozowick exhibited prints, paintings, and drawings with a wide
variety of organizations, and the numbers of exhibitions have
continued to grow since his death. In Germany in the early 1920s,
he exhibited at Grosse Berliner Kunstaustelung, Berlin (1922); the
Juryfreie Kunstshau, Berlin (1922); the International Exhibition,
Düsseldorf (1922); the First Zenit International Exhibitiion of
New Art, Belgrade (1924); and the New Objectivity exhibition at
Mannheim in 1925. In the United States, Lozowick's paintings
were shown regularly in exhibitions of the Salons of America,
Society of Independent Artists, John Reed Club, the American
Print Makers, the American Institute of Graphic Arts' Fifty Prints
of the Year, the Society of American Graphic Artists, An American
Group, Educational Alliance Art School, the Whitney Studio
Club, and the Whitney Museum of American Art. His works
were also regularly accepted for the large annual and biennial
shows held at the Carnegie Institute, Pittsburgh; the Corcoran
Gallery, Washington, D.C.; The Pennsylvania Academy of Fine
Arts, Philadelphia; and The National Academy of Design, New
York City. During the 1930s and early 1940s, there were numerous
group exhibitions organized on behalf of the New Deal projects,
the American Artists' Congress, Inc., and Artists for Victory.
Lozowick's prints were consistently chosen for, and often awarded
major prizes in, international and national competitions such as
those held at the Art Institute of Chicago, the Cleveland Museum
of Art, the Library of Congress, and The Brooklyn Museum. As a
member of the Audubon Artists and the National Society of
Painters in Casein, he exhibited regularly with these groups.

Represented

The works of Louis Lozowick are represented in most of the major
museums and collections nationally. These include National Mu-
seum of American Art; Brooklyn Museum; Carnegie Institute;
Cleveland Museum of Art; Hirshhorn Museum and Sculpture
Garden; Jersey City Museum; Library of Congress; Los Angeles
County Art Museum; Montclair Art Museum, Montclair, New
Jersey; Museum of Fine Arts, Boston; Museum of Modern Art,
New York; New York Public Library at 42nd Street, Newark
Library and Museum; University of Massachusetts, Amherst;
University of Texas, Austin; Victoria and Albert Museum; Walker
Art Center; Whitney Museum of American Art; Art Gallery,
Yale University.

CHRONOLOGY

1892
Born December 10 in Ludvinovka, Ukraine, son of Abraham and Mary (Tafipolsky) Lozowick.

1896
Mother dies.

1903
Moves to Kiev with his brother and begins studies at the Kiev Art Institute.

1901–1905
Attends Kiev Art Institute.

1906
Leaves Russia and joins his brother in the United States.

1907–1911
Lives in New Jersey; supports himself with a variety of jobs while attending Barringer High School, Newark.

1907–1908
Attends National Academy of Design, receiving Silver Medal for Antique Figure Class in 1908.

1912–1915
Attends National Academy of Design, New York City, where he studies with Leon Kroll, George Willoughby Maynard, Ivan Olinsky, Douglas Volk, and others.

1915–1918
Attends Ohio State University, completing his degree in three years and graduating Phi Beta Kappa. Volunteers for U.S. Army

in June 1918; assigned to Medical Corps, Charleston, South
Carolina.

1919

Discharged from army June 23, though continues to work with
Medical Corps until August. Travels across country, visiting Pitts-
burgh, Chicago, Minneapolis, and several other cities. Granted
U.S. citizenship.

1920

Teaches the history of art at the Educational Alliance Art School in
the winter. Leaves for Paris in spring or summer, arriving in Paris
by the fall 1920. Enrolls in French language classes at the Sorbonne.

1922

Moves to Berlin in winter (probably February or March). Enrolls
in Friedrick Wilhelms Universität. Begins to paint seriously; paints
first of his "City" compositions and begins semiabstract ink drawings, which become known as "Machine Ornaments." Establishes
close friendships with Russian artists in Germany, especially El
Lissitsky. On a brief trip to Russia in summer, meets Malevich,
Tatlin, Al'tman, Shterenberg, Puni. Contributes articles and translations to *Broom*. Exhibits in the Juryfreie Kunstschau in Berlin,
with the Novembergruppe at the Grosse Berliner Kunstausstellung,
and at the International Exhibition in Düsseldorf. First one-person
exhibition at K. E. Twardy Book Shop, Berlin, in June.

1923

Makes his first lithographs, *Cleveland* and *Chicago*. Second one-
person exhibition at the Gallerie Alfred Heller, Berlin, in August.
Returns to Paris for a short visit in the fall.

1924

Returns to New York City by February. Lectures on modern
Russian art for Société Anonyme and the Educational Alliance Art
School. In April (9–19), three of Lozowick's works are included in
the First Zenit International Exhibition of New Art, mounted by
Zenit Galerie in Belgrade.

1925

With the encouragement of Carl Zigrosser, director of the Weyhe
Gallery, resumes work in lithography. Begins painting second
series of "Cities." Included in the New Objectivity exhibition,
Mannheim, Germany. His lectures on modern Russian art for the
Société Anonyme are published by the Société Anonyme as *Mod-*

ern Russian Art. Joins the organizational staff of the *New Masses* as a contributing editor.

1926

Exhibition of "Cities" and "Machine Ornaments" at J. B. Neumann's New Art Circle in New York City (January–February). Designs sets for Georg Kaiser's *Gas,* produced by Marion Gering at the Kenneth Sawyer Goodman Memorial Theatre of the Art Institute of Chicago in January–February. In March designs window display and backdrop and platform for fashion show for centennial celebration of Lord & Taylor department store, New York. Included in the International Theatre Exhibition held in February, organized by the Little Review Gallery, and in the Société Anonyme's International Exhibition of Modern Art held at the Brooklyn Museum in November. Joins executive board of *New Masses.*

1927–1928

Exhibits in the Machine-Age Exposition in May 1927; his article, "The Americanization of Art," is included in the exhibition catalogue. Lectures and designs posters for the Workers' Drama League and the New Playwrights' Theatre. Leaves for Europe and U.S.S.R. in the fall of 1927 in connection with his one-person exhibitions at the Museum of Western Art in Moscow in January 1928 and at the Galerie Zak in Paris in July 1928. During trip, visits Chagall and Léger in Paris and Moholy-Nagy at the Bauhaus in Dessau. Returns to New York in the summer of 1928.

1929

First major one-person print exhibition of lithographs at Weyhe Gallery. Lives next door to Weyhe Gallery at 792 Lexington Avenue. Summers at the Yaddo Art Colony. *Still Life #2* (lithograph) awarded Brewster Prize at the First International Lithography and Wood Engraving Exhibition, Art Institute of Chicago. Helps organize the John Reed Club and becomes a charter member, remaining active in the Club until its dissolution in 1934.

1930

Brooklyn Bridge awarded first prize for lithography at the Third Exhibition of American Lithography, Philadelphia Print Club. Summers at the Yaddo Art Colony.

1931

City on a Rock (lithograph) receives first prize of $1,000 at the International Print Competition, Cleveland Print Club. Executive

secretary of the John Reed Club and art editor of *New Masses.*
Tours Soviet Central Asia (Tajikistan) with an international group
of writers, which also includes his friend Joshua Kunitz. Meets
Adele Turner, whom he marries later in the year.

1932
Exhibits at Stendahl Gallery in Los Angeles and Courvoisier Galleries in San Francisco in connections with a lecture tour through
California, followed by a trip to Mexico. Elected international secretary of the John Reed Club at its national convention. Summers
at the Yaddo Art Colony, where he completes many of his lithographs of Tajikistan.

1933
Included in the "Social Viewpoint in Art" exhibition sponsored
by the John Reed Club; leads tour of the Soviet Union in the
summer.

1934
Employed briefly by the Public Works of Art Project, New York
City. Lectures and teaches lithography with Jacob Friedland at the
John Reed Club School of Art. Included in the "Revolutionary
Front—1934" exhibition sponsored by the John Reed Club.

1935
Travels to U.S.S.R. in the summer. Participates in the organization
of the first American Artists Congress. Employed by Graphic Arts
Division of the Works Progress Administration late in year.

1936–1937
Transferred to Treasury Relief Art Project early in 1936; begins
work on two large paintings of Manhattan for New York City Post
Office. Becomes executive secretary of the American Artists'
League and delivers an address at the first American Artists' Congress in February 1936. A member of the Board of Control and an
instructor of lithography at the newly founded American Artists
School. His *Five Year Plan Comes to a Caucasian Village,* a lithograph
of 1932, was included in the school's print series of 1936.

1938
Returns to Graphic Arts Division, WPA; employment terminates
October 25, 1940.

1943
Included in the exhibition American Realists and Magic Realists at
the Museum of Modern Art, New York City. Teaches at the Edu-

cational Alliance Art School, New York City. Lives in Croton-on-Hudson, New York. His son Lee is born November 18.

1945
Moves to South Orange, New Jersey.

1948
Nuns on Wall Street (lithograph) awarded prize by Rochester Print Club. For the next decade, works independently; lectures, writes, and travels extensively while continuing to participate in numerous group exhibitions.

1954
Travels to Israel, Greece, and Turkey.

1956
Travels to Guatemala and Mexico, primarily in Yucatan.

1959
Trip around the world, including Japan and Central Asia.

1960
Included in "The Precisionist View in American Art" exhibition organized by the Walker Art Center, Minneapolis.

1961
One-person exhibition at the Zabriskie Gallery, New York City; several "City" paintings purchased by Joseph Hirshhorn.

1962
Travels to Peru and Bolivia.

1964
Travels to Israel, Egypt, Cambodia, and Africa.

1965
Visits U.S.S.R.

1968
Travels to Israel and Europe.

1969
Travels to Portugal and Spain.

1971
Visits Yugoslavia. Elected to membership in the National Academy of Design as Associate National Academician (A.N.A.) in the Graphic Arts Section.

1972

Elected to rank of National Academician (N.A.) in Graphic Arts Section of the National Academy of Design. Makes a cross-country trip to California in an automobile. Major retrospective of his lithographs at the Whitney Museum of American Art, New York City.

1973

Important one-person exhibition at Seton Hall University, South Orange, New Jersey. Dies September 9 in South Orange, New Jersey.

NOTES

Prologue

1. L. Lozowick, *Survivor from a Dead Age.*

2. Ibid.

3. Ibid.

4. Ibid.

5. Ibid.

6. P. Florensky, "Khramovoe deistvo kak sintez iskusstva," in *Makovets,* Moscow, No. 1 (1922): 28–32.

7. Lozowick, *Survivor from a Dead Age.*

8. See K. Malevich: "O poezii" in *Izobrazitel'noe iskusstvo,* Petrograd, No. 1 (1919): 31–35.

9. Lozowick, *Survivor from a Dead Age.*

10. Ibid.

11. Malevich, "O poezii," 31.

12. A. Kruchenykh, untitled leaflet published in Baku in 1921. Republished in V. Markov (ed.), *Manifesty i programmy russkikh futuristov* (Munich: Fink, 1967), 180.

13. Letter from Kazimir Malevich to Mikhail Matiushin dated July 3, 1913. Translated in *K.S. Malevich. Essays,* Vol. 4, T. Andersen, ed. (Copenhagan: Borgen, 1978), 204.

14. "Pervyi Vserossiisskii s'ezd baiachei budushchego" in *Zhurnal za sem' dnei,* St. Petersburg, No. 29 (1913): 606.

15. Quoted in T. Loguine, *Gontcharova et Larionov* (Paris: Klincksieck, 1971), 132.

16. V. Val'ter: "Rassuzhdeniia o muzyke. Skriabin i Stravinsky" in *Zhar-ptitsa,* Berlin, No. 6 (1922): 39–40.

17. Lozowick, *Survivor from a Dead Age.*

18. Ibid.

19. Such was the sentiment and purpose of the exhibition "5 x 5 = 25" organized in Moscow in 1921 and mentioned by

Lozowick. Rodchenko gave Lozowick a copy of the "5 x 5 = 25" catalogue.

20. "Deklaratsiia Associatsii khudozhnikov revoliutsionnoi Rossii" (1922). Translated in *Russian Art of the Avant-Garde,* John Bowlt, ed. (London: Thames and Hudson, 1988), 266.

21. Lozowick, *Survivor from a Dead Age.*

22. "OST. Platforma" (1929). Translation in Bowlt, *Russian Art of the Avant-Garde,* 281.

23. L. Lozowick, "Amerikanizatsiia iskusstva" in *Vestnik inostrannoi literatury,* Moscow, No. 1 (1928).

24. B. Rapoport, Introduction to *Vystavka risunkov sovremennogo amerikanskogo khudozhnika Lui Lozovika* (catalogue of Lozowick's one-man exhibition at the Museum of New Western Art, Moscow, 1928). Quoted in *Iz istorii khudozhestvennoi zhizni SSSR. Internatsional'nye sviazi v oblasti izobrazitel'nogo iskusstva 1917–1940,* L. Aleshina and N. Yavorskaia (compilers) (Moscow: Iskusstvo, 1987), 131.

25. Dzh. Friman (Joseph Freeman), "Amerikanskii khudozhnik Lui Lozovik" in *Vestnik inostrannoi literatury,* No. 12 (1928): 103–109.

26. Lozowick, *Survivor from a Dead Age.*

27. Lozowick wrote on the John Reed Club for the catalogue. See L. Lozowick, "Klub Dzhona Rida v SASSh" in *Antiimperialisticheskaia vystavka,* Moscow (1931): 29–31.

28. The exhibition opened in March 1931, even though the catalogue is dated 1931.

29. S. An-ski, "Evreiskoe narodnoe tvorchestvo" in *Perezhitoe,* Vol. 1 (St. Petersburg, 1909), 297.

30. Lozowick, *Survivor from a Dead Age.*

31. Ibid.

32. L. Lozowick, "What, Then, Is Jewish Art?" in *Menorah Journal,* New York (January–March 1947): 103–110.

33. B. Aronson and I. Rybak, "The Path of Jewish Painting," in *Oifgang* (1919) (in Yiddish). Quoted in G. Kazovsky, "Evreiskoe iskusstvo v Rossii. 1900–1948. Etapy istorii" in *Sovetskoe iskusstvoznanie,* Moscow, No. 27 (1991): 247.

34. Lozowick, *Survivor from a Dead Age.*

35. Ibid.

Chapter 1

1. The first name, "Nikolai," refers to Tsar Nicholas II (Nikolai Aleksandrovich); the last name, "Pavlovich," refers to Tsar Nicholas I (Nikolai Pavlovich).

2. Here and elsewhere, Lozowick speaks of "Jewish" as a language; clearly, Yiddish is meant.

3. It is unclear if Lozowick's statement that Lev Kupernik defended the victims of the Kishinev pogrom is accurate. Kupernik was best known in the Jewish community for his defense the Jewish villagers accused of murdering a Christian girl in the blood libel suit of 1879 in Kutaisi, Georgia, and his defense of the Jews accused of mounting pogroms against the Russian population in Gomel in the summer of 1903. The latter trial occurred in 1904. Lozowick certainly would have known Kupernik's role in the 1904 trial of those Jews accused of the Gomel pogrom. ("Blood Libel," *Encyclopaedia Judaica,* vol. 4 [Jerusalem: Keter Publishing; New York: Macmillan, 1971], 1130; "Gomel," ibid., vol. 7, 767–768.)

There were two Kishinev pogroms: April 6 to 7, 1903, and October 19 to 20, 1905. Because Kupernik died in 1905, he would probably have been involved with the trial of the 1903 Kishinev pogrom, if Lozowick is accurate. ("Kishinev," ibid., vol. 10, 1063–1066.)

Chapter 2

1. Lozowick's phraseology is somewhat misleading. In Jewish culture the Sabbath is anthropomorphized and is generally known as "Queen Sabbath" or "Sabbath, the Queen." Although the term *Malkah Shabbos* appears in Yiddish literature of the early 1900s, more common contemporary usage is *Shabbos Ha-malkah*. (I thank Rabbi Samuel Klein for clarifying this distinction.)

2. In speaking of the "Passover service," Lozowick means the family's Passover Seder at which the Haggadah is read. (I thank Rabbi Klein for this clarification.)

3. *Zeinah* is a local pronunciation of the more standard *zonah*. (I thank Rabbi Samuel Klein for his clarification.)

4. It is believed that the locusts that John the Baptist ate (Matthew 3:4; Mark 1:6) were in fact the pods of the carob tree, also known as the locust tree. Hence, the fruit of the carob tree is often called "St. John's bread." (*Dictionary of the Bible,* ed. James Hastings, rev. Frederick C. Grant and H.H. Rowley [New York: Charles Scribner's Sons, 1963], 778.)

5. Bar Kokhba was the Hebrew military leader who revolted successfully against the Romans, A.D. 132–35. ("Bar Kokhba," *Encyclopaedia Judaica,* vol. 10, 228–239.)

6. Akiva (ca. 50–135) was a Hebrew teacher, scholar, and helper of the poor during the Roman era. He was one of the members of a deputation to the emperor who pleaded for recision of decrees forbidding the practice and teaching of Judaism. He was imprisoned by the Romans for openly teaching the Torah in defiance of their edict. He was tortured to death by the Romans ("Akiva," *Encyclopaedia Judaica,* vol. 2, 488–492).

7. Lozowick's description of *hamanataschen* as "pies" is misleading. These are pastries that are made in a great variety of sizes and shapes. (I thank Rabbi Samuel Klein for this distinction.)

8. Hasidism arose in the context of persecution by Jews in Poland and Ukraine and of internal dissension within the Jewish community during the eighteenth century. Haidamack bands of peasant serfs robbed and murdered Jewish travelers and assaulted Jewish tenant farmers living in small towns. These attacks culminated in 1768 in the massacres of thousands of Poles and Jews in the city of Uman, where reportedly 20,000 people were murdered by Cossack Haidamacks. In addition to attacks from Haidamacks, the false messianic movements of Shabbetai Zevi and Jacob Frank raised questions about the rabbinical leadership within the Jewish community. In response, individualistic and charismatic leaders in Poland and Lithuania formed Hasidic groups practicing an ascetic life style. ("Hasidism," *Encyclopaedia Judaica,* vol. 7, 1390–1432.)

9. The Baal Shem Tov (1700–1760), born Israel Ben Eliezer, is the founder of Hasidism.

10. According to Rabbi Samuel Klein, only the Baal Shem Tov was believed to have had the ability to leap over distances through thought.

11. The standard Hasidic practice of obtaining an audience with the zaddik begins with making a charitable donation *(pidyon)* in the hope that this deed will offset any sins the visitor has committed that might block the efficacy of the zaddik's prayers on his or her behalf. The visitor enters the zaddik's presence with a *kvitl,* a note or brief account of his name and that of his family members and sometimes a mention of his problem. The visitor gives the zaddik the *kvitl.* He looks at it, perhaps prays on the visitor's behalf, and speaks with him briefly. (I am indebted to Rabbi Samuel Klein for elucidating this Hasidic practice.)

12. See Chapter 2, note 1.

Chapter 3

1. Though Lozowick describes *kasha* as made from barley, it is commonly made from buckwheat. (I thank Rabbi Samuel Klein for this information.)

Chapter 4

1. See Chapter 2, note 7.

2. "Sheenie" is an archaic pejorative term for a Jew.

3. The relation of *"vakhalaklakes"* to the rest of the jingle is, in fact, clear. The full sentence from Psalm 35:6 reads: "Let their way be dark and slippery, the angel of the Lord pursuing them." "Them" refers to them "that seek after my soul," an obvious refer-

ence to the goyim. (I thank Stephen Lewis for his research of this reference.)

Chapter 5

1. The Pharaoh's Third Plague was the plague of lice (Exodus 8:16–19), an appropriate reference for Lozowick's description of the consequences of poor hygiene and uncleanliness.

2. In this context, *gilgul* means a forlorn soul, sometimes evil, which is doomed to travel from body to body—sometimes assuming an animal shape, sometimes entering a living human being. (I thank Rabbi Samuel Klein for this information.)

3. The text is somewhat unclear here. The tallith katan (small tallith) is a short scarf or shawl worn all day, not just for prayers; the longer tallith is worn only for prayers and is known as the prayer scarf or shawl. Lozowick is speaking of the tallith katan, which he wore throughout the day. (I thank Rabbi Samuel Klein for this information.)

Chapter 6

1. Prince Oleg ruled Kievan Russia from 882 to 913.

2. Babi Yar is a site of a massacre of Jews and others by the Nazis in 1941.

3. Prince Vladimir ruled Kievan Russia from 980 to 1015. According to legend, in 988 the newly baptized ruler forced his subjects into a mass baptism in the Dnieper River. After his death, Vladimir was canonized and became known as Saint Vladimir.

4. Baccio Bandinelli (1493–1560) was an Italian Renaissance sculptor who worked principally in Florence. Lozowick's mention of Bandinelli most likely is a reference to the role of Italian Renaissance artists in building projects undertaken by Ivan III (Ivan the Great, 1440–1505) and Peter the Great (1728–1762).

5. For information on the Wanderers, see Elizabeth Valkenier, *Russian Realist Art: The State and Society: The Peredvizhniki and their Tradition* (New York: Columbia University Press, 1989) and *The Wanderers: Masters of 19th-Century Russian Painting,* ed. Elizabeth Kridl Valkenier (InterCultura of Fort Worth, Dallas Museum of Art, Ministry of Culture of the USSR, 1990). For a general introduction to the Wanderers, see Dmitri V. Sarabianov, *Russian Art: From Neoclassicism to the Avant-Garde, 1800–1917* (New York: Harry N. Abrams, 1990), 111–132.

6. For a thorough analysis of the World of Art, see Janet Elspeth Kennedy, *The "Mir iskusstva" Group and Russian Art 1898–1912* (New York and London: Garland Publishing, 1977); for a more succinct history, see Sarabianov, *Russian Art,* 222–231.

7. Lozowick may be referring to Lunacharskii's *Faust and the City,* a play begun in 1908 and finished in 1916. For an English translation, see *Three Plays by A. V. Lunacharski,* translated by L. A. Magnus and K. Walter (London: Routledge and Sons, 1923), 3–134.

8. "Bloody Sunday" refers to January 9, 1905, when Tsarist police fired on a peaceful demonstration by workers led by Father Grigorii Gapon who carried a petition to the Tsar. Several workers were killed. (I thank Benjamin J. Salzano for this information.)

9. Aleichem initially published his story as a serial titled *Der Mabl* (The deluge), which appeared in the periodicals *Varheit* (Truth) and *Unzer Lebn* (Our life) in 1907. He later published the story as a book, *In Shturm* (In the storm). Hence the numerous titles associated with the same story.

Chapter 7

1. The Black Hundreds *(Chernosotentsy)* were members of a reactionary secret police organization established to counter revolutionary activity during 1905–1907. (Ivan Avakumovic, "Black Hundreds," *The Modern Encyclopedia of Russian and Soviet History,* Vol. 4, ed. Joseph L. Wieczynski [Gulf Breeze, Fla.: Academic International Press, 1977], 197–200.)

2. The Beilis Trial is a celebrated case of a Jew, Mendel Beilis (1874–1934), charged with ritual blood libel. On March 20, 1911, a 12-year-old Christian boy, Andrei Yustchinskii, was found murdered in a cave outside Kiev. An anti-Semitic campaign led by the Black Hundreds alledged that the boy's death was part of a blood ritual practiced by Jews. A lamplighter testified that he had seen the victim playing with two other boys on the premises of the brick kiln owned by a Jew. Beilis, the Jewish superintendent of the kiln, was arrested on July 21, 1911, and imprisoned for two years before the case went to trial, despite the fact that the police investigation traced the murder to the gang headed by Vera Cheberiak, a known criminal. The trial of Beilis was held from September 25 to October 28, 1913. As the civil prosecutor representing the mother of the murdered boy, Chmakov worked with the state prosecutors who charged that the murder was a blood murder by Jews. The charge was successfully refuted, and Beilis was acquitted. For accounts of the trial, see Mendel Beilis, *Scapegoat on Trial: The Story of Mendel Beilis* (New York: C.I.S. Publishers, 1992); Albert S. Lindemann, *The Jew Accused: Three Anti-Semitic Affairs (Dreyfus, Beilis, Frank), 1894–1915* (Cambridge; New York: Cambridge University Press, 1991); and Maurice Samuel, *Blood Accusation* (Philadelphia: Jewish Publication Society of America, 1966).

Chapter 8

1. James Fenimore Cooper wrote five *Leatherstocking Tales: Pioneers* (1823), *The Last of the Mohicans* (1826), *The Prairie* (1827), *The Pathfinder* (1840), and *The Deerslayer* (1841).

2. Captain Mayne Reid (1818–1883) wrote many adventure stories for young readers. Among those set in America are: *The Desert Home,* or *The Adventures of a Lost Family in the Wilderness* (London: D. Bogue, 1852); *Blue Dick,* or *The Yellow Chief's Vengeance: A Romance of the Rocky Mountains* (New York: Beadle and Adams, 1879); and *Wild Life,* or *Adventures on the Frontier: A Tale of the Early Days of the Texan Republic* (New York: G.W. Dillingham, 1889).

Part Two. 1906–1920

1. Louis Lozowick, interview with Seton Hall University students, April 26, 1973.

2. Ibid.

3. Louis Lozowick, interview with Barbara Kaufman, August 30, 1973.

4. Louis Lozowick, interview with William C. Lipke, January 11, 1970.

5. Lozowick, interview, August 30, 1973.

6. Ibid.

7. *The Sansculotte* (one word) was a name taken by young rebellious populists during the French Revolution; its literal translation is "without pants." There were only three issues: January, February, and April 1917. Lozowick was on the editorial board along with Louis Rich, Boris Glossman, N. J. Donner, and Jack Lewis; James Light was editor-in-chief. I thank Malcolm Cowley and Professor Lewis C. Branscomb of Ohio State University for their kind assistance in locating and obtaining photocopies of *The Sansculotte.*

8. Lozowick, interview, April 26, 1973.

9. Ibid.

10. For an excellent account of the Educational Art Alliance, see Norman L. Kleeblatt and Susan Chevlowe, eds., *Painting a Place in America: Jewish Artists in New York, 1900–1945. A Tribute to the Educational Alliance Art School* (New York: The Jewish Museum, in cooperation with Indiana University Press, 1991).

11. Louis Lozowick Papers, Archives of American Art, Smithsonian Institution.

12. Lozowick, interview, April 16, 1973.

13. Louis Lozowick, "William Gropper," unpublished manuscript (1935–1936), Louis Lozowick Papers, Archives of American Art.

14. Harold E. Stearns, *America and the Young Intellectual* (New York: George H. Doran Co., 1921), 168. Also see, Harold E. Stearns, "The Harsher Feminism," *Freeman 3* (May 11, 1921): 200–201.

15. For discussions of the impact of Stearns' books, see Samuel Putnam, *Paris Was Our Mistress* (New York: Viking Press, 1947), 27–28; and Malcolm Cowley, *An Exile's Return: A Narrative of Ideas* (New York: W. W. Norton & Co., 1934), 116, 118.

16. Edmund J. Wilson, Jr., "The Aesthetic Upheaval in France," *Vanity Fair 17* (February 1922): 49.

17. Harold E. Stearns, "So, This is Paris!," *Freeman 5* (July 5, 1921): 398. Also see: Emmy Veronica Sanders, "America Invades Europe," *Broom 1* (November 1921): 89–93.

18. Malcolm Cowley, *An Exile's Return,* 118.

19. Ibid.

20. *Broom* was published by Americans living abroad. From November 1921 to October 1922, it was published in Rome, where it was edited by Harold A. Loeb and Alfred Kreymborg. From December 1922 to March 1923, it was published in Berlin, where it was edited by Loeb and Matthew Josephson. From August 1923 to January 1924, it was published in New York, where it was edited by Loeb, Josephson, Malcolm Cowley, and Slater Brown.

21. Matthew Josephson, "Made in America," *Broom 2* (June 1922): 280.

22. Matthew Josephson, "The Great American Billposter," *Broom* 3 (November 1922): 305.

23. Ibid.

24. Josephson, "Made in America," 270.

25. Harold A. Loeb, "Mysticism of Money," *Broom 2* (September 1922): 115.

26. Loeb concludes a letter to Lozowick dated July 22, 1922, with the remark, "I look forward to a Russian mail," indicating that Lozowick's departure was imminent. On September 12, 1922, Lozowick writes Loeb that he is "just back from Russia" (The Broom Correspondence of Harold A. Loeb, Box 1. Manuscripts Division, Department Rare Book and Special Collections, Princeton University Libraries. Published with permission of the Princeton University Libraries).

Chapter 9

1. Monsieur Jourdain is the principal character of Molière's popular farce *La bourgeois gentilhomme* of 1670. He is an enriched but ignorant bourgeois who makes a fool of himself by assuming the manners and airs of a gentleman. "Monsieur Jourdain" came to be known for making prose without knowing it. ("Monsieur Jour-

dain," *Pierre Larousse: La grande dictionnaire universel du XIXe siècle*
[Geneva-Paris: Slatkine, 1982], vol. 2, 1122–1123.)

2. *La vie des lettres et des arts* (October 1920): 172.

3. "A trois plans" refers to Beauduin's "L'homme cosmogonique
(poèmes synoptiques à trois plans," a copy of which Beauduin gave
to Lozowick. This poem also appeared in *La vie des lettres et des arts*
(October 1921): 762–796.

4. Nicholas Beauduin, "Lettre ouverte, à Pierre Chapka-
Bonniere," *La vie des lettres et des arts,* October 1920, 173–175.

5. Rudolf Blümner, "Die absolute Dichtung," *Der Sturm* 12, no.
7 (July 1921): 121–123. The quotations are from page 121.

6. Rudolf Blümner, "Ango Iaïno: Eine absolute Dichtung," *Der
Sturm* 12, No. 7 (July 1921): 123–126. The cited lines are from
page 126.

7. In this passage, Lozowick provides a loose translation of por-
tions of Malevich's *O poezii* (On poetry). I have corrected the lines
of poetry at the end of the passage to reflect Lozowick's published
article, "A Note on the New Russian Poetry," *Broom* 1 (February
1922): 311.

8. The Works Projects Administration (WPA) employed artists
under its Federal Arts Project (WPA/FAP) from 1935 to World II.
It was the major relief program of the New Deal during the 1930s.
For a history of WPA/FAP, see William F. McDonald, *Federal Relief
Administration and the Arts; The Origins and Administrative History of
the Arts Projects of the Works Progress Administration* (Columbus:
Ohio State University Press, 1969) and Marlene Park and Gerald
E. Markowitz, *New Deal for Art* (New York: The Gallery Associa-
tion, 1977).

9. The *Khlysty* is a Christian sect that broke away from the
Orthodox Church in the eighteenth century. Their services were
marked by ecstatic frenzies of singing, wild dancing, and flagella-
tion, giving rise to unintelligible utterances—glossolalia—that the
sect's adherents believed were divine prophecies. Central to the
Khlysty's break with the Church was its Christology, by which they
believed that Christ was the spirit of God, not the son of God, and
that this spirit resided in cult leaders, who, hence, were "christs."
The sect was opposed by the *Raskol,* the Old-Believers, who asserted traditional Orthodox beliefs. (George E. Munro, "Khlysty,"
The Modern Encyclopedia of Russian and Soviet History, vol. 16,
150–154.)

10. "Néantisme," *La vie des lettres et des arts* (February 1922): 67.

11. Lozowick's comment indicates that he was writing his account prior to the year of death given by Zdanevitch.

12. Italian Futurism, which was announced by Marinetti in
1909, asserted that speed and dynamism characterized the modern
age and should be the subject matter of art (including theatre and

music) and poetry. Rejecting both the subject matter and formal conventions of past art, Futurist artists (Giacomo Balla, Umberto Boccioni, Carlo Carrà, Gino Severini, and others) depicted subjects such as racing cars, speeding trains, humans in dynamic activities, whereas Futurist poets (Marinetti and others) attempted to simulate the noise of speeding forms through syllabic repetition and innovative typography and page layout. The Futurist aesthetic had a profound and far-reaching influence on progressive art movements in Western Europe, Russia, England, and the United States, especially during the 1910s. For further discussion of Italian Futurism, see Pontus Hulten, *Futurism and Futurisms* (New York: Abbeville Press, 1986); Marianne W. Martin, *Futurist Art and Theory, 1909–1915* (New York: Hacker Art Books, 1978); and Caroline Tisdall and Angelo Bozzolla, *Futurism* (New York and London: Oxford University Press, 1978).

13. For studies on Marinetti's *parole in libertà*, see *The Futurist Imagination: Word + Image in Italian Futurist Painting, Drawing, Collage and Free-Word Poetry*, ed. Anne Coffin Hanson (New Haven: Yale University Press, 1983); especially relevant are Christine Poggi's essay, "Marinetti's *Parole in libertà* and the Futurist Collage" (2–15) and Antonella Ansani, "Words-in-Freedom and Cangiullo's Dancing Letters," translated by Darby Tench (50–59).

14. The *Union Bulletin* issued Lozowick an identification card designating him "European Correspondant" for a term ending "January 30, 1923." The card was signed "Louis Rich, editor." (Louis Lozowick Papers, Archives of American Art.)

15. Most of the scholarship on Zenithism and *Zenit* may be attributed to Zoran Markuš and Irina Subotić. The most comprehensive bilingual source is Irina Subotič, *Zenit i avan garda 20ih godina/Zenit and the Avant-Garde of the Twenties* (Belgrade: National Museum and Institute of Literature and Art, 1983). Micić regarded Lozowick's work highly. Four of Lozowick's compositions were reproduced in *Zenit:* a decorative composition, No. 12 (March 1922); *Russian Church* (drawing), No. 14 (May 1922); an untitled Machine Ornament, No. 23 (April 1923); and *Raumgestaltung,* No. 26–33 (March–October 1924). In addition, in the important First Zenit International Exhibition of New Art held in Belgrade from April 9–19, 1924, American art was represented by three works by Lozowick. (I am especially grateful to Irina Subotić for researching Lozowick's works in Belgrade collections.)

16. Valentin Parnac, *Histoire de la danse* (Paris: Les Editions Rieder, 1932).

17. Marranos were Spanish Jews in medieval times who professed Christianity to avoid persecution.

18. The *Murs de Fedérés* is a wall in the Père Lachaise Cemetery in which the Communards were executed in 1871.

19. Giorgio de Chirico, "Gustave Courbet" (Rome: "Valori plastici," 1925).

20. Cendrars wrote *La fin du monde, filmée par l'Ange Notre Dame* in 1917; Léger's illustrations appeared in the 1919 edition.

21. *Mother Earth,* published by Emma Goldman and Alexander Berkman from March 1906 to April 1918, was a magazine espousing anarchist ideas.

22. Guignol, or Grand Guignol, is a French marionette drama.

Chapter 10

1. This is probably Arnold Ludwig Mendelssohn (1855–1933), son of a second cousin of Felix Mendelssohn-Barthody, who was a composer and an organist. (Edward F. Kravitt, "Mendelssohn, Arnold Ludwig," *The New Grove Dictionary of Music and Musicians,* vol. 12, ed. Stanley Sadie [London: Macmillan, 1980], 133–134)

2. See Louis Lozowick, "Modern Art in Germany," *Nation* 127 (November 7, 1928): 494.

3. De Stijl (1917–1931) was a Dutch modernist style that was based on Mondrian's neo-plastic ideas of primary colors and rectilinear construction. In addition to Mondrian and Van Does-burg, the primary group included the painters Bart van der Leck and César Domela, the interior designer Vilmos Huszar as well as the architects Gerrit Rietveld, Robert van't Hoff, J. J. P. Oud, and Cornelis van Eesteren, and the sculptor Georges Vantongerloo. For information on De Stijl, see H. L. C. Jaffé, *De Stijl* (Cambridge, Mass. and London: Belknap Press of Harvard University Press, 1986) and *De Stijl: 1917–1931 Visions of Utopia* (New York: Abbe-ville, 1982).

Van Doesburg was also a Dadaist poet for a brief time, publish-ing under two pseudonyms, K. I. Bonset and Aldo Corrini. For a full discussion of Van Doesburg's participation in the Dada move-ment, see Hanna L. Hedrick, *Theo van Doesburg: Propagandist and Practitioner of the Avant-Garde, 1909–1923* (Ann Arbor, Mich.: University Microfilms International Research Press, 1980).

4. Lissitzky made two portfolios of *Khad Gadya* (One kid) in 1917 (watercolors) and 1919 (lithographs), illustrated Moshe Broderson's *Sikhes Khulin. A Prager legende* (An everyday conversa-tion. A legend of Prague) in 1917 and R. Kipling's *Elfandl* (The lit-tle elephant) in 1922, and made two series of ink drawings entitled *Vaysrusische folkmayses* (Belorussian folk tales) in 1919–1922 and *Ukraynische folymayses* (Ukrainian folk tales) in 1922.

5. Lissitzky's *Prouns* represent an intermediate between pure painting and the more utilitarian and applied arts of architecture and industrial design stage within the evolution of the Russian avant-garde. For Lissitzky's writings on art, see Sophie Lissitzky-

Küppers, ed., *El Lissitzky: Life, Letters, Text* (London: Thames and Hudson, 1968).

6. Lozowick refers to some of Lissitzky's *Proun* installation and exhibition spaces. These included: a room of the *Erste Russische Kunstausstellung* (First Russian Art Exhibition) in 1922; *Prounen-raum (Proun* room) at the Grosse Berliner Kunstausstellung in 1923, in which *Proun* reliefs were both hung on the flat walls as well as positioned so that a single relief spanned adjoining walls, visually uniting the discrete surfaces of the room into a uninterrupted continuum; *Raum für konstruktive Kunst* (Room for constructive art) at the Internationale Kunstausstellung in Dresden in 1926; *Abstraktes Kabinett* (Abstract cabinet) at the Niedersächsische Landesgalerie in Hanover in 1927, an exhibition space for abstract art in which the wall surfaces were covered by closely spaced vertical strips of wood; the Soviet pavilion at the *Pressa-Köln* (International Press Exhibition-Cologne) in 1928; and the Soviet pavilion at the International Hygiene Exhibition in Dresden in 1930.

7. *Izvestiia ASNOVA* (Moscow, No. 1, 1926) was the publication of ASNOVA *(Assotsiatsiia novykh arkitektorov,* Association of New Architects). Only one issue was produced; it appeared in mid-1926.

8. In his article "Seriia neboskrebov dlia Moskvi" (Series of skyscapers for Moscow), which appeared in *Izvestiia ASNOVA,* Lissitzky introduced his *Wolkenbügel* (Cloud-prop), to which Lozowick alludes. For further explanation and illustration of the *Wolkenbügel,* see *El Lissitzky (1890–1941)* (Cambridge, Mass.: Harvard University Art Museums, 1987), 32–34. (I thank Gail Harrison Roman for her help in understanding this structure.)

9. Although it is not clear what painting by Ryback Lozowick is referring to, there was an exhibition of Ryback's works in Berlin in 1923/1924. The exhibition catalog includes the reproduction of *Stilleben mit Alef-Beth* (Still life with *Alef-Beth),* with *"Alef"* and *"Beth"* being the first and second letters of the Hebrew alphabet. The painting includes Hebrew letters. It is most likely that Lozowick would have seen this exhibition of Ryback's work.

10. The painting referred to is Chagall's *Self-Portrait with Seven Fingers* (1912).

11. It is likely that Lozowick is probably referring to Eduard Fuchs's *Geshichte der erotishchen Kunst* (Munich: A. Langen, 1922–1924).

12. Georg Kaiser's *Gas* is a trilogy: *Die Koralle* (The coral) (1917), *Gas I* (1918), and *Gas II* (1920). The plots are sequential: In *Die Koralle,* the utopian theme of the "new man," one who asserts a humane society as an alternative to capitalism, is introduced. In *Gas I,* a billionaire offers his workers the opportunity for a more humane life if they will abandon the production of gas on which the machinery of capitalism depends; the workers choose to main-

tain the industrial society. *Gas II* presents an apocalyptic destruction of both capitalism and socialism. Lozowick probably saw *Gas II.*

13. Grosz's *Face of the Ruling Class* was a book of 55 drawings, issued as volume 4 of *The Little Revolutionary Library,* published by Malik Verlag in Berlin in 1921. (I thank Sherwin Simmons for this information.)

14. Iwan Goll edited a bilingual journal, *Hémisphères: Revue franco-américaine de poésie/Hemispheres: Franco-American Quarterly of Poetry,* vol. 2, no. 6 (Brooklyn; summer 1943–v. 2, n. 6 [ca. 1946]).

15. Lozowick's one-person exhibition at K. E. Twardy Book Shop, which was held in June 1922, included fifteen paintings and five drawings. Among the paintings were *Chicago* and *Spiegel und Fenster* (Mirror and window).

16. Lozowick's exhibition at the Gallerie Alfred Heller, which was held from August 1 to September 1, 1923, included eight paintings and eight drawings. The paintings included *New York, Chicago, Cleveland, Pittsburgh,* two compositions, and two constructions; the drawings included *New York, Chicago, Cleveland,* two constructions, a portrait, and two sketches for theatre decorations.

17. Bruno W. Reimann, "Louis Lozowick," *Jahrbuch des jungen Kunst* (Leipzig: Verlag Kinkhardt und Biermann, 1923), 312–325. Illustrations of Lozowick's *Raumgestaltung* and *New York* (third version), *Chicago,* and *Cleveland* accompanied this article. The original article had appeared in *Der Cicerone 15* (1923): 955–957.

18. John Garfield, "Louis Lozowick," *Zelt* 1, No. 9 (1924): 330–331. Four of Lozowick's "City" paintings were reproduced: *Pittsburgh, Oklahoma, New York,* and *Chicago.*

19. *Cleveland* was illustrated in *L'Esprit nouveau,* No. 21 (1924), no pagination.

20. *The Machine-Age Exposition* (New York: The Little Review, 1927), 18–19.

21. Lozowick's *Oklahoma* and *Painting* (actually *Raumgestaltung)* were reproduced in the spring 1925 issue of *Little Review.*

22. This exhibition was titled "The Responsive Eye."

23. Like Lozowick, I have been unable to determine if Berlewi published the mentioned book.

24. Lozowick alludes to Alfred Kreymborg's characterization of himself as a troubadour in *Troubadour: An Autobiography* (New York: Boni and Liveright, 1925). Actually Kreymborg and Loeb were editors of *Broom* from its first issue of November 1921 to February 1922, when Kreymborg resigned as editor. Loeb remained editor until its last issue of June 1924.

25. Lozowick is referring to his first article for *Broom,* "A Note on New Russian Poetry," which appeared in the February 1922 issue (306–311); his article on Russian art, "A Note on Modern Russian Art," appeared in the February 1923 issue (200–204).

26. A black and white abstract drawing, later given the generic name "Machine Ornament," was reproduced in the March 1923 issue of *Broom* on page 247. It was the same design that appeared on the cover of the pamphlet to Lozowick's exhibition at the Galerie Alfred Heller in Berlin in August 1923 (see Figure 8). For references to Lozowick's translations that appeared in *Broom,* see the bibliography in this book.

27. Riurik is the legendary Norseman who was invited by the Slavs in 862 to end their strife and to rule over them. He is considered the founder of Russia.

28. Mayakovsky wrote two versions of his *Mystery-Bouffe.* The first (1918) was produced by Meyerhold in 1918 in Petrograd; the second (1921) was produced by Meyerhold in 1921 in Moscow. Most likely Lozowick read the second version.

29. Louis Lozowick, "Russian Berlin," *Broom 3* (August 1922): 78–79.

30. The exhibition "Dada, Surrealism, and Their Heritage" was held at the Museum of Modern Art from March 27 to June 9, 1968.

31. Held in conjunction with the Museum of Modern Art's exhibition "Fantastic Art, Dada, Surrealism" (December 7, 1936–January 17, 1939), the symposium organized by the American Artists' Congress took place on January 13, 1937. The speakers were Walter Quirt, Salvador Dalí, Richard Huelsenbeck, Meyer Schapiro, and Jerome Klein. (The Museum of Modern Art Archives: A. Conger Goodyear Papers, vol. 53. I thank Michelle Elligott of the Museum of Modern Art Archives for her research assistance.)

32. Dr. Auguste Henri Forel (1848–1931) wrote many books on the topic of sex. Lozowick may be referring to Forel's *Die sexuelle Frage. Eine naturwissenschaftliche, psychologische, hygienische und soziologische Studie (The Sexual Question: A Scientific, Psychological, Hygienic and Sociological Study),* which was originally published in 1905 and subsequently was translated, revised, and enlarged.

Chapter 11

1. The Erste Russische Kunstausstellung opened at the Galerie Van Diemen in October 1922.

2. The full title of this important pamphlet is *From Cubism and Futurism to Suprematism: The New Painterly Realism.* It the first appeared in conjunction with the "0.10: The Last Futurist Exhibition" held in Petrograd in December 1915. For an English translation, see John E. Bowlt, ed. *Russian Art of the Avent-Garde: Theory and Criticism, 1902–1934* (New York: Viking, 1976), 116–135.

3. Malevich's backdrops for the 1913 production of *Victory over the Sun* are considered the first manifestations of the nonobjective

geometric imagery that characterized Suprematism. For an informative analysis of this opera, see Charlotte Douglas, *Swans of Other Worlds: Kazimir Malevich and the Origins of Abstraction in Russia* (Ann Arbor, Mich.: University Microfilms International Research Press, 1980), chap. 3.

4. For discussion of Malevich's development of Suprematism, see Douglas, *Swans of Other Worlds;* W. Sherwin Simmons, *Kasimir Malevich's "Black Square" and the Genesis of Suprematism, 1907–1915* (New York & London: Garland Publishing, 1981); and *Kazimir Malevich* (Los Angeles: Armand Hammer Museum of Art and Cultural Center, 1990).

5. The "Exhibition of Petrograd Artists of All Trends 1918–1923" was held at the Academy of Arts of Petrograd in May 1923. In "The Suprematist Mirror" Malevich announced the "zero" of art, the culmination of his Suprematist aesthetic. Lozowick's translation differs only slightly from the translation by Xenia Glowacki-Prus and Arnold McMillin in K. S. Malevich, *Essays on Art,* vol. 1, ed. Troels Andersen (London: Rapp and Whiting; Chester Spring, Penn: Dufour Editions, 1968), 224–225.

6. The painting described is Malevich's *Self-Portrait* (1933).

7. The exhibition "5 x 5 = 25" was held in Moscow in September 1921. It included five works by five INKhUK artists—Aleksandra Exter, Liubov Popova, Aleksandr Rodchenko, Varvara Stepanova, and Aleksandr Vesnin. The artists devoted themselves to an examination of color and to the creation of color constructions based on the objective laws of color.

8. Tairov was the director of the Kamernyi Theatre, which opened in Moscow in December 1914. For a history of Tairov's production, see Konstantin Rudnitsky, *Russian and Soviet Theatre 1905–1932,* trans. Roxane Permar, ed. Dr. Lesley Milne (New York: Harry N. Abrams, 1988), 15–19, *passim.*

9. The film *Aelita* was made in 1924 by Yakov Protazanov.

10. Louis Lozowick, "Alexandra Exter's Marionettes," *Theatre Arts Monthly* 12 (July 1928): 514–519.

11. For studies on Constructivism, see Christina Lodder, *Constructivism* (New Haven: Yale University Press, 1983); idem, "The Transition to Constructivism," *The Great Utopia: The Russian and Soviet Avant-Garde, 1915–1932* (New York: Solomon R. Guggenheim Museum, 1992), 267–281; and *Art into Life: Russian Constructivism, 1914–1932* (New York: Rizzoli, 1990).

12. For discussion of Tatlin's *Project for a Monument to the Third International* (1920), see John Milner, *Vladimir Tatlin and the Russian Avant-Garde* (New Haven and London: Yale University Press, 1983), chap. 8. For critical reaction to the *Monument* both in Russia and in the West, see Gail Harrison Roman, "Tatlin's Tower: Revolutionary Symbol and Aesthetic," *The Avant-Garde Frontier:*

Russia Meets the West, 1910–1930, ed. Gail Harrison Roman and
Virginia Hagelstein Marquardt (Gainesville: University Press of
Florida, 1992), 45–64.

13. For the full text of Punin's "The Monument to the Third
International," published in 1921, see *Tatlin,* ed. Larissa Alekseevna
Zhadova (New York: Rizzoli, 1984), 344–347.

14. Lozowick's translation of Ehrenburg's "Vitrion" appeared in
Broom 3 (September 1922): 83–94.

15. For the text of Shklovskii's "The Monument to the Third
International," published in 1921, see *Tatlin,* 342–343.

16. For a thorough study of Tatlin's *Letatlin* (1929–1932), see
Milner, *Vladimir Tatlin,* 217–225.

17. The use of "Futurism" for Russian art and poetry is fraught
with problems. Progressive artists and writers used the term in
varying contexts during the 1910s and early 1920s. Despite their
protestations to the contrary, Russian poets and artists were influenced by Italian Futurism (see Chapter 9, note 12), which
Marinetti announced in 1909 and lectured on in Moscow and
St. Petersburg in the winter of 1914. Adopted by Mayakovsky and
his circle, "Futurism" was used to describe transrational *zaum*
poetry, which, although sharing innovative typography and nonsensical, phonetic sounds with Marinetti's *parole in libertà,* was not
used principally to articulate, either graphically or audibly, the
themes of speed and dynamism (see Chapter 9, note 13). Instead,
the Russian Futurist poets were equally interested in exploring the
spiritual dimension suggested by sound and glossolalia. In painting
of the 1910s, artists such as Malevich and Goncharova developed a
"Cubo-Futurist" style using cylindrical shapes and moving forms
for a synthesis of the Cubists' geometric vocabulary and the Italian
Futurists' theme of motion. For his part, Mikhail Larionov, in his
Rayonist paintings, attempted to show spatial relationships constructed by the intersection of rays reflected from forms, a goal that
alludes to the nonobjective implications of Italian Futurism. Later,
after the Revolution, the theoreticians of Constructivism used
"futurism" to mean art intended to contribute to the rebuilding of
society—i.e., future-oriented. They used the term to describe their
objective of uniting art with life through industrial application, a
union that they believed would occur in the near future. For more
information on Russian Futurism, see Vladimir Markov's ground-
breaking study, *Russian Futurism: A History* (London: McGibbon
and Gee, 1969). (I thank Gail Harrison Roman for her assistance
in clarifying the complexity of Russian Futurism.)

18. Viktor Shklovskii, *Erinnerungen an Maiakovskii* (Frankfurt:
Insel-Verlag, 1966).

19. *"Zorved"* is the union of the roots of words dealing with
sight and intellectual cognition: *"zor"* from *"zret',"* meaning physi-

cal sight, and *"zorkii,"* meaning sharp-sightedness; and *"ved"* from *"vedat',"* meaning seeing in the manner of knowing. Christina Lodder, thus, gives the English translation as "see-know" *(Constructivism,* 297 n. 5). Lozowick quotes from Matiushin's article on *zorved* in *Zhizn' iskusstva,* No. 20 (1923): 15. Briefly, Matiushin sought to express the full 360 degrees of ambient space and believed that such vision would reveal the fourth dimension. For further explanation, see Lodder, *Constructivism,* 206; and Linda Dalrymple Henderson, *The Fourth Dimension and Non-Euclidean Geometry* (Princeton, New Jersey: Princeton University Press, 1983), 292–293.

20. For further explanation of biomechanics, see Konstantin Rudnitsky, *Russian and Soviet Theatre 1905–1932,* trans. Roxane Permar, ed. Dr. Lesley Milne (New York: Harry N. Abrams, 1988), 93–94.

21. VKhUTEMAS is the acronym for *Vysshie gosudarstvennye khudozhestvenno-tekhnicheskie masterskie.* For information on the development and curriculum at the VKhUTEMAS, see Christina Lodder, *Constructivism* (New Haven and London: Yale University Press, 1983), chap. 4; Szymon Boijko, "Vkhutemas," *The Avant-Garde in Russia: New Perspectives, 1910–1930* (Los Angeles: Los Angeles County Art Museum, 1979), 78–90; and Natalia Adaskina, "The Place of VKhutemas in the Russian Avant-Garde," *The Great Utopia,* 283–294.

22. For discussion of Mayakovsky's poetry, see Juliette R. Stapanian, *Mayakovsky's Cubo-Futurist Vision* (Houston: Rice University Press, 1986).

23. For Brik's ideas on the utilitarian direction of art, see his "From Pictures to Textile Prints," 1924, in Bowlt, *Russian Art of the Avant-Garde,* 244–249. This direction, which was never fully attained, was called "Production Art" or "Productivism." For the distinction between Constructivism and Productivism, see Lodder, *Constructivism,* 75–76.

24. These terms refer to the typical work of key Constructivists: Tatlin produced his three-dimensional constructions of wood, metal, and wire known as "counter-reliefs" during 1915–1916; Lissitzky made his *Prouns* (see Chapter 10, note 5) from 1919 to 1924; Rodchenko and other members of the OBMOKhU *(Obshchestvo molodykh khudozhnikov,* Society of Young Artists) made space constructions, which were exhibited in an important exhibition in Moscow in May 1921; and Popova and others painted compositions of colored planes and volumes.

25. For similar views, see Kushner's "The Divine Work of Art," 1919, in Bowlt, *Russian Avant-Garde Art,* 166–170.

26. For extracts from Gan's *Constructivism,* see Bowlt, *Russian Art of the Avant-Garde,* 214–225.

27. The concepts of *tektonika, faktura,* and *konstruktsiia* are complex. *Tektonika* (tectonics) emerges from the ideological tenets of Communism and from the appropriate use of the industrial material; *faktura,* though "texture" in translation, is the working of the material in an expedient manner without hampering *tektonika* and *konstruktsiia; konstruktsiia* (construction) is the process of structuring and organizing the material for the formation of the concept through material (Lodder, *Constructivism,* 94–95, 99).

28. For the full declaration, see AKhRR, "Declaration of the Association of Revolutionary Artists," in Bowlt, *Russian Art of the Avant-Garde,* 265–267. AKhRR is the acronym of *Assotsiatsiia khudozhnikov revoliutsionnoi Rossii.*

29. The production of *Gas* staged at the Kenneth Sawyer Goodman Memorial Theatre in January–February 1926 was a four-part adaptation of Kaiser's plays.

30. Sheldon Cheney, *Stage Decoration* (New York: John Day Co., 1928), plate 121.

31. GOSET is the acronym of *Gosudarstvennyi evreiskii teatr.*

32. See Chapter 10, note 4.

33. Lozowick would have seen Meyerhold's production during his 1927–1928 to Moscow.

34. Louis Lozowick, "Chagall's 'Circus,'" *Theatre Arts Monthly* 13 (August 1929): 593–601.

Part Four. 1924–1945

1. Louis Lozowick, letter to Harold A. Loeb, September 12, 1922, The Broom Correspondence of Harold A. Loeb, Box 1.

2. Lozowick's stay in Paris lasted until at least November 27, 1923, when he received a letter addressed "Louis Lozowick, Paris" (Louis Lozowick Papers, Department of Special Collections, Syracuse University Library).

3. Louis Lozowick, letter to Katherine S. Dreier, February 2, 1924, Katherine S. Dreier Papers, Yale Collection of American Literature, Beinecke Rare Book and Manuscript Library, Yale University.

4. Concerning *Modern Russian Art,* see correspondence between Lozowick and Dreier, Katherine S. Dreier Papers.

5. Dreier selected Lozowick's *Work* and *Play* for exhibition (Dreier, letter to Lozowick, November 19, 1926, Katherine S. Dreier Papers).

6. Louis Lozowick, letter to Dreier, October 25, 1926, Katherine S. Dreier Papers.

7. On December 18, Lozowick gave the third and last lecture, which was entitled "Certain Aspects of Modern Art." The other speakers were Alfred Stieglitz (December 4) and David Burliuk (December 11). For Lozowick's review of the exhibition, see

"Modern Art: Genesis or Exodus," *Nation* 123 (December 22, 1926): 672.

8. For sources on the machine age in America and Precisionism, see Milton Brown, "Cubist-Realism," *Marsyas* 3 (1943–1945): 139–160; idem, "Precisionism and Mechanism," in *The Modern Spirit: American Painting, 1908–1935* (London: Arts Council of Great Britain, 1977), 52–55; Susan Fillin-Yeh, *The Precisionist Painters 1916–1949: Interpretations of the Mechanical Age* (Huntington, New York: Heckscher Museum, 1978); Martin L. Friedman, *The Precisionist View in American Art* (Minneapolis, Minn.: The Walker Art Center, 1960); Susan Lubowsky, *Precisionist Perspectives: Prints and Drawings* (New York: Whitney Museum of American Art, 1988); Merrill Schleier, *The Skyscraper in American Art, 1890–1931* (New York: DA CAPO Press, 1986); Dickran Tashjian, *Skyscraper Primitives: Dada and the American Avant-Garde* (Middletown, Conn.: Wesleyan University Press, 1975); *Precisionism in America 1915–1941: Reordering Reality* (New York: Harry N. Abrams, in association with The Montclair Art Museum, 1994); Richard Guy Wilson, Dianne H. Pilgrim, and Dickran Tashjian, *The Machine Age in America* (New York: The Brooklyn Museum in Association with Harry N. Abrams, 1986); Barbara Zabel, "The Machine as Metaphor, Model, and Microcosm: Technology and American Art, 1915–1930" *Arts Magazine* 57 (December 1982): 100–105.

9. Louis Lozowick, interview with William C. Lipke, January 11, 1971.

10. Ibid.

11. For discussion of this and other projects of applied design, see Virginia Hagelstein Marquardt, "From 'Machine Ornaments" to Applied Design, 1923–1930," *The Journal of Decorative and Propaganda Arts (DAPA)* 8 (Spring 1988): 40–57.

12. Louis Lozowick, "'Gas': A Theatrical Experiment," *Little Review* 2 (Winter 1926 [special theatre number]: catalog of International Theatre Exposition): 58.

13. Lozowick, interview with Lipke, January 11, 1971.

14. For a history of *The Masses,* see Rebecca Zurier, *Art for The Masses: A Radical Magazine and Its Graphics, 1911–1917* (Philadelphia: Temple University Press, 1988). For a discussion of the *Liberator* and *New Masses,* see Virginia Hagelstein Marquardt, "Art on the Political Front in America: From *The Liberator* to *Art Front,*" *Art Journal* 52, No. 1 (Spring 1993): 72–81.

15. Louis Lozowick, interview with Gerald M. Monroe, April 24, 1972. I am indebted to Gerald M. Monroe for allowing me to listen to his taped interview with Lozowick.

16. The approximate time-frame of Lozowick's second trip abroad is established by Marc Chagall's letter of "Sun-9-27"—presumably September 1927—addressed to Lozowick in Paris

(Louis Lozowick Papers, Syracuse University) and Lozowick's letter of July 10, 1928, to Dreier in which he writes that he has just returned from Europe (Katherine S. Dreier Papers).

17. For discussion of the ideologic and aesthetic evolution of the *New Masses,* see Virginia Hagelstein Marquardt, *"New Masses* and John Reed Club Artists, 1926–1936: Evolution of Ideology, Subject Matter, and Style," *The Journal of Decorative and Propaganda Arts (DAPA)* 12 (Spring 1989): 56–75.

18. Lozowick, interview with Monroe, April 24, 1972.

19. Louis Lozowick, (reply), *New Masses,* February 1931, 31.

20. For a discussion of workers' theatre groups in America, see Virginia Hagelstein Marquardt, "Centre Stage: Radical Theatre in America, 1925–1934," *Revue d'art canadienne/Canadian Art Review (RACAR)* 19, No. 1–2 (1992): 112–121.

21. The John Reed Club was founded by staff members of *New Masses* in October 1929 in an effort to become more actively involved in promoting proletarian culture in America. The group took the name of John Reed, a Bolshevik sympathizer and journalist who wrote *Ten Days that Shook the World,* a firsthand account of the Russian Revolution. For discussion of the programs and activities of the John Reed Club and its art school, see Virginia Hagelstein Marquardt, *"New Masses* and John Reed Club Artists, 1926–1936: Evolution of Ideology, Subject Matter, and Style," 67–73.

22. Louis Lozowick, letter to Lincoln E. Kirstein, December 14, 1933, *Hound & Horn* Papers, Yale Collection of American Literature, Beinecke Rare Book and Manuscript Library, Yale University.

23. For studies of the Artists' Union, see Gerald M. Monroe, "The Artists' Union of New York," Ed.D. dissertation, Department of Art and Art Education, New York University, 1971, and Francine Tyler, "Artists Respond to the Great Depression and the Threat of Fascism: The New York Artists' Union and Its Magazine *Art Front* (1934–1937)," Ph.D. dissertation, Department of American Civilization, New York University, 1991.

24. For the history of the American Artists School, see Virginia Hagelstein Marquardt, "The American Artists School: Radical Heritage and Social Content Art," *Archives of American Art Journal* 26, No. 4 (1986): 17–23.

Appendix

1. "Jumper" is a nonstandard term that is not used in contemporary lithography. It is unclear what type of instrument Lozowick alludes to. I am indebted to Clinton Adams for sharing his knowledge of lithographic practices with me and to Robert Conway for referring me to Mr. Adams.

SELECTED BIBLIOGRAPHY

Writings by Louis Lozowick (In Chronological Order)

"Tentative Attitudes," *Sansculotte* 1 (January 1917): 14

"The Russian Dadaists," *Little Review* 7 (September–December 1920): 72–73.

"Numa Patlagean, The Artist of Spiritual Synthesis," *Union Bulletin* 11 (May 1921): 6, 22, 26.

"Éphraïm Mikhaël, A French Poet," *Union Bulletin* 11 (August–September 1921): 8, 17.

"Camille Pissaro: The Great Impressionist Artist," *Union Bulletin* 11 (October 1921): 8, 22.

"Ivan Goll; An Expressionist Poet," *Union Bulletin* 11 (November 1921): 15–16.

"Néantisme," *La vie des lettres et des arts* 8 (February 1922): 67.

"A Note on the New Russian Poetry," *Broom* 1 (February 1922): 306–311.

"The Poet in Architecture: A Study of the Work and Ideas of Erich Mendelsohn," *Union Bulletin* 12 (April–May 1922): 7, 19.

"Russian Berlin," *Broom* 3 (August 1922): 78–79.

"Tatlin's Monument to the Third International," *Broom* 3 (October 1922): 232–234.

"Max Liebermann," *Union Bulletin* 13 (January 1923): 14–15.

"Max Reinhardt," *Union Bulletin* 13 (February 1923): 16–17, 31.

"A Note on Modern Russian Art," *Broom* 4 (February 1923): 200–204.

"Jewish Artists of the Season," *Menorah Journal* 10 (June 1924): 282–285.

"Marc Chagall," *Menorah Journal* 10 (August–September 1924): 343–346.

Fig. 30 Ralph Steiner, Lozowick, photograph, 1930.

"A Jewish Art School," *Menorah Journal* 10 (November–December 1924): 465–466.

Modern Russian Art. (New York: Museum of Modern Art and Société Anonyme, 1925).

"Dorothea A. Dreier," *Little Review* 2 (Spring 1925): 33–34.

"Fernand Léger," *Nation* 121 (December 16, 1925): 712.

"'Gas': A Theatrical Experiment," *Little Review* 2 (Winter 1926; special theatre number: catalogue of International Theatre Exposition): 58–60.

"Art of Nathan Altman," *Menorah Journal* 12 (February 1926): 61–64.

"Marc Chagall," *Nation* 122 (March 17, 1926): 294–295.

"Eliezar Lissitzky," *Menorah Journal* 12 (April 1926): 175–176.

"Some Artists of Last Season," *Menorah Journal* 12 (August 1926): 401–405.

"Modern Art: Genesis or Exodus?" *Nation* 123 (December 22, 1926): 672.

"The Americanization of Art," In *The Machine-Age Exposition* (New York: Little Review, 1927): 18–19.

"In the Midwinter Exhibitions," *Menorah Journal* 13 (February 1927): 48–50.

"Eugene Zak," *Menorah Journal* 13 (June 1927): 283–286.

"Russia's Jewish Theatres," *Theatre Arts Monthly* 11 (June 1927): 419–422.

"Books" (Review of *Nach-Expressionismus* by Franz Roh), *The Arts* 12 (August 1927): 115–116.

"Marc Chagall," *Young Israel* 20 (March 1928): 3–4.

"The Moscow Jewish State Theatre," *Menorah Journal* 14 (May 1928): 478–482.

"Moise Kisling," *Young Israel* 20 (June 1928): 7, 22.

"Modern Art in Germany" (Review of *Bauhaus Bücher), Nation* 127 (November 7, 1928): 494.

"Jewish Artists in Paris," *Menorah Journal* 15 (July 1928): 62–67.

"Alexandra Exter's Marionettes," *Theatre Arts Monthly* 12 (July 1928): 514–519.

"Moise Kisling," *Menorah Journal* 15 (September 1928): 227–230.

"Jacques Lipschitz," *Menorah Journal* 16 (January 1929): 46–48.

"Tairov," *Theatre* 1 (January 1929): 9–11.

"A Century of French Painting," *Nation* 128 (January 2, 1929): 24–26.

"A Decade of Soviet Art," *Menorah Journal* 16 (March 1929): 243–248.

"Honoré Daumier, 1808–1879," *Nation* 128 (April 24, 1929): 505–506.

"Numa Patlagean," *Menorah Journal* 16 (May 1929): 420.

"Chagall's 'Circus,'" *Theatre Arts Monthly* 13 (August 1929): 593–601.

"The Soviet Cinema: Eisenstein and Pudovkin," *Theatre Arts Monthly* 13 (September 1929): 664–675.

"The Theater Is for the Actor: An Iconoclast's Methods in Moscow," *Theatre Guild Magazine* 7 (October 1929): 34–35.

"El. Lissitsky," *transition,* No. 18 (November 1929): 284–286.

Freeman, Joseph, Joshua Kunitz, and Louis Lozowick, *Voices of October: Art and Literature in Soviet Russia* (New York: Vanguard Press, 1930).

"Lithographs," *Forums* 83 (February 1930): 88, 92–93.

"Lithography: Abstraction and Realism," *Space* 1 (March 1930): 31–33.

"Theatre Chronicle: V.E. Meyerhold and His Theatre," *Hound & Horn* 4 (October–December 1930): 95–105.

"What Should Revolutionary Artists Do Now?" *New Masses* (December 1930): 21.

"Art in the Service of the Proletariat," *Literature of the World Revolution* No. 4 (1931): 126–127.

"New World in Central Asia," *Menorah Journal* 20 (July 1932): 167–173.

"The Artist in Soviet Russia," *Nation* 135 (July 13, 1932): 35–36.

"Hazardous Sport in Tajikistan: The Dare-Devil Horsemen of Central Asia," *Travel* 61 (September 1933): 14–17, 38.

"Theatre of Turkestan: Old Forms Serve New Needs," *Theatre Arts Monthly* 17 (November 1933): 885–890.

"John Reed Club Show," *New Masses* (January 2, 1934): 27.

"Aspects of Soviet Art," *New Masses* (January 29, 1935): 16–19.

"The Independent Art Show," *Daily Worker* (April 19, 1935): 5.

"Government in Art: Status of the Artist in the U.S.S.R." In *Proceedings I* (New York: American Artists' Congress, 1936), 70–71.

"Lithography." In *America Today; A Book of 100 Prints Chosen and Exhibited by the American Artists' Congress* (New York: Equinox Cooperative Press, 1936), 10.

"Soviet Gypsy Theatre," *Theatre Arts Monthly* 20 (April 1936): 282–287.

"The Artist in the U.S.S.R.," *New Masses* (July 28, 1936): 18–20.

"Towards a Revolutionary Art," *Art Front* 2 (July–August 1936): 12–14.

"William Gropper." In *William Gropper* (New York: A.C.A. Gallery, March 1937).

"Revolutionary Artist," *New Masses* (January 31, 1939): 22–23.

"Hitler Calls It Art," *New Masses* (July 29, 1941): 26–28.

"The Jew in American Plastic Arts." In *100 Contemporary American Jewish Painters and Sculptors.* (New York: Yiddisher Kultur Farband, Art Section, 1947), ix–xv.

"Soviet Art." In *Understanding the Russians: A Study of Soviet Life and Culture,* ed. Bernard Stern and Samuel Stern (New York: Barnes and Noble, 1947), 143–145.

"What, Then, Is Jewish Art?" *Menorah Journal* 35 (January–March 1947): 103–110.

Introduction to *A Treasury of Drawings from Pre-History to the Present,* ed. Louis Lozowick (New York: Lear, 1948), 1–10.

"Katherine S. Dreier, 1870–1923," "Ivan Puni," and "Udalzova."
  In *Collection of the Société Anonyme: Museum of Modern Art 1920.*
  (New Haven, Conn.: Yale University Art Gallery for the Associ-
  ates in Fine Arts, 1950).
"When the U.S.S.R. Was Radical" (Review of *The Great Experiment*
  by Camilla Gray), *Art News* 61 (December 1962): 47, 67–68.
"Russian Art." In *Encyclopedia Americana* (International Edition),
  Vol. 24. (New York: Americana Corporation, 1966).
"Lithography," *New Jersey Music and Arts* (January 1971): 20–21.
"William Gropper." In *Louis Lozowick* (New York: Associated Uni-
  versity Presses, 1983). Foreword by Milton W. Brown.

Translations by Louis Lozowick (In Chronological Order)

Rémy de Gourmont. *Three Stories from Colors.* In *Mr. Antiphilos,
  Satyr,* translated by John Howard with introduction by Jack
  Lewis. (New York: Lieber & Lewis, 1922).
Maryngoff, Anatoly. "October," *Broom* 2 (May 1922): 164–165.
Pilniak, Boris. "At the Doors," *Broom* 3 (August 1922): 57–75.
Ehrenbourg, Ilya. "Vitrion," *Broom* 3 (September 1922): 83–94.
Shershenyevitch, Vadim. "A Toast to Ourselves," *Broom* 3 (Septem-
  ber 1922): 102.
Ivanov, Vsevolod. "The Kid," *Broom* 4 (February 1923): 188–198.
Granovsky, Naum. "Aesthetics and Utility," *Little Review* 2 (Spring
  1925): 28–29.

**Selected Sources on Louis Lozowick
(In Alphabetical Order)**

Angermayer, Fred Antoine. "Introduction." In *Louis Lozowick,
  New York: Ausstellung* (Berlin: Gallerie Alfred Heller, August 1–
  September 1, 1923).
American Artists Group. *Original Etchings, Lithographs and Woodcuts
  by American Artists.* (New York: American Artists Group, 1936).
"Art across North America," *Apollo,* No. 111 (May 1980): 402.
Bainbridge, Diana. "Art Reviews and Commentaries," *New Jersey
  Music and Arts* 23 (January 1968): 11.
Biographical Encyclopedia of American Jews. (New York: M. Jacobs and
  L. M. Glassman, 1935).
Bowlt, John. "Introduction." In *Louis Lozowick: American Precision-
  ist Retrospective.* (Long Beach, Calif.: Long Beach Museum of
  Art, 1978).
Brown, Gordon. "Arts Reviews," *Arts* 51 (December 1976): 42.

Brown, Milton W. *American Painting from the Armory Show to the Depression.* (Princeton, N.J.: Princeton University Press, 1955).

———. "Cubist-Realism: An American Style," *Marsyas* 3 (1943–1945): 139–164.

Cahill, Holger. "American Art Today." In *America as Americans See It,* ed. Fred J. Ringel. (New York: Harcourt, Brace & Co., 1932).

Cahill, Holger, and Alred H. Barr, Jr., eds. *Art in America in Modern Times.* (New York: Reynal and Hitchcock, 1934).

Campbell, Lawrence. "Reviews and Previews: Louis Lozowick," *Art News* 59 (January 1961): 13.

Cary, Elisabeth Luther. "Reflections on Modern Prints," *Parnassus* 8 (April 1936): 12–15.

Celender, Donald D. "Precisionism in Twentieth-Century American Painting." Ph.D. dissertation, Frick Fine Arts Department, University of Pittsburgh, 1963.

Crawford, Andrew Wright. "A National Exhibition of Prints," *Prints* 3 (March 1933): 23–31.

Cummings, Paul. *Dictionary of Contemporary American Artists,* 3rd ed. (New York: St. Martin's Press, 1977).

Current Biography. (New York: H. W. Wilson Co., 1942).

Current Biography Yearbook 1973. (New York: H. W. Wilson Co., 1974).

de Furia, Louis A. "The Lozowick Mystique," *New Jersey Music and Arts* 26 (June 1971): 30–31.

Dictionnaire biographique des artistes contemporains, Vol. 2. (Paris: Art & Edition, 1931).

Dieterich, Redigiert von. "Louis Lozowick," *Farbe und Form* 8 (January 1923): 4–5.

Encyclopedia of American Biography. (New York: American Historical Company, 1934).

"Exhibitions: American Print Makers, The Downtown Gallery," *Art News* 29 (December 20, 1930): 59.

Flint, Janet A. "Louis Lozowick: Drawings and Lithographs." In *Louis Lozowick: Drawings and Lithographs* (Washington, D.C.: National Collection of Fine Arts, Smithsonian Institution, 1975).

———. *The Prints of Louis Lozowick: A Catalogue Raisonné.* (New York: Hudson Hill, 1982).

Francis, Henry Sayles. "The International Exhibition at Cleveland," *American Magazine of Art* 23 (July 1931): 25.

Frank, Peter. "New York Reviews: Louis Lozowick's New York," *Art News* 75 (March 1976): 138.

Friedman, Martin L. *The Precisionist View in American Art*. (Minneapolis: The Walker Art Center, 1960).

Lloyd Goodrich. "New York Exhibitions," *Arts* 9 (June 1926): 345.

Gaer, Yossef. "Louis Lozowick; An Artist Who Presents the Soul of America." *B'nai B'rith Magazine* 41 (June 1927): 378–379.

Garfield, John. "Louis Lozowick," *Das Zelt* 1, No. 9 (1924): 330–331.

Georges, Valdemar. "Paysages d'Amérique." In *Exposition de dessins et gravures de Louis Lozowick* (Paris: Galerie Zak, July 11–25, 1928).

Gerdts, William H., Jr. *Painting and Sculpture in New Jersey*. New Jersey Historical Series. (Princeton: D. Van Nostrand Co., 1964).

Gilbert, Haynes A. "Louis Lozowick," *The Jewish Tribune,* September 19, 1930, p. 52.

Gropper, William. "Louis Lozowick," In *The Universal Jewish Encyclopedia*. 10 vols. Edited by Isaac Landman. (New York: The Universal Jewish Encyclopedia, 1948).

Gutman, Walter. "American Lithography," *Creative Art* 5 (November 1929): 800–804.

Hanley, F. "'La Vie Boheme' is 'La Vie de Machine' in America," *The American Hebrew,* 118 (January 15, 1926): 323.

The Index of Twentieth Century Artists, 1933–1937. Reprint ed. (New York: Arno Press, 1970.)

Joffe, Harriette N. "Louis Lozowick: The Creative Artist As Social Critic." Masters thesis, Art Department, City College of The City of New York.

Kainen, Jacob. "Prints of the Thirtes: Reflections on the Federal Art Project." *Artist's Proof* 11 (1971): 34–41.

Kaye, S. A., ed. *Biographical Encyclopedia of the World*. 4th ed. (Bethpage, New York: Institute for Research in Biography, 1947).

Kistler, Aline. "The National Survey," *Prints* 6 (June 1936): 241–250.

Lewis, Jo Ann. "Immigrant Artists: Who They Were and What They Did," *Smithsonian Magazine* 7 (May 1976): 92–100.

Lipke, William C. "Abstraction and Realism: The Machine Aesthetic and Social Realism." In *Abstraction and Realism: 1923–1943 Paintings, Drawings and Lithographs of Louis Lozowick* (Burlington: Robert Hull Fleming Museum, The University of Vermont, 1971.)

"Louis Lozowick: Graphic Artist Honored by Whitney Show Dies." *New York Times,* September 10, 1973, p. 24.

Marquardt, Virginia Hagelstein. "The American Artists School:
Radical Heritage and Social Content Art," *Archives of American
Art Journal* 26, No. 4 (1986): 17–23.

————. "Introduction." In *Louis Lozowick: A Centennial Exhibition.*
(New York: Associated American Artists, 1992).

————. "Louis Lozowick: An American's Assimilation of Russian
Avant-Garde Art of the 1920s." In *The Avant-Garde Frontier:
Russia Meets the West, 1910–1930* (Gainesville: University Press
of Florida, 1992), 241–274.

————. "Louis Lozowick: Development from Machine Aesthetic
to Social Realism, 1922–1936." Ph.D. dissertation, Department
of Art, University of Maryland, 1983.

————. "Louis Lozowick: From 'Machine Ornaments' to Applied
Design, 1923–1930." *The Journal of Decorative and Propaganda Arts*
(DAPA) 8 (Spring 1988): 40–57.

————. *"New Masses* and John Reed Club Artists, 1926–1936:
Evolution of Ideology, Subject Matter, and Style." *The Journal of
Decorative and Propoganda Art (DAPA)* 12 (Spring 1989): 56–75.

Marquardt, Virginia Hagelstein, and Sylvan Cole. "American
Artists Schools Print Series of 1936," *Print Quarterly* 6 (December 1989), 413–421.

Miller, Dorothy C., and Alred Barr, Jr. eds. *American
Realists and Magic Realists.* (New York: The Museum of Modern
Art, 1943).

Potamkin, Harry Alan. "Louis Lozowick," *Young Israel* 26(January
1934): 3–4.

Prasse, Leona E., "International Competitive Print Exhibition,"
The Bulletin of the Cleveland Museum of Art (April 1931): 62–64.

Preston, Stuart. "Early 20th Century Revolution in Art and Its
Effects," *New York Times,* September 3, 1961, sec. 11, p. 8.

Putnam, Samuel. "Of Waffles, Skyscrapers, Muscovites, and 'Gas',"
Chicago Evening Post Magazine of the Art World, December 29,
1925, 3–4.

Rashell, Jacob. *Jewish Artists in America.* (New York: Vantage Press,
1967).

Reimann, Bruno W. "Louis Lozowick," *Der Cicerone* 15 (1923):
955–957.

————. "Louis Lozowick." In *Jahrbuch der Jungen Kunst.* (Leipzig:
Verlag Kinkhardt et Biermann, 1923), 312–315.

Rich, Louis. "Soul of Our Cities: A Painter's Interpretation of the
Expression of Civilization through Machinery." *New York Times
Magazine,* February 17, 1924, p. 3.

Roth, Cecil. *The Jewish Contribution to Civilization.* (Cincinnati,
   Ohio: The Union of Amerian Hebrew Congregations, 1940).

Rothchild, Lincoln. "Louis Lozowick (1892–1973)," *The Pragmatist
   in Art* 7 (Fall 1973): 3.

Savitt, Mark. "Shapes of Industry," *Arts* 50 (November 1975): 9.

Singer, Esther Forman. "The Lithography of Louis Lozowick,"
   American Artist 37 (November 1973): 36–41, 78, 83.

Solomon, Elke M. Introduction to *Louis Lozowick: Lithographs*
(New York: The Whitney Museum of American Art, November
   21, 1972–January 1, 1973).

Taylor, Joshua C. *America as Art.* (Washington, D.C.: Smithsonian
   Institution Press, 1976).

Who's Who in American Jewry. (New York: National News Associations, 1938).

Williams, Ruthann. "Louis Lozowick at the Whitney Museum,"
   New Jersey Music and Arts 28 (November 1972): 25–30.

Wolf, Robert. "Louis Lozowick," *Nation* 122 (February 17, 1926):
   186.

"The World of Art: The Beginning of the Season," *New York
   Times Magazine,* October 12, 1924, p. 10.

Zabel, Barbara Beth. "The Machine as Metaphor, Model, and
   Microcosm: Technology and American Art 1915–1930," *Arts
   Magazine* 57 (December 1982): 100–105.

———. "Louis Lozowick and Technological Optimism of the
   1920s." Ph.D. dissertation, McIntire Department of Art, University of Virginia, 1978.

———. "Lozowick and Urban Optimism of the 1920." *Archives of
   American Art Journal* 14, No. 2 (1974): 17–21.

———. "The Precisionist-Constructivist Nexus: Louis Lozowick
   in Berlin," *Arts Magazine* 56 (October 1981): 123–127.

Zigrosser, Carl. "Modern American Graphic Art," *Creative Art* 9
   (November 1931): 368–374.

Archival Material (In Alphabetical Order)

Carbondale, Illinois. Morris Library, Southern Ilinois University,
   Special Collections: Samuel Putnam Papers.

Chicago, Illinois. Chicago Public Library, Special Collections Division: Goodman Theatre Archives.

Chicago, Illinois. University of Illinois Library, Archives Division:
   Alfred P. Maurice, "Checklist of Fifty Years of Lithographs by
   Louis Lozowick," 1973.

Milwaukee, Wisconsin. Golda Meir Library, University of Wisconsin-Milwaukee, University Manuscript Collections: *Little Review* (Chicago, Ill.) Records, 1914–1964.

New Haven, Connecticut. Beinecke Rare Book and Manuscript Library, Yale University: Katherine S. Dreier Papers; and *Hound & Horn* Papers.

Philadelphia, Pennsylvania. Charles Patterson Van Pelt Library, University of Pennsylvania, Rare Books Collection: Carl Zigrosser Collection.

Princeton, New Jersey. Princeton University Library. Rare Books and Special Collections: The *Broom* Correspondence of Harold A. Loeb.

Syracuse, New York. George Arents Research Library, Manuscript Division, Syracuse University: Louis Lozowick Papers.

Tucson, Arizona. University Library, The University of Arizona, Special Collections: Thomas Woods Stevens Collection.

Washington, D.C., Archives of American Art, Smithsonian Institution: Louis Lozowick Papers.

Interviews with Louis Lozowick

January 11, 1971, South Orange, New Jersey. Conducted by William C. Lipke.

April 24, 1972, South Orange, New Jersey. Conducted by Gerald M. Monroe.

April 26, 1973, South Orange, New Jersey. Conducted by Seton Hall University students.

August 30, 1973, South Orange, New Jersey. Conducted by Barbara Kaufman.

INDEX